A Brief Introduction to Psychoanalytic Theory

Also by Stephen Frosh:

Feelings

*Psychoanalysis outside the Clinic: Interventions in Psychosocial Studies**

For and Against Psychoanalysis

*Hate and the Jewish Science: Anti-Semitism, Nazism and Psychoanalysis**

Critical Narrative Analysis in Psychology (with Peter Emerson)*

Key Concepts in Psychoanalysis

*After Words: The Personal in Gender, Culture and Psychotherapy**

Young Masculinities: Understanding Boys in Contemporary Society
  (with Ann Phoenix and Rob Pattman)*

*The Politics of Psychoanalysis**

Sexual Difference: Masculinity and Psychoanalysis

Child Sexual Abuse (with Danya Glaser)*

*Identity Crisis: Modernity, Psychoanalysis and the Self**

*Psychoanalysis and Psychology**

*Also published by Palgrave Macmillan

A Brief Introduction to
Psychoanalytic Theory

Stephen Frosh

palgrave
macmillan

First published 2012 by
PALGRAVE MACMILLAN

Palgrave Macmillan in the UK is an imprint of Macmillan Publishers Limited,
registered in England, company number 785998, of Houndmills, Basingstoke,
Hampshire RG21 6XS.

Palgrave Macmillan in the US is a division of St Martin's Press LLC,
175 Fifth Avenue, New York, NY 10010.

Palgrave Macmillan is the global academic imprint of the above companies
and has companies and representatives throughout the world.

Palgrave® and Macmillan® are registered trademarks in the United States,
the United Kingdom, Europe and other countries.

ISBN 978-0-230-36930-6   ISBN 978-0-230-37177-4 (eBook)

DOI 10.1007/978-0-230-37177-4

This book is printed on paper suitable for recycling and made from fully
managed and sustained forest sources. Logging, pulping and manufacturing
processes are expected to conform to the environmental regulations of the
country of origin.

A catalogue record for this book is available from the British Library.

A catalog record for this book is available from the Library of Congress.

10 9 8 7 6 5 4 3 2 1
21 20 19 18 17 16 15 14 13 12

Contents

Acknowledgements

I would like especially to thank Catherine Gray at Palgrave Macmillan, who insisted that I write this book and provided an extraordinary editorial service. Most of the good things in the book are a result of her advice.

Thanks also to Joel and Alec, who encouraged me to produce this book for people like them.

PART I
Freudian theory

1
The appeal of psychoanalysis

Why psychoanalysis matters

Psychoanalysis can claim to be one of the most influential intellectual and practical projects of modern times. It was invented by Sigmund Freud and others towards the end of the nineteenth century, during the same period that other major social sciences (including psychology and sociology) were coming into being. It rapidly became prominent in clinical, academic and artistic circles and in some branches of commerce, notably advertising and public relations (Zaretsky, 2004). Psychoanalysis was also a major spur to the professions of psychotherapy and counselling that grew up in the twentieth century. It had a dramatic impact on treatment methods and was especially important in advancing the psychological therapy of 'shell-shocked' patients during both World Wars. Many of its ideas became part of the taken-for-granted psychological understanding that people have about themselves and others. This applies especially to the proposal that people's behaviour is strongly affected by 'unconscious' impulses about which they know little and over which they have only limited control. The belief that talking about psychological problems might help a person deal with them, or that our dreams might reveal something about our 'deep' wishes and conflicts, or that slips of the tongue might have significance, is premised on a generally psychoanalytic understanding about how the unconscious works. Ways of thinking about child development, about intimate relationships and about the meaning of psychological symptoms have all been profoundly affected by psychoanalytic theories.

Despite this extensive influence, the *standing* of psychoanalysis as a discipline possessing valid knowledge about human psychology remains uncertain. Freud claimed that psychoanalysis was a *science* and that its value lay in the way in which it identified the real sources of psychological life. This has always been heavily debated, with several writers raising serious doubts about whether psychoanalysis ever fulfilled the requirements of scientific practice (for example Borch-Jacobsen and Shamdasani, 2012) or whether it has been supported or disproven by evidence (Grünbaum, 1984). Defenders of psychoanalysis have argued that many of these critics have used a very idealized version of science in order to make their point, and also that psychoanalysis actually does have rational and testable approaches to knowledge, shown in the 'laboratory' of the consulting room and in its growing openness to scrutiny in terms of reports and discussions of its clinical work (Frosh, 2006). For yet others, psycho-analysis is seen more as an artistic or 'humanistic' approach to imaginative understanding, and does not need to pretend to be a science in order to have validity.

There is also something more general to say about the standing of psychoanalysis. This is a slightly complicated idea that has to do with what is called the *reflexivity* of human beings. What this refers to is the way in which people seek meaning through interpreting their own actions and thoughts and those of others. Humans can perhaps be seen as 'meaning-making machines'. The argument here is that one universal characteristic of people is that they try to find ways to work out what they are 'about' and – on the whole – that they do this in the context of their relationships with others. We go through life reflecting on ourselves to a greater or lesser extent; and it not only a psychoanalytic truism to think that the depth and extent of someone's capacity for such reflection might be a measure of their standing as a person.

How do we make sense of ourselves? It has to be through drawing on our experiences and our behaviour and employing the ideas that can be found around us in our culture to help us interpret these. Among these ideas are some that derive from psychoanalysis, which we might use even if we have never read any psychoanalytic theory. For instance, the notion that childhood experiences matter for the way in which we later form relationships as adults is a very wide-spread one. The failure to make good relationships might be interpreted as a consequence of difficulties we had with our parents, maybe because we had an abandoning and rejecting father or a depressed and unresponsive mother. It is not necessary to know any psychoanalytic theory to hold this view; but psychoanalysis speaks cogently to it and provides a framework to support and consolidate such 'lay' understandings.

Even more generally than this, the extent to which western culture is permeated by psychological assumptions, many with their roots in psychoanalysis, is very striking. The idea that childhood determines or at least strongly influences adulthood has already been mentioned. The central psychoanalytic notion that we have unconscious motivations that drive our behaviour and are often not understood by us is perhaps just as pervasive. When people ask of themselves why they did something, or accuse a friend of self-deception, or of not being able to see the 'real' reasons for their actions, they are drawing on what can be called a psychoanalytic 'discourse' to make sense of their social environment. This suggests that culture is 'saturated' by psychoanalytic assumptions in ways that are not obvious because they are so taken-for-granted.

The reflexivity of humans also means that the psychological theories that take hold in a culture are not just *descriptions* of what people are like; they also *produce* people in their own image. If we hold a theory about the stars, it could be completely wrong and this would mean that many predictions and calculations made by scientists would be incorrect (perhaps disastrously so); but it would not actually affect the stars. They would continue in the firmament, twinkling away, and it would not matter what people thought of them. This is often referred to as the *material resistance* of the objective world (Borch-Jacobsen and Shamdasani, 2012): if our ideas about the properties of material objects are wrong, those objects have a habit of refusing to fit in with them. If, however, we have a powerful theory about *people*, it affects the way its subjects think about themselves, and actions follow – so it has a real impact on the thing it is studying. Social theories can work in this way. For instance, Marxist theory was taken up in a manner that produced actual revolutions because it promoted new ways in which people could understand themselves and their situation. Psychoanalysis is another such theory. If the unconscious had never existed before Freud invented it, there is a sense in which it would exist now, because we understand and treat ourselves and others in accordance with the idea that we have unconscious lives. It is very difficult to escape this: try denying that you have an unconscious, or that this denial is anything other than a form of what psychoanalysts would call a 'defence'. Psychoanalysis therefore matters greatly both as an intellectual discipline and as a way of comprehending what people make of themselves.

Psychoanalysts and others: a guide to terminology

Not all who use elements of psychoanalytic thought in their intellectual or clinical work are actually psychoanalysts. In fact, there is a huge range of activities that derive from or are connected in some way with psychoanalytic ideas and practices. A necessarily approximate way of dividing up the different groupings is in the following 'guide to terminology'.

Psychoanalysis: (1) The body of theory derived from the work of Sigmund Freud emphasizing the existence and workings of a 'dynamic' unconscious. (2) The clinical practice of psychoanalysis as a several-times-a-week encounter between an analyst and an 'analysand' (patient).

Psychoanalyst: Someone formally trained in psychoanalysis by one of the institutes laying claim to that term, most of which are recognized in some way by the International Psychoanalytic Association.

Psychoanalytic psychotherapy: A less intensive form of psychotherapeutic work based on psychoanalytic principles.

Psychodynamic theory and psychotherapy: A broad approach to psychology using the concept of a dynamic unconscious but including ideas and techniques that deviate from or extend psychoanalysis in important ways. Group analysis, transactional analysis, Jungian analytical psychology and some types of couple and family therapy might be included here.

Psychodynamic counselling: A more focused form of psychoanalytic psychotherapy.

Psychotherapy: A broad range of approaches to the treatment of psychological problems, including but not restricted to psychoanalytic and psychodynamic psychotherapy.

These different terms are ways of distinguishing psychoanalysis from its close colleagues and competitors, but in truth there is a great deal of overlap between them. There is also, as laid out below, a significant amount of variation and disagreement among psychoanalysts themselves, sometimes concerning quite fundamental ideas.

Variations in psychoanalysis

From the very start of psychoanalysis' history, which now dates back over a hundred years, there have been disputes about the core concepts of psychoanalysis and about what counts as genuine psychoanalysis and what does not. These disputes will be outlined in the next chapter, when we deal with a 'family tree' of psychoanalysis, and the main issues will each be elaborated in more detail later in this book. However, a brief list of major controversial areas within psychoanalysis includes:

- *Unconscious*

Psychoanalytic theory takes as axiomatic the existence of ideas that are 'in' the mind yet are not available to introspection and hence are hidden away from conscious knowledge. This basic premise lies at the heart of most of the concepts described in this book. In addition, the unconscious phenomena with which psychoanalysis is concerned are *dynamic* in the sense that they have force and motion – they are not just stored in some archive where they are not used. Despite the universal acceptance of these fundamental assumptions by psychoanalysts, there is a great deal of variation in their understanding of the nature of unconscious ideas, the way they are formed and the different channels through which their effects are felt.

- *Sexuality*

Freud was insistent on psychosexuality as the core psychoanalytic explanatory concept, at least until after the First World War, when he became more openly accepting of the idea that a destructive or aggressive drive might also be important. Other early psychoanalysts, notably Jung and Adler, reduced the importance of sexuality, at least outside the neuroses. This was a major source of early schisms in the movement. In post-Freudian psychoanalysis (meaning psychoanalysis after Freud's death in 1939), the quality of intimate relationships has become more important, leading to a relative downplaying of the role of sexuality in psychic life. There is a lot of dispute over whether this means that psychoanalysis has lost its edge, or whether it rather indicates a maturing of the discipline alongside a recognition that the psychological issues facing people have changed. Perhaps repressed sexuality is less of a problem now, and the difficulty of forming fulfilling relationships is a more pressing concern.

- *Drive theory*
Freudian theory was basically organized around the idea that people are 'driven' by internal forces (mainly sexuality) and that psychology is a matter of tracing the ways in which these drives are expressed and satisfied. Not only is the nature of drives controversial among different schools of psychoanalysis, but the very idea of a drive-based psychology is also disputed. For instance, instead of seeing relationships primarily as a means of expressing sexual impulses, perhaps it is more accurate simply to say that humans are relationship-oriented beings. Forming relationships of dependency, mutuality and love (and reacting aggressively when the opportunities for this are blocked) might be simply what people do.

- *Developmental theory*
Freud laid down the general structure of a theory that assumed that the sexual drive operated from birth but was expressed in different ways during the course of development. He suggested these ways could be coded according to the pleasure-sites of the body – oral, anal and genital. He argued that a central feature of human psychosexual development is the way in which what he termed the Oedipus complex is negotiated: that is, how infants manage the restrictions placed on their sexuality by society, and especially by their parents. While most psychoanalysts accept some of this, there have been many revisions of psychosexual developmental theory and a good deal of controversy within psychoanalysis itself about when the Oedipus complex occurs and what form it actually takes.

- *Defence mechanisms*
As noted above, Freud presented unconscious phenomena as a dynamic force in the sense that unconscious ideas are always trying to make themselves heard and felt. This means that unconscious

ideas are always in motion and would appear openly except for the fact that they are opposed by various strategies of the mind. These strategies are termed 'defence mechanisms', understood broadly as those psychological acts that prevent disturbing ideas coming into conscious awareness. This general idea is more or less universally held by contemporary psychoanalysts, but the types of defence they emphasize vary greatly. There is likewise much variety in the psychological disturbances that they take to be characterized by each defence. For example, the Freudian focus on repression ('motivated forgetting') seems to be much less widely shared than it once was. On the other hand, projection (experiencing one's own feeling or thought as if it belongs to someone else) and splitting (separating out ambivalent ideas into their 'positive' and 'negative' aspects) are now much more commonly highlighted in clinical reports.

- *Mental structure*
Quite late in his life, Freud described a structure of the mind which has become very well known, distinguishing between the I ('ego'), the It ('id') and the Over-I ('superego') – ideas I will discuss in more detail in Chapter 7. While this structure is still very influential, its relationship to the distinction between conscious and unconscious mental phenomena has never been clear-cut. Many psychoanalysts from the 1920s onwards saw their craft as one of working with the 'I'/ego. They mostly became known as 'ego psychologists' because of this, and in their theory as well as their practice they paid little attention to the id. This has generally speaking also been true for another major group of psychoanalysts, the 'object relations' group, which portrays mental structure as made up primarily of ego–object relationships (that is, internalized versions of self–other relations) in complex arrays.

- *Psychoanalytic technique*
It took a long time for psychoanalytic technique to become relatively standardized, and even now there are significant differences between practitioners. Some psychoanalysts are very careful with interpretations, preferring to form a positive 'therapeutic alliance' with a patient before moving to interpret at a 'depth' level, and to focus on the interpretation of defences before tackling underlying conflicts. Others argue that this can mean that nothing happens in analysis, and that

the patient has the experience of a therapist who seems frightened of handling difficult issues. They prefer to go straight for what they see as the primary anxiety that a patient is bringing, however disturbing that might be. Most analysts and psychodynamic psychotherapists work in one way or another with what they call the 'transference' (the way in which patients will incorporate important features of their past life into the relationship with the analyst), but how they do this and in particular what emphasis they put on the analyst's response to the patient (the 'countertransference') varies greatly.

• *Applications of psychoanalysis*
The tradition of applying psychoanalysis to areas outside the consulting room was enthusiastically embraced by Freud and his early followers, many of whom were social critics and artists rather than clinicians (Makari, 2010). Freud wrote on literature and art as well as on social phenomena such as religion and war, and believed psychoanalysis could offer unrivalled insights into these areas (as well as sometimes learning from them). Subsequent psychoanalysts and writers on psychoanalysis have continued this tradition with great verve, but not without contention. Political thinkers have used psychoanalysis to promote conservative or radical agendas; psychoanalysts interested in the arts have had very different ways of understanding them, producing a vivid but incoherent field of thought. There is also a worry about what happens when psychoanalytic ideas are taken out of the 'clinic' where they originate and are most easily tested. For instance, what does it mean to make a psychoanalytic interpretation of a literary 'text' that cannot, like a live patient, answer back?

Two core assumptions of psychoanalysts

It should be clear by now that it is not sufficient to define psycho-analysts and psychoanalytic psychotherapists as 'followers of Freud', because many of them work in ways that Freud would not have approved of or even recognized. The simplest definition of psycho-analysis, as the 'science of the unconscious' is also difficult to sustain, partly because of the controversial status of psychoanalysis as a 'science' – a label that many social and natural scientists would deny it.

However, it is fair to argue that what unites psychoanalysts is:

1. A shared belief that unconscious phenomena exist.

2. A practice that is geared to understanding those phenomena and exploring what happens to them in the context of the live encounter between analyst and patient (or 'analysand').

What this means for those who use psychoanalysis outside the clinic is a matter for considerable debate; but even here one might agree that there is something specific about the application of concepts such as unconscious fantasy or defences that characterizes these applications as psychoanalytically informed.

Precarious psychoanalysis

This book presents some of the major theoretical ideas of psychoanalysis from a largely sympathetic point of view. However, it is worth noting at the outset that there is a lot of uncertainty about the future of psychoanalysis, and that this might have to do not only with how useful it is as a theory and a practice, but also with cultural factors such as the patience people have for relatively long-drawn-out, expensive ways of offering psychotherapy. In the UK, for example, the preferred mode of therapy for psychological problems, supported actively by government through funding to the National Health Service, is cognitive behaviour therapy. Even where psychoanalysis gets a look-in, it is in a diluted form, for instance as 'dynamic interpersonal therapy', which is a focused, attachment-based version of brief psychotherapy. Several of the psychoanalytic psychotherapy training organizations are struggling to find sufficient trainees, and in many ways this is not surprising. Not only is the training very long and expensive, mainly because it requires several years of personal therapy usually three to five times weekly, but also, with some exceptions (for instance in child psychotherapy), there is very little by way of a career structure for those who emerge with a psychotherapy qualification. *Psychoanalysis*, which is the 'strongest' form of psychoanalytic psychotherapy, requires the most devotion to the training and still maintains a certain amount of clinical prestige. But investing tens of thousands of pounds in a training taking several years to complete, and then making one's way in life mainly through the uncertainties of private practice, is not always an attractive prospect.

Around the world, the situation is more varied. In the USA, where psychoanalysis was dominant in psychiatry and clinical psychology for a long period after the Second World War, many of the same pressures operate as in the UK. There too, varieties of cognitive and cognitive behavioural therapy are in the ascendant, and insurance companies have for a long time now placed restrictions on how much psychoanalysis they will pay for. Europe is similar, although there are pockets of psychoanalytic strength in certain areas in France and Italy. In South America, on the other hand, psychoanalysis seems to be thriving. There are very large numbers of trainees in Argentina and Brazil, for example, and a culture of psychological therapies that is much more welcoming to psychoanalytic ways of working. In other countries, psychoanalysis suffers from its roots in European culture, although there is also considerable interest in some surprising places, Japan being the most prominent.

Outside the therapeutic clinic, psychoanalysis is in a more promising situation, although still showing important weaknesses. In the 1970s and 1980s there was a resurgence of interest in how psychoanalysis could be applied to historical, cultural and political issues, with striking work in film studies and literature being good examples. Perhaps as a vestige of the emergence of a sexually fuelled counterculture in the 1960s, it was also drawn on to help people understand both what the effects of sexual repression might be, and the possibilities for sexual emancipation. This was linked with politics, for example in the impact of certain forms of psychoanalytic thinking on the work of some major Marxist, feminist and (later) postcolonial writers. Since then, psychoanalysis' star has waxed and waned in these fields too. For instance, feminist *criticism* of its patriarchal assumptions about women and about 'sexual difference' has been matched by feminist *use* of psychoanalytic ideas to help understand sexuality, sexual violence and the continuing oppression of women in many societies (for example Mitchell, 1974). Psychoanalytic approaches to *literature* were ridiculed in the 1970s because of the tendency to treat fictional characters as if they were real, and to read literary works as if they were straightforwardly the product of their authors' unconscious lives. Nevertheless, since then there has

been a varied and imaginative use of psychoanalysis to expand understanding of literature in terms of the effects of language, memory and
desire as they are played out across the workings of texts. This means
that psychoanalysis has been developed as a way of attending to the
specific forms that the literary imagination takes, rather than by reducing
poetry or novels to the neurotic musings of the author. Some of psychoanalysis' more transparently reactionary aspects have also given way to
new forms of thinking. For example, psychoanalysts were among the
last group of mental health professionals in the USA to agree that
homosexuality is not a mental disorder, and for a long time it was impossible for openly gay people to train as psychoanalysts. This situation has
now changed dramatically, although as ever unevenly, and psychoanalysis has offered a great deal of explanatory leverage on *homophobia*,
including the homophobic attitudes and anxieties of psychoanalysts and
psychotherapists themselves.

Defending psychoanalytic values

This kind of list could be extended greatly. My summary position with
regard to criticisms of psychoanalysis, and some responses to these,
is as follows.

- Psychoanalysis has been required to weather various storms
  throughout its history, but it has established itself both as a professional practice and as a legitimate intellectual discipline active in
  a wide area of the humanities and social sciences.
- This position has been under attack for various reasons. Some critics
  have stressed the difficulty of establishing the effectiveness of
  psychoanalysis as a therapy; the way in which it has often arrogantly
  pronounced on fields of work (for example literature and politics)
  that have their own complex traditions requiring specialist knowledge; and the frequently conservative assumptions that many
  psychoanalysts have had about sexuality, family forms and the like.
  These assumptions have placed them at odds not only with progressive thinkers, but also with the realities of social change in the late
  twentieth and early twenty-first centuries.

- While there is some basis for these criticisms, many of them also reveal the difficulties people have with some of the *values* that psychoanalysis stands for.
  - Psychoanalysis promotes a rigorous practice of thinking that cannot be rushed, that demands time and patience, and that is based on a kind of ethical assumption that it is worth pursuing what one might call a 'truthful' approach to living even if this is difficult and at times painful to do. Consequently, psychoanalysis has never been satisfied with 'quick fix' cures for psychological symptoms.
  - While some of its adherents have been rather prone to generalizing about the world from their 'expert' position as psychoanalysts, at its best psychoanalysis is curious and provocative, analysing what is going on without falling into the trap of making simplistic prescriptions for change.
  - Psychoanalysis stands for something serious, slow, thoughtful, uncertain and complicated. This does not always go down well in rushed societies demanding instant solutions, and characterized by short attention spans and a tendency to want to control dissent and disagreement.
- Psychoanalysis continues to influence therapeutic and counselling practice even where it is not the therapy of choice. There are some approaches that deliberately incorporate versions of psychoanalysis; but even among those that do not, its conceptualization of the therapeutic process is one that has to be engaged with. For instance, assumptions about the importance of the therapeutic relationship, or of the value of 'talking cures' involving interpretation of underlying mental states, derive in large part from psychoanalysis (though they have other sources too).
- Psychoanalysis is of such cultural significance that it also influences many intellectual disciplines in their attempts to conceptualize their own areas. This is the case even where there has been much criticism of psychoanalysis within the disciplines. One needs to know about psychoanalysis in order to understand what attitudes are taken towards it, and how to evaluate these debates.

The areas of dispute outlined above also constitute a map of some of the major concepts of psychoanalysis. This book offers a guide through these concepts. After Chapter 2, which gives a more detailed historical account of how psychoanalysis emerged, the book devotes several chapters to Freud's original ideas, as these continue to provide the basis for contemporary psychoanalytic theorizing. The second part of the book looks at some of the major developments since Freud, explaining the ideas of some of the main psychoanalytic schools and evaluating what they might mean. Finally, the third part offers two chapters outlining applications of psychoanalysis in the arts and social sciences.

Summary

- Psychoanalysis continues to have importance in the contemporary world, despite the emergence of new therapies that have severely constricted its role in psychotherapy, and also despite many criticisms of how it has been applied outside the clinic.
- This importance is due in large part to its impact on how people experience themselves, especially in western culture. In addition, many taken-for-granted elements of psychotherapy and counselling practice are derived from psychoanalysis, as are widely held assumptions about human psychology.
- There are many ways of doing psychoanalysis and many competing theories within it. However, what all psychoanalysts share is a commitment to exploring the workings of the unconscious.
- Many psychoanalytically informed scholars are also interested in how the basic tenets of psychoanalysis might offer new insights in the broad field of the humanities and social sciences.

2
A family history of psychoanalysis

Psychoanalytic history as myth

All academic disciplines have their histories in which certain central figures inspire others, who take their discoveries and their methods and develop them. Many disciplines trace their histories so far back that the founding figures have a mythological rather than an actual status, and most active workers in the field know little about them. Even some relatively recent fields are neglectful of their past and see it as of little relevance to the progress of the discipline. Psychology students, for example, are given very little background, either historical or philosophical; the tendency is instead to promote psychology as a branch of science, following scientific methodology and emerging somehow fully formed into the modern world. The founders of modern psychology such as Wilhelm Wundt and William James might be mentioned in passing in psychology textbooks, but few contemporary psychology students would call on them as authorities to justify the way in which they work.

Psychoanalysis is very different, and very peculiar. One might even suggest (as has often been done) that the structure of psychoanalytic history is much more like the history of a religious sect than that of a science or social science, or indeed any conventional discipline. Like a religion, there was a founding father who had a revelation (the existence of the unconscious); he struggled to have the truth of this revelation recognized by a hostile world, and gradually gathered around him a group of followers. There were early schisms and betrayals until a loyal second generation arose that started to establish an orthodox position. A canon of set (sacred) texts emerged, mostly penned by (or attributed to) the founder and studied continuously down the generations. Fundamentalist groups then formed that took the sacred texts literally, while more progressive groups believed the truth can be reinterpreted in each generation. These different groups turned on one another but were all united in their opposition to the growing lack of religiosity around them. Today, regular rituals are performed, for instance coming together for meetings in which the original truths are reiterated, and these have the effect of cementing the movement. What is especially noticeable is that the texts of the founder are actually read and studied by trainees and students, not only as historical relics but as the source of insights that may have been developed greatly in later years, but have rarely been surpassed.

In the case of psychoanalysis, Freud obviously performed the role of founder. He had many precursors and many influences operated on him. Principal among these were his scientific teachers, some of whom were the most significant medical and psychological researchers of his day. Freud was also well educated in the humanities, and drew widely on his knowledge of classical literature to help him think through his ideas. There were also some very specific social circumstances that affected Freud greatly. Importantly, he was a member of a generation of European Jews who had benefitted from emancipation in the nineteenth century, but who still found themselves coming up against deeply engrained antisemitism in their everyday professional and personal lives. This created a large group of highly educated secular Jews who shared in the ambitions of the enlightenment and of modernity, but who were also, because of antisemitism, excluded from the mainstream of society and made to struggle for acceptance. Freud was thus both an insider and an outsider, and psychoanalysts from the start took up a position as members of a marginal discipline capable of seeing the foibles of their social milieu more clearly than those who were immersed fully within it. Freud was also responding to a broad contemporary interest in what might be termed 'occult' phenomena – suggestion, hypnosis, telepathy and the like – which raised questions about the limits of rational understanding (Luckhurst, 2002). For Freud, these things were slightly unholy bedfellows, contesting the role of psychoanalysis as the primary explanatory system for irrational ideas. While maintaining an interest in them (for example, he accepted the reality of telepathy), Freud was at pains to distance himself from occultism on the grounds that psychoanalysis was actually a science, a rational discipline and not something that celebrated irrationality itself.

Whatever Freud's sources and influences, whatever cultural cross-currents his work might have responded to, the mythical presentation of him is as the great explorer and founding hero, the one who discovers the true nature of the unconscious and invents psychoanalysis as the system through which it can be studied, understood and appeased. This discovery came after a period of wandering in the professional wilderness, supposedly rejected by his scientific contemporaries. During this time (the last years of the nineteenth century), Freud experimented with apparently outlandish ideas and methods in an effort to understand psychological disturbances. In particular, he turned his attention to the then-prevalent disorder of hysteria, in which patients (mostly women) presented physical symptoms such as fainting or paralysis that seemed to have no organic origins, but rather to have psychological causes. According to the myth, Freud experimented with different healing techniques including hypnosis and a kind of sugges-tive 'pressure technique' (laying his hand on the patent's forehead and encouraging or demanding them to recall forgotten trauma) and making wrong theoretical turns. These included the infamous 'seduction theory', in which Freud proposed that the source of hysteria was actual sexual abuse in childhood, usually by the father – an idea he aban-doned when he came to believe that the sheer frequency of abuse entailed (including by his own father) was untenable. The relinquish-ment of the seduction theory has been a source of great controversy among Freud scholars. The positions taken on it range from Jeffrey Masson's (1984) claim that it was the point where Freud and psychoa-nalysis turned away from truth (that is, Freud denied the existence of sexual abuse that had actually happened); through Borch-Jacobsen and Shamdasani's (2012) criticism that Freud always found what his current theory predicted so it is impossible to know what actually happened to his patients; to the psychoanalytically orthodox assertion that the abandonment of the seduction theory was the founding moment for psychoanalysis itself, because it introduced the idea that patients' *fantasies* might be the key element in their psychopathology (for example Anzieu, 1986).

Following the mythological path, as psychoanalytic history has often done, the abandonment of false theories is followed by the revelation of the truth. In most accounts (for example Gay, 1988), the medium for this revelation was the 'self-analysis' that Freud undertook in the 1890s. This 'heroic' self-analysis (the extent of which has been challenged by Borch-Jacobsen and Shamdasani, 2012) was based on Freud's supposedly unflinching investigation of his own dreams. The reward for his bravery was that the meaning of dreams came to him, and in so doing revealed the operations of the unconscious. After one particular dream, that of 'Irma's Injection' which formed an important element in his book *The Interpretation of Dreams* (Freud, 1900a), Freud wrote to his friend Wilhelm Fliess wondering if some day a marble tablet might be placed on the house in which he dreamt it – a tablet inscribed with the words, 'Here, on July 24, 1895, the secret of the dream revealed itself to Dr Sigm. Freud' (Freud, 1900b, p. 417).

All this might seem very strange as an account of the origins of a sophisticated intellectual movement. Revelations come in science as well as in religion, and dreams are often part of this, so in itself this does not mean that psychoanalysis is unscientific. However, the intensity with which Freud's personal psychology was bound up with the advance of psychoanalysis is unusual, and the degree to which it still continues to be so, more than a century after the founding dream, may be unique.

The unconscious of the psychoanalytic movement

This peculiarity of psychoanalysis is of crucial significance in understanding how psychoanalysis is transmitted across its generations. What is most striking about it is that the subject matter of psychoanalysis – the unconscious, repressions, transference and so on – is played out in the actual relations between psychoanalysts and in its institutional history. One could argue that the involvement of personal issues in intellectual work is true of other disciplines as well. For instance, science does not advance progressively, and much of what happens within it is fuelled by rivalries and ambitions, hopes and acts of generosity, and by irrational aspects of the psychological and social make-up of the scientific community. The same is true of the arts and humanities – how people feel about things is enormously important in determining what work is valued and what ideas take hold. But perhaps it is only really in psychoanalysis that *exactly the same* processes that are studied are also enacted in how the discipline is pursued.

The 'unconscious', first and foremost, is a term applied to the tendency of unacknowledged wishes to break through into consciousness through indirect means. Psychoanalysis claims that people's behaviour is governed in large part by impulses about which they have little awareness and over which they have little control. These impulses are observable when people act in ways that are apparently irrational. Such acts include overemotional responses to things, oddly self-destructive decisions, compulsions, weird slips, bombastic or denigrating self-presentations, or an attraction towards wrong turns and blind alleys. In addition, the unconscious underpins what seems to be the most rational activity of all – the drive to knowledge, including psychoanalytic knowledge itself. Why are people so heavily invested in establishing the truth of their ideas and their superiority over others? Why do they argue with such intensity and fall out with one another, making lasting feuds over what Freud called 'the narcissism of small differences'? Not just, one might suggest, because they have built their reputations on the truth of their ideas, although this is obviously very important; but also because they are emotionally over-involved with them. The ideas mean something more than they appear to mean. They might represent success and self-worth, or a way to deal with a deficiency or trauma. They might even stand in for something else, for example sexual knowledge. In his case study of the teenage girl he called 'Dora', Freud describes her using an encyclopaedia for sexual enlightenment: this might be one source of all drives to knowledge – and certainly one can often see, in the exhibitionism attached to being an expert, a wish to be admired and desired.

If the unconscious infiltrates the pursuit of knowledge, then psychoanalysts will themselves show the workings of the unconscious in the development of their own practices. And while this is true for all disciplines, it is particularly strongly enacted in psychoanalysis for two major reasons. One is the point about reflexivity made in the previous chapter. Psychoanalysts use notions of the unconscious not only to study the minds of their *patients*, but also to understand themselves and their professional colleagues (and, indeed, everyone else, including their parents and children, their friends and partners, their managers and employers and supervisees). For instance, they might interpret people's criticisms as if they are due to the critic's own anxieties or neurotic inhibitions, in which case the response to critics would be that they need more personal analysis. This has historically been a common form of character assassination in the psychoanalytic movement, used by Freud himself. They might also see criticisms as stemming from personal hostility or rivalry (which, of course, they often are). Or they might understand theoretical innovations as manifestations of the unconscious of the theorist involved, and not solely as new ideas. The consequence of this is a movement that is saturated with emotion, sometimes making it immensely exciting and creative, and at other times producing schisms and personal antagonisms far in excess of what might seem 'reasonable'. Many psychoanalytic institutes around the world have shown these tendencies, making them more like religious or political societies than supposedly scientific ones.

The second reason for the strength of the emotional undercurrents in psychoanalysis' institutional development has to do with the way in which psychoanalysts are trained. In every school of psychoanalysis, whatever their other differences, the core of the training is the personal 'training analysis'. Fundamentally, this means being in psychoanalysis oneself as a patient with an officially approved analyst (a 'training analyst') for the entire duration of the training, and normally for some time before the training starts and after it ends. The rationale for this is very strong. Not only does it give the newly hatched analyst a clear experience of what it is like to be a patient, but it is also the liveliest way imaginable to demonstrate the workings of the unconscious and of the psychodynamic mechanisms that surround it. One can talk or read about the unconscious, but *experiencing* it is another matter, and it is that experience that is crucial to understanding the essence of psychoanalysis. In addition, there is the argument that dealing with one's own neuroses is important if one is going to treat other people through the use of an intimate personal relationship that can stir up all sorts of feelings. Even if one does not believe that it is possible to be perfectly 'mentally healthy', one might still accept that gaining a clearer understanding of one's own beliefs, prejudices and emotional responses is likely to be a very good thing.

All this is fair and convincing, but a further effect of the training analysis lies in what could be termed, using psychoanalytic language, the *unresolved transferences* of the trainee. At its simplest, what this means is that through the process of personal analysis, the trainee forms a strong emotional relationship with the analyst which is examined and worked on, but never fully removed. Because the analysis serves the dual function of therapy and training, the professional activities of trainees are heavily influenced by their experiences in the training analysis; indeed, this is part of the point. Whether analysts intend this to happen or not, their influence over their trainees is likely to be profound – not just a matter of teaching skills or ideas, but a deeply emotional and personal formation of the personality around what is taken in from the training analyst. Institutionally, this means that psychoanalysis breeds new generations that are even more indebted to their seniors than is the case for other professions, and that frequently replay the disputes of previous generations. It also means that when analysts break from their trainers it is a highly emotional affair, often producing polarization rather than a gentler form of intellectual development. When one adds to this the dependence that trainees and younger analysts have on older ones for acceptance into the movement (the criteria for approving someone as an analyst have always had a great deal of subjective judgement about them) and for patient referrals, teaching positions and reputation, one can see perhaps why there has been a history of intense rivalries, internecine disputes, and general overemotionality in the psychoanalytic movement as a whole. Again one might argue that this intensity is a source of psychoanalysis' creativity, and this is certainly true; but it does not make for an easy life.

Schools of psychoanalysis

All this is by way of explanation as to why it makes sense to think of a kind of family tree of psychoanalysis, in which there are marriages and divorces and a genealogy identified both by intellectual affinity and by the fact of who analysed whom. The story of course starts with Sigmund Freud, who analysed himself. The next generation was mostly analysed by him (including his daughter, Anna, in a move that would now be deemed more or less incestuous) or by those close to him. Adherents came and went, the most famous early example being Carl Jung. Freud had initially seen Jung as the one who would inherit his mantle as leader of psychoanalysis and had made him the first president of the International Psychoanalytical Association (IPA), the initial proposal being that this should be his job for life. However, Freud and Jung broke up painfully. This break-up was ostensibly over the centrality of sexuality in psychoanalytic theory, but each of the protagonists interpreted it as due to unconscious complexes in the other – Jung's Oedipal rivalry with Freud (his 'father-fixation'), Freud's inability to cope with being displaced by a younger man. Jung then moved out of psychoanalysis completely, forming his own school of thought (Analytical Psychology), something that also happened with some other early analysts such as Alfred Adler. After the first painful schisms, the psychoanalytic movement showed a greater capacity to retain its rebellious sons and daughters, although there were other examples of analysts leaving to form their own non-psychoanalytic schools (Karen Horney in America after the Second World War is one important instance of this). What has tended to happen instead is that different views have been managed within the movement, with the IPA recognizing some and blocking others, but with everyone still wanting to claim the title 'psychoanalysis' on the grounds of their continuing fealty to what they see as the truths of Freud's basic insights – although of course they differ substantially on what these truths might be.

One example will suffice here, from British psychoanalysis. Before the Second World War it was dominated by the theories and followers of Melanie Klein, who had come to London from Berlin in 1926. Unfortunately, Klein herself, as well as Kleinian theory, was at logger-heads with Freud's daughter Anna. Like Klein, Anna was a non-medical analyst working with children as well as adults, but unlike Klein she had developed a very empirical, 'ego-oriented' way of working (see Chapter 10). When Anna arrived in London with her father in 1938 it sparked a rift in the British Psychoanalytical Society that threatened to destroy the integrity of psychoanalysis in Britain, with secessions plotted and emotional withdrawals and accusations abounding. That the Second World War was raging and bombs were falling over London at the same time is an ironic and possibly not irrelevant feature of this dispute. Over the course of the first few years of the 1940s, the Society staged a series of 'Controversial Discussions' from followers of Klein and Anna Freud. These were highly emotional and at times bitter affairs revealing all the complexities of psychoana-lytic overindulgence. For example, one of Klein's bitterest critics was her daughter Melitta Schmideberg. The attacks Schmideberg made on her mother's ideas about early infant and child development have all the passion and poignant family violence one might ever want to read. The end result of these discussions, however, was productive for the Society and demonstrated a capacity for containing dissension that was not so obvious earlier on in psychoanalytic history. The Society split its training into two main streams, A (the Kleinians) and B (the Freudians), allowing students to train in one school or another, but also insisting that they had one supervisor from a third group, the 'independents', who in a time-honoured British tradition did not want to commit themselves to either extreme. Gradually, these independents forged their own main way of looking at things, known as object relations theory, but the general split has continued, although without as much acerbity as was the case in the past and with a high degree of overlap in training experiences. This agreement between the Kleinians and Freudians allowed a new school of British psychoanalysis to emerge, as well as preserving a tendency towards empirical studies of child development that has flowered again in recent years through adaptations of attachment theory (see Chapter 11).

In other parts of the world there have been equivalent splits, some more vituperative and others less so. In post-war USA there was a division between those who followed a kind of orthodox ego psychology that emphasized 'internal' and biological factors in unconscious life, and those more interested in the impact of social and cultural forces. These differences plus various personal rivalries resulted in there being numerous IPA-recognized societies across America, and some cities (notably New York) have more than one such group. In France there was a famous 'expulsion' of Jacques Lacan from the IPA in the 1950s, resulting from a split in the French society and opposition in the IPA to Lacan's clinical and training techniques. The refusal of the IPA to recognize a French society that allowed Lacan to train others resulted in the formation of a separate Lacanian movement, which now has more affiliates across the world than any other single psychoanalytic group. This does not mean that there is no opposition to Lacanian psychoanalysis even within France; but there is at least some evidence that the conflicts between groups are less visceral than they once were, and more like other differences between people working on roughly the same projects as one another.

We are left with a number of relatively easily differentiated schools, which can be placed in very approximate relationship with one another as shown in Figure 2.1.

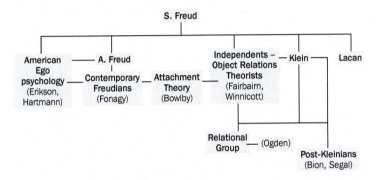

Figure 2.1 Schools of psychoanalysis

The ideas of some of these schools will be described in more detail later on in this book, especially in Part II. However, as a very brief guide, the main assumptions that distinguish them are as follows:

- *Ego psychology* was the dominant form of psychoanalysis in the USA after the Second World War. As its name suggests, it concentrated on understanding the workings of the 'ego' or 'I', understood as that element of the mind that mediates between the demands of the unconscious and the 'real' outside world. It drew heavily on the work of *Anna Freud*, whose groundbreaking volume *The Ego and the Mechanisms of Defence* formulated an empirically oriented approach to psychoanalytic treatment focused on how defence mechanisms operate and how they should be analysed. In the UK in particular, this work has now developed into a 'Contemporary Freudian' school that still gives priority to how people adapt constructively to reality and that is heavily impacted upon by recent developments in attachment theory and neuroscience.
- *Kleinian psychoanalysis* has as its main sphere of interest unconscious *phantasies* (the specifically Kleinian spelling is meant to indicate a difference from conscious fantasies such as daydreams).

These arise from inner drives and their relationships with the 'objects' to which they become attached. These objects are people or parts of people (the mother's breast is the primary one); the drives are divided into loving and destructive ones, arising from the life and death drives described by Freud and discussed in Chapter 5. What distinguishes Kleinian psychoanalysis is an emphasis on 'id' impulses and on very early, 'primitive' developmental issues, linked with a relational orientation that means it often gets classed as an object relations theory.

- *Object relations theory* is an approach that takes as primary not inner drives, but rather the impulse towards forming relationships with other people. It is a major contributor to what has come to be called the relational perspective in psychoanalysis, which itself covers analysts working in more 'intersubjective' and 'interpersonal' ways as well as in object relations theory proper. There has also been some crossover in recent years with adherents of American self psychology, which is concerned with how people develop secure inner structures as a consequence of their early relational context, much as is the work of the British 'independent' Donald Winnicott. Some of the similarities and differences between these generally relational psychoanalysts will be addressed later in this book.

- *Lacanian psychoanalysis* is possibly the most radically distinct of the main theoretical groups, and has historically been opposed to many of the assumptions of ego psychology and of object relations theory. It has produced its own vocabulary and theoretical notions, many of them very complex in their full formulation. Perhaps its strongest claims to be included in an introductory account of this kind are as follows. First, it has become immensely influential both in clinical work and in the wider world of psychoanalytic 'applications' to culture, politics and social science. Secondly, its focus on psychoanalysis as a 'practice of speech' offers a radical alternative to more emotion-oriented psychoanalytic and psycho-therapeutic approaches. This particular focus produces quite a distinctive understanding of the unconscious and of transference as products of the clinical encounter rather than as permanent 'things' that are always operating and can be uncovered wherever one looks for them. While there are various influences on Lacanian psychoanalysis, these have tended to be philosophical and artistic rather than coming from other psychoanalytic schools.

These are by no means the only psychoanalytic approaches worth knowing about, but between them they represent the main trends and networks of debate within the psychoanalytic movement, covering ego adaptation, object relations, drive theory; different models of transference and interpretation, and different approaches to the understanding of unconscious life. In the rest of Part I of this book, the basic ideas outlined by Freud will be described, before returning to their elaboration in more recent theories. We begin in Chapter 3 with a brief look at what Freud was aiming at in developing his new science – with the question of what psychoanalysis is *about*.

Summary

- Psychoanalysis has had a turbulent history of transmission and dissension fuelled not only by the intellectual task of developing a new discipline, but also by emotional and relational investments.
- While other disciplines show similar patterns, psychoanalysis is unusual in that its object of study (the unconscious) is enacted in the institutional relations between psychoanalysts and particularly in the training situation, where a personal analysis is central.
- The various schools of psychoanalysis that have developed since Freud's early work have at times been intensely rivalrous with one another. Although there are still very clear differences between these schools, there are also some noticeable moves towards more conciliatory attitudes and more sharing of ideas.
- The major schools of thought differ in their views on ego adaptation, object relations, unconscious fantasy, the mechanisms of psycho-analytic therapy, and many other things. These differences are largely represented in the variations between some well-established schools – ego psychology, object relations, Kleinian and Lacanian. While other important approaches to psychoanalysis exist, these schools cover the range of different issues sufficiently to form the basis of a comprehensive account.

3

What Freud was trying to do

Freud's ambition

As I have already hinted, Freud's emergence as a major intellectual and cultural figure was by no means a straightforward affair. Not only did controversy surround him throughout his life, but there was an ambiguity in his thinking that meant that the Freudian project was always a complex and uncertain one. Was it a science or an art? Was it a way of treating people or an investigative procedure with few therapeutic aspirations? Freud himself is reputed to have said that, 'We do analysis for two reasons: to understand the unconscious and to make a living' (Jacoby, 1975, p. 124). This does not suggest that he was overly enamoured of the business of making people feel better. But what he does seem to have wanted to do was to make discoveries, to answer big questions and consequently to become someone who would be well known. In his account of a memory that he mentions in *The Interpretation of Dreams*, produced in response to what is known as the 'Count Thun' dream, Freud himself suggested that there might have been a personal motivation of a psychoanalytic kind at work here. At the age of 'seven or eight', Freud tells us, he urinated in his parents' bedroom. Angered, his father dismissed all previous intimations of greatness with the prophecy, 'The boy will come to nothing'. Freud comments,

> This must have been a frightful blow to my ambition, for references to this scene are still constantly recurring in my dreams and are always linked with an enumeration of my achievements and successes, as though I wanted to say: 'You see, I *have* come to something'. (Freud, 1900a, p. 216)

This dream and the interpretation Freud gives it lead one to assume that the major driving force behind his work was not so much sexuality (though competitive masculine potency might be an issue), but rather the wish to show that he had in fact 'come to something'. Driven by an ambition to be a great man, Freud eventually became exactly that.

There is indeed some evidence that Freud looked to make his mark wherever he could, rather than being first and foremost devoted to psychology. In fact, his early interests were in philosophy – he commented to his friend Wilhelm Fliess in 1895 that 'I most secretly nourish the hope of arriving ... at my initial goal of philosophy. For that is what I wanted originally, when it was not yet at all clear to me to what end I was in the world' (Freud, 1895, p. 159). Psychology was until the late nineteenth century seen as a branch of philosophy, so Freud's statement here is not particularly decisive. Nevertheless, in many later works he refers to philosophy as a good grounding for psychoanalysis as well as a kind of non-empirical rival to psychoanalytic thinking. For example, discussing the relationship between the ideas of the Greek philosopher Empedocles and his own theory of the life and death drives, Freud (1937, p. 245) comments, 'we should be tempted to maintain that the two are identical, if it were not for the difference that the Greek philosopher's theory is a cosmic phantasy while ours is content to claim biological validity.'

Psychoanalysis as science

This last quotation points to a set of issues that have surrounded psychoanalysis from its earliest Freudian days and that continue to lap around it. These centre on the question of the extent to which psychoanalysis can be thought of as a science. Freud's view on this, expressed most firmly in his New Introductory 'Lecture' on *The Question of a Weltanschauung*, was unequivocal. A *Weltanschauung* is 'an intellectual construction which solves all the problems of our existence uniformly on the basis of one overriding hypothesis, which, accordingly, leaves no question unanswered and in which everything that interests us finds its fixed place' (Freud, 1933, p. 158). Having defined it in this way, Freud then asserts (p. 181), 'Psychoanalysis, in my opinion, is incapable of creating a *Weltanschauung* of its own. It does not need one; it is a part of science and can adhere to the scientific *Weltanschauung.*' Psychoanalysis is 'a specialist science, a branch of psychology,' (p. 158) unfit to create its own attitude towards or view of the world. The fact that it deals with subjective issues – what Freud calls the 'mental field' – makes no difference, 'since the intellect and the mind are objects for scientific research in exactly the same way as any non-human things' (p. 160). What psychoanalysis contributes is an application of the scientific method and point of view to wishes and other unconscious mental events, but it can adopt the ways neither of art nor of religion, though it can be used to analyse these. Science, and with it psychoanalysis, must contest the ground of explanation, and triumph. 'It is simply a fact that the truth cannot be tolerant, that it admits of no compromises or limitations, that research regards every sphere of human activity as belonging to it and that it must be relentlessly critical if any other power tries to take over any part of it' (p. 160).

Given Freud's very strong view on the superiority of the scientific perspective, it is ironic that one of the strongest criticisms of psychoanalysis has been over its *lack* of scientific standing. Hans Eysenck (1985, p. 208), an irrepressible debunker of psychoanalysis, pronounced of Freud:

> He was, without doubt, a genius, not of science, but of propaganda, not of rigorous proof, but of persuasion, not of the design of experiments, but of literary art. His place is not, as he claimed, with Copernicus and Darwin, but with Hans Christian Anderson and the Brothers Grimm, tellers of fairy tales.

For Ernest Gellner (1985), a major figure in twentieth-century anthropology, psychoanalysis is a 'mystical' practice. For the philosopher Karl Popper (1959), psychoanalysis was unscientific because its basic assertions are untestable, or at least 'non-falsifiable'. For example, an interpretation cannot be proved wrong because whatever happens (say, a patient denying the truth of what has been said or going off onto a tangential subject after the interpretation has been made) can itself be interpreted, by the tenets of psychoanalysis, as a form of resistance. For Adolf Grünbaum (1984), on the other hand, Freud's claims concerning interpretation can be tested – and when they are, they are found wanting. Grünbaum's argument is in a long tradition seeing psychoanalytic practice as a mode of *suggestion*, in which the persuasive power of the analyst subtly or directly influences the patient to think in certain ways. This may at times be therapeutically helpful, but it is not tenable as evidence of the truthfulness of psychoanalytic claims about the existence of the unconscious or the accuracy of interpretations.

Explanations and causes

There are numerous responses to these accusations of scientific inadequacy, ranging from claims that empirical studies can be found that do in fact support many psychoanalytic theories, to assertions that the issue of whether or not it is scientific misses the main point. One important distinction is between an *explanatory* or *causal* approach and an *interpretive* or *hermeneutic* one. Freud certainly saw himself as seeking the former, in the sense that the concept of the unconscious was drawn on to explain behaviour or experiences that could not otherwise be made sense of. A dream could be explained by the unacknowledged wish to which it gave disguised expression; a slip of the tongue would arise from an unacceptable unconscious impulse; a neurotic symptom might be due to an irresolvable conflict between the urge to express something and the anxiety to which that urge gives rise. In each of these cases, uncovering the unconscious underpinnings of the observed behaviour (the dream, slip or symptom) explains it not just by making sense of it, but specifically by pointing to its *cause*. The dream happens *because of* the wish, the slip *because of* the impulse, the symptom *because of* the conflict. Identifying the unconscious source of a phenomenon is the same thing as explaining it; removing that source would remove the phenomenon itself.

While this 'strong' account of the role of the unconscious in determining psychological events was Freud's aspiration, it has numerous difficulties. One was clearly recognized by Freud himself, under the term *over-determination*. This means that any single event might have multiple causes. In Freud's account, this refers to multiple *unconscious* causes, but one could equally well argue that an unconscious idea might always be necessary but not sufficient to explain something. For instance, a dream might be explained by a current conscious worry due to 'real world' events which have triggered an unconscious anxiety left over from childhood; both the conscious and the unconscious factors would then be different kinds of causes of the dream. More importantly, however, it may be that the unconscious 'sense' of something is not exactly its cause, but rather is what it 'signifies' to the subject. The dream might not be caused by the unconscious wish in a straightforward way; it might just indicate that this wish exists.

There is also a difference between what might be termed 'retrospective' and 'prospective' accounts. The former try to identify the previous events that gave rise to something; the latter are more interested in what the phenomena in question produce. It might be easier to follow this if one considers the role of interpretation (interpretation is discussed in more detail in Chapter 17). One view is that an interpretation names something that already exists and is the actual cause of an event – for instance a feeling of having been rejected by one's parents, or of being haunted by some trauma from long ago. In naming this, the interpretation identifies the actual cause of, say, a neurotic symptom. An alternative is to see what happens when one uses an interpretation to open out a new way of thinking. The interpretation could explore the unconscious resonance of the event – for instance what a slip of the tongue makes the speaker think of. This means that the interpretation does not have to be 'accurate'. It is more important that it is 'productive', leading to more elaborate and complex thinking that can enable the person concerned to escape their tired and self-defeatingly repetitious usual ways of being.

In line with these notions, the psychoanalytic method has been seen by some as a mode of hermeneutics, which basically means that it offers ways to interpret material that comes from the unconscious. This idea is perhaps now the dominant view. It makes fewer claims than does the causal model, but again one has to say that it is not wholly what Freud might have liked. The question is in part whether psychoanalysis retains its power if it no longer claims that the unconscious is a real discovery rather than, less ambitiously, a way of elaborating meaning.

The occult side of Freud

The emphasis on Freud the scientist is one side of the reality of Freud. It certainly reflects his context in the second half of the nineteenth century, in which scientific advances were enormous and were highly celebrated, and in which it seemed possible that scientific progress might produce a newly advanced state of civilization freed from the neuroses of the past. Freud shared this hope. In his major work on religion, tellingly entitled *The Future of an Illusion*, Freud (1927) was particularly clear on this: psychoanalysis would be the rational science that would reveal the sources of the religious impulse and hence transcend it. This was always Freud's attitude towards religion. He was a hard-line atheist, and his interest in religion was due to its power over its adherents, not because he believed in its truths.

Nevertheless, while Freud might have been a devotee of rationalism and scientific progress, this does not mean that he had no links with the other side of things – the irrational and even the occult. To a considerable extent this was presented as applying the methods of 'psychoanalytic science' to areas usually given up to occultism, in order to make better sense of them. However, even where Freud wrote in this vein, there is a sense that something else might be at work. For instance, in his text *Psycho-Analysis and Telepathy*, Freud (1921) provides a clear exposition of what psychoanalysis has to do with the occult. He argues (pp. 178–9) that there are links between psychoanalysis and occultism not only in how they are treated as outsiders by 'official science', but also because they are concerned to understand the 'unrecognized characteristics' of mind and spirit. This suggests an affinity between the two that speaks sufficiently strongly to Freud to make occultism of interest to him. However, the difference between occultism and psychoanalysis is a profound one, rooted in the difference between 'convinced believers who are looking for confirmation' and the openness of a critical scientific mind, which is 'incorrigibly' materialist. But Freud also showed that he was rather impressed with the materiality of the claims occultists might make, at least in some areas. In particular, Freud thought telepathy might be genuine and might well be linked to the kind of phenomena that were turning up in the psychoanalytic situation. This can be seen, for instance, in a passage from the lecture called *Dreams and Occultism* in the 1933 *New Introductory Lectures on Psycho-Analysis*. First, Freud acknowledges his own temptation towards the 'dark side', stating (p. 53), 'It may be that I too have a secret inclination towards the miraculous which thus goes half way to meet the creation of occult facts.' Freud proceeds from here to argue that the existence of what he calls 'thought-transference' and hence of telepathy is an 'objective possibility' and indeed that psychoanalysis might provide an explanation of it. Throwing caution to the wind, he then goes so far as to suggest that telepathy might be 'phylogenetically' (that is, in the origin of the species) the fundamental form of communication.

> If only one accustoms oneself to the idea of telepathy, one can accomplish a great deal with it – for the time being, it is true, only in imagination. ... One is led to a suspicion that this is the original, archaic method of communication between individuals and that in the course of phylogenetic evolution it has been replaced by the better method of giving information with the help of signals which are picked up by the sense organs. But the older method might have persisted in the background and still be able to put itself into effect under certain conditions – for instance, in passionately excited mobs. All this is still uncertain and full of unsolved riddles; but there is no reason to be frightened by it. (p. 55)

What is instructive about this is how it combines Freud's wish to place everything on a scientific basis with his willingness to make himself open to any kind of experience, and his tendency from time to time to give credit to the existence of material that is usually seen as disreputable and at odds with scientific progress. This might seem like an aberration, and to protect his followers Freud did state clearly that his belief in telepathy should be seen as his own personal affair, and not essential to psychoanalysis. However, it is reasonable to claim that in being open to the reality of at least some occult phenomena, Freud was displaying some important aspects of psychoanalysis itself.

Psychoanalysis deals with many of the same issues that occultism did – suggestion, hypnotism, thought transference, the weird way in which people would act as if under the control of forces that they could not name. It was not accidental in this respect that British psychoanalysis had roots in the Society for Psychical Research, of which Freud was a corresponding member (Hinshelwood, 1995): the question of *influence* in the sense of transmission of forces 'unconsciously' between people (and between the living and the dead) was a major one in late Victorian society. Perhaps this represented the underside of the advance in scientific knowledge, as people struggled both to retain a sense of the spiritual and also to account for things that science could not understand. In any event, Freud's work was of great interest to psychic researchers, and seemed to offer a lot of additional explanatory power to their own theories.

This relates to a more general issue. Freud's openness to the occult, understood as what cannot be easily understood or explained away, was of a piece with his approach to the *psychiatric* conundrums of his day. Hysteria, for example, had been described and explained in many ways, none of them satisfactory. Freud showed himself willing to think some unthinkable things: for instance, that male hysteria might exist, that hysteria might have psychological origins, that sexuality might be of central importance, and that the talk of hysterics might have meaning. Perhaps we can go so far as to say that in his approach to hysteria he revealed exactly the tension that has surrounded psychoanalysis from its beginnings. On the one hand, it is a scientific approach that attempts to make rational sense of apparently irrational events. Consequently, it aims to make the unconscious conscious, so that it can be better understood and mastered – exactly as science tries to do with all other natural phenomena. On the other hand, rather like those romantic poets who celebrate the wildness of nature and seek to allow it expression in their work, Freud *gave voice* to hysteria, allowing the wishes and fantasies of his patients space in the pages of his texts as well as in the consulting room. This means that there is a sense in which Freud let the genie of the unconscious out of its bottle in order to view it fully; but like all such genies, once it was free it was never quite possible to keep it under control. Psychoanalysis is thus not an occult practice, but in its readiness to let the unconscious speak, it acknowledges the reality and significance of the irrational in human life. In the next chapter, we shall look at what this unconscious has to say.

Summary

- Freud aspired to creating psychoanalysis as a scientific practice that would bring rational order to the understanding of internal psychological events.

4

The Freudian unconscious

Discovering the unconscious

Ask someone to free associate to the word 'Freud' and the likelihood is that there will be a small number of words that will come to that person's mind rapidly and predictably. 'Sex' is one, 'dreams' another; maybe even some apparently esoteric terms such as 'Oedipus complex' will appear. High up on the list, however, will be 'the unconscious', for it was with the discovery of a particular kind of 'unconscious mind' that Freudian psychoanalysis came into its own. In essence, the discovery or invention of the unconscious arose from Freud's clinical work. Observing how his patients behaved, Freud found himself forced to speculate that behind otherwise inexplicable gaps in awareness or in their ability to make sense of their own actions, there must be something lurking. This 'something' is the unconscious, or more accurately (as there is no 'place' called the unconscious) it is a system of unconscious ideas. Freud describes his own thought processes here in terms of an inescapable logic, even an understanding that he did not necessarily want to have. 'We have found,' writes Freud (1923, p. 14), 'that is, we have been obliged to assume – that very powerful mental processes or ideas exist ... which can produce all the effects in mental life that ordinary ideas do ... though they themselves do not become conscious.' The phrase 'obliged to assume' presumably means that he could think of no other explanation for what he was hearing in his consulting room and that he therefore hypothesized the existence of unobservable things, a common practice in science generally (nobody can actually *see* the force of gravity, but postulating its existence explains events that are definitely observable, and predicts others). But it also has another resonance, well in tune with the characteristics of unconscious life: that *despite himself* Freud had to assume the existence of the unconscious, that somehow he did not wish to do this, but could not avoid it.

This idea that the unconscious is an unwelcome notion is a useful one for understanding arguments about resistances to psychoanalysis itself and about the controversial nature of its history. The problem with unconscious ideas is that no one can catch them; they can only be assumed to exist because without them nothing would make sense. For Freud, it is in this production of 'sense' that the best evidence for the unconscious actually exists. In his *Introductory Lectures on Psycho-Analysis* (1917a, p. 288), he states, 'the possibility of giving a sense to neurotic symptoms by analytic interpretation is an unshakeable proof of the existence – or, if you prefer it, of the necessity for the hypothesis – of unconscious mental processes.' 'Sense' here is a particular kind of meaning; it not only allows one to understand a psychological event, but it explains that event in a causal way, and in so doing it also makes a difference to it.

An obsessional case

A famous example from Freud's exposition of 'the sense of symptoms' might help here (Freud, 1917a, pp. 261–3). Incidentally, it reveals a lot about the social situation in which Freud worked, with its assumption of a bride's virginity, separate bedrooms for husband and wife, and a cast of servants whose expectations of appropriate behaviour have to be met. Freud describes a female patient of nearly 30 with obsessional symptoms including the following action, which she had to perform several times a day.

> She ran from her room into another neighbouring one, took up a particular position there beside a table that stood in the middle, rang the bell for her housemaid, sent her on some indifferent errand or let her go without one, and then ran back into her own room.

Freud comments, 'This was certainly not a very distressing symptom, but was nevertheless calculated to excite curiosity.' He reports that whenever he asked the patient 'Why do you do that?

What sense has it?' she answered, 'I don't know.' But one day, after Freud 'had succeeded in defeating a major, fundamental doubt of hers, she suddenly knew the answer.'

> More than ten years before, she had married a man very much older than herself, and on the wedding-night he was impotent. Many times during the night he had come running from his room into hers to try once more, but every time without success. Next morning he had said angrily: 'I should feel ashamed in front of the housemaid when she makes the bed,' took up a bottle of red ink that happened to be in the room and poured its contents over the sheet, but not on the exact place where a stain would have been appropriate. I could not understand at first what this recollection had to do with the obsessional action in question; the only resemblance I could find was in the repeated running from one room into the other, and perhaps also in the entrance of the housemaid. My patient then led me up to the table in the second room and showed me a big stain on the tablecloth. She further explained that she took up her position in relation to the table in such a way that the maid who had been sent for could not fail to see the stain. There could no longer be any doubt of the intimate connection between the scene on her wedding-night and her present obsessional action, though all kinds of other things remained to be learnt.

Freud notes that the patient was identifying herself with her husband and also that the table and tablecloth in her ritual took the place of the bed and sheet. As 'table and bed together stand for marriage ... the one can easily take the place of the other,' he comments. This makes sense of the patient's action, with one addition that Freud is alert to and that explains its *intention*, that is, what unconscious psychological wish it is aiming to fulfil.

> Its kernel was obviously the summoning of the housemaid, before whose eyes the patient displayed the stain, in contrast to her husband's remark that he would feel ashamed in front of the maid. Thus he, whose part she was playing, did not feel ashamed in front of the maid; accordingly the stain was in the right place. We see, therefore, that she was not simply repeating the scene, she was

continuing and at the same time correcting it; she was putting it right. But by this she was also correcting the other thing, which had been so distressing that night and had made the expedient with the red ink necessary – his impotence. So the obsessional action was saying: 'No, it's not true. He had no need to feel ashamed in front of the housemaid; he was not impotent.' It represented this wish, in the manner of a dream, as fulfilled in a present-day action; it served the purpose of making her husband superior to his past mishap.

Just as a dream is fuelled by an unconscious wish, so the explanation of the woman's bizarre ritual is understandable in terms of the wish to make good her wedding night and to protect her husband from gossip. There are other complications in this case that Freud goes on to describe, but the main point for us is that in offering an account of these unconscious wishes, Freud has made previously 'mad' behaviour comprehensible. In this way, the unconscious is an explanatory device that makes convincing narrative sense of psychological phenomena. Without it, psychoanalysts would argue, there are too many such phenomena that are left making no sense at all.

The nature of the unconscious

According to Freud, the unconscious is one of three ways in which ideas can be expressed. Thoughts can be:

1. *Conscious*, which means they are in awareness.
2. *Preconscious*, which indicates that they are not conscious but are nevertheless available for thinking, should the person concerned need them (for instance words one knows, or a memory of something such as where one has parked one's car).
3. *Unconscious*, which means they are repressed and inaccessible.

These types of ideas are also contained in different *systems*, initially called by Freud the 'systems Cs., Pcs. and Ucs.' each with its own laws (these will be described in more detail in Chapter 7). In the case of the system Ucs, these laws are at odds with the usual parameters of everyday life. 'There are in this system,' writes Freud (1915c,

p. 186), 'no negation, no doubt, no degrees of certainty.' The unconscious dispenses with time, with the need to avoid contradiction, with normal reality and judgement processes. Dreams, which are relatively uncensored expressions of unconscious ideas, are a good example here: in dreams, past, present and future combine, and all sorts of impossible things can be experienced. Anything can happen, yet unconscious ideas do follow certain laws of their own, in that they express wishes and intentions and deploy symbols in relatively predictable ways. On the other hand, the unconscious is not directly knowable. In ways that are not completely dissimilar to some religious views of God, psychoanalysis asserts that the unconscious can only be known negatively. It is seen by its effects in what appears unexpectedly in someone's speech or in the bungled actions, dreams or symptoms of a person as they blunder through life. It is knowable only in this secondary way because it is defined basically as *what is not accessible to consciousness*, as that which functions as 'other' to the norm, as a great 'negation'. Once we try to describe it, it wriggles away; so we are left only saying that unconscious ideas are not rational or time-bound or logical.

This all sounds quite mystical, but thankfully there are other things to say about the Freudian unconscious. The main one is that it is a *dynamic* system, in the sense that it is understood as designating a set of psychological forces that are *active*, as opposed, for example, to simply being in a kind of long-term store from which they can be removed to be used when needed. The Freudian unconscious is a motivational system in which ideas that are pressing for expression are held back by an opposing force (generically called 'repression') because they are too unsettling or anxiety-producing. This means that in an important sense, repression causes the unconscious. Because certain ideas cannot be allowed full flow, yet are of central significance to the person, there has to be a place or (better) a state in which they can be stored. 'The repressed is the prototype of the unconscious for us', Freud (1923, p. 15) writes, highlighting how unconscious material is actively kept out of consciousness by a process or force that refuses it entry. So the model is that there are unconscious ideas – wishes, in the main – which actively press for expression but which for one reason or another are too dangerous to countenance. An opposing, repressing force therefore operates on them to keep them in check.

This vision of the unconscious as a space of dynamic activity has given rise to the general term *psychodynamic* to refer to theories and therapies based on this idea. Although there is considerable variation among these approaches, they share the notion that there are unconscious ideas operating at some kind of 'depth', which means they are not visible directly on the 'surface' of psychological functioning, yet they are always looking for ways to break through. They are in motion, hidden from awareness yet still active ('dynamic') and pushing for release. Repressed, unconscious material has not been destroyed or put to sleep, but has a life of its own, with its own build-ups and releases of tension. This does not mean it loses its power; quite the contrary, in fact, in that as certain ideas become hidden from the light of consciousness they actually become more difficult to manage, and keep seeping out or breaking through in peculiar ways. This is why a deeply repressed idea, such as the memory of a trauma, might be the source of powerful effects many years after the event. *Because* it is hidden, it cannot be properly dealt with.

Freud notes that, if anything, unconscious material develops more energetically than material governed by conscious thought, which always has to take into account the constraints imposed by reality or social respectability. Unconscious material 'proliferates in the dark' (Freud, 1915c, p. 149), where it is freed from these constraints; this makes it more exciting but also more anxiety-provoking. In relation to neurosis, for instance, what he calls the 'instinctual representative' (by which he means the psychological expression of biological drives) 'takes on extreme forms of expression, which when they are translated and presented to the neurotic are not only bound to seem alien to him, but frighten him by giving him the picture of an extraordinary and dangerous strength of instinct' (ibid.). Dreams and nightmares demonstrate the exaggerated nature of fantasy; the very fact of an idea being unconscious encourages it to become stronger and harder to control.

Working with the unconscious

The obvious implication of all this is that in order to understand a person fully, one needs to trace the unconscious sources of their actions; and once one has done this, one might be in a position to make them conscious and help the person move away at least from the nightmarish elements of their situation. Freud himself was not very optimistic about this process. Early on, in his 1895 book with Josef Breuer, *Studies on Hysteria*, he describes a challenge from an imaginary patient:

> Why, you tell me yourself that my illness is probably connected with my circumstances and the events of my life. You cannot alter these in any way. How do you propose to help me then?

Freud's reply is a very clear statement of what the limits of therapy might be:

> No doubt fate would find it easier than I do to relieve you of your illness. But you will be able to convince yourself that much will be gained if we succeed in transforming your hysterical misery into common unhappiness. (Breuer and Freud, 1895, p. 305)

And very late in life he said something not that radically different: 'Our impression is that we must not be surprised if the difference between the person who has not and the person who has been analysed is, after all, not so radical as we endeavour to make it and expect and assert that it will be' (Freud, 1937, p. 383). These limits are due both to the impact of external circumstances, which cannot be changed by psychoanalysis, and also to the strength of the urge towards *repetition*; caught up in unconscious conflicts, people are very much attached to their continuing mistakes. Psychoanalysis can help, but it is never going to be an easy task to free people from long-standing ways of being and behaving that even when they appear self-destructive, might be protecting them from what they imagine would be worse.

Despite the difficulty of bringing about change, the psychoanalytic belief that there is something in the nature of an unconscious idea that resists words suggests that if that idea can be named it might become easier to deal with. Freud (1915c, p. 201) argues that the difference between a conscious and an unconscious idea is that the former 'comprises the presentation of the thing plus the presentation of the word belonging to it, while the unconscious presentation is the presentation of the thing alone.' Unconscious ideas, lying outside language, act in an unmediated 'thing-like' way. This is part of the sense one has of them: how often do people feel that something unknown and thing-like is acting inside them? It may even be part of the attraction of films like Ridley Scott's (1979) *Alien*. There are strange and vicious things in the universe, but perhaps these are only external reflections of the strange, vicious and alien aspects of ourselves. Once these internal 'things' are named, however, there is the possibility that they can be brought into the light of consciousness. Seeing them clearly in this way, having the words to control and express them, is precisely what makes them no longer unconscious. This emphasis on finding the right words to name what is unconscious and call it one's own is why psychoanalysis is fairly dubbed 'the talking cure' and, it is claimed, is also the reason why, from time to time, psychotherapy might work.

Freud expresses this very clearly in a late work in which he also uses the terminology of the 'id', 'ego' and 'superego' to refer to different structures in the mind. This 'structural model' will be described more fully in Chapter 7, as it complicates things by not overlapping straightforwardly with the earlier division between the unconscious, conscious and preconscious. Put simply, the ego (the Latinized translation of Freud's 'Ich', better thought of as the 'I') is the centre of perception and consciousness, while the id (the 'Es' or 'it') is the structure in which unconscious drives and thing-like impulses reside. The superego is the internalized set of judgements and punishments that govern much of the psychic economy of guilt within each of us. Using this nomenclature, Freud (1933, p. 80) describes the aims of therapy revealingly in terms of how ideas get translated from one structure to another. The intention of psychoanalysis, he says, is 'to strengthen the ego, to make it more independent of the super-ego, to widen its field of perception and enlarge its organization, so that it can appropriate fresh portions of the id. Where id was, there ego shall be. It is a work of culture – not unlike the draining of the Zuider Zee.' Here the sea is drained in order to make it available for human use, a 'work of culture'. Similarly, the unconscious is drained or rather channelled into consciousness so that its energy can be more easily used for the work of human activity, again for 'culture'. Psychoanalysis makes this possible, to some degree anyway, by giving voice to the unconscious. This will always challenge everyday norms, but it also allows unconscious ideas to be better managed, indeed to become what one might term 'cultivated' desires.

The unconscious as portrayed by Freud is thus a powerful, active state in which important, emotionally charged ideas are held. One question that arises from this is what it is that 'fuels' unconscious material, in the sense of giving it the energy that it uses in motivating and disrupting people's lives. Freud's own suggestion, that at the root of the unconscious lies a set of biological *drives*, has become one of the more controversial aspects of psychoanalytic theory. It is to describing what he means by this that the next chapter is devoted.

Summary

- The unconscious is an explanatory concept deployed to make sense of psychological phenomena.
- Identifying the unconscious wish out of which an action arises means that one has explained that action and has also made it more amenable to conscious control.
- The unconscious is also a system (the system Ucs) with its own attributes, mostly defined negatively as 'other than' conscious rational thought.
- The key characteristic of the Freudian unconscious is that it is dynamic. Unconscious ideas are pushing for expression and are being kept out of awareness by a set of opposing forces. The dynamic nature of unconscious ideas explains how they can be causal in their effects.
- Unconscious ideas are more like 'things' than words, and feel that way when they express themselves. This links with the psychoanalytic perspective on therapy, which aims to give voice to unconscious ideas so that they can be brought into consciousness and better managed or used in the service of the person and of culture.
- Freud was pessimistic about how successfully this therapeutic ambition could be carried out.

5
Sex, aggression, life and death

What drives us on

The concept of a drive has immediate appeal as a way of describing what it feels like to be under the sway of the unconscious. Sometimes we are 'driven' to do things that do not seem to be within our control. We might feel an impulse to damage something, or be overwhelmed by anger, or fall in love, or be inescapably sad. These things have the sense of being unwilled – they come upon us not necessarily as a response to external circumstances (though this might happen), but as a result of a pressure from within. While Freud's ideas about the nature and centrality of drives were theoretically derived and fitted into a widely held set of ideas of his time, this 'phenomenological' element, in which what is being captured is the *experience* of being compelled to do something, is also quite close to the concerns of psychoanalysis.

What is a drive? For one thing, it is not an 'instinct', despite the decision by Freud's early translators to render his German word 'trieb' as 'instinct'. An instinct is an automatic response of some kind to an environmental stimulus; it is biologically programmed but specific and limited in its zone of activity. *Drives*, however, are basic biological forces operating all the time and fuelling the psychological activities of the mind. In what are known as his 'metapsychological' series of papers, published in 1915, Freud offers two slightly different definitions of a drive. On the one hand, in *Instincts and their Vicissitudes* (in the original German, *Triebe Und Triebschicksale*), he says it is 'a concept on the frontier between the mental and the somatic' (Freud, 1915a, p. 122), and suggests it can be thought of as something that operates in the mind. This implies that the drive itself is a psychological entity. In his paper on *The Unconscious*, however, written at about the same time, Freud clearly differentiates between drives and the ideas that symbolize them.

> An instinct [drive] can never become an object of consciousness – only the idea that represents the instinct can. Even in the unconscious, moreover, an instinct cannot be represented otherwise than by an idea. (Freud, 1915c, p. 177)

This inconsistency seems to be a real one and to reveal Freud's uncertainty about the exact connection between body and mind (or brain and mind, in today's neuroscientific framework). In turn, this reflects a complicated relationship between what is unconscious and what is conscious. Perhaps the most satisfactory way of thinking about it is that there are basic biological urges operating within the individual, and these are expressed in psychological and behavioural ways. Some of these expressions are conscious, some unconscious. So, to take the most prominent example, there is a drive, developed through evolutionary processes, which gives rise to the fantasies and behaviours associated with sexuality. It thus makes sense to call it a 'sexual' drive, but the point is that it is a biological *tendency* which is expressed in various ways in the actual unconscious and conscious life of individuals. There is unlikely ever to be a 'pure' expression of this drive and a sexual fantasy cannot be seen as the same as the underlying drive, as it is affected by processes of socialization and by the broad range of experiences a person might have. But every activity is fuelled at least in part by this drive. What then makes it sexual? This is one of the more profound and controversial elements of the Freudian scheme.

The sexual drive

Freud decided early on that the roots of psychological life would have to reside in conflict – that only conflict between different forces could explain the ways in which people tie themselves in knots. After all, why would hysterical symptoms have to substitute for sexual desires if it were not the case that those sexual impulses were in conflict with other forces? For Freud, these 'other forces' were not solely those put in place by a sexually repressive society, but were internal to the person her or himself.

Throughout his psychoanalytic career, Freud assumed that the conflict would be between two major classes of drive, although in 1920 he made a radical revision in his thinking about what exactly these drives were. The initial dichotomy was between what he called 'sexual' and 'ego-preservative' drives, which he loosely translated as 'love and hunger', and this division served psychoanalysis well for quite a long time. Although these two elements are formally equal in status, in fact most of the attention of early psychoanalysis was focused on sexuality. The central claim here is simply that sexuality is the fundamental driving force behind psychic life. It is sexual energy and the sexual drive that is at the source of human behaviour and unconscious conflict. Sexuality is biologically rooted, but it does not *reduce* to biology: that is, the sexual drive is somehow *excessive*, more than is needed simply to keep the species going. Sexuality, according to psychoanalysis, works in the service of pleasure rather than of reproduction. Freud believed that this claim was one reason for opposition to psychoanalysis, and it is certainly the case that psychoanalysis very quickly polarized people because of its commitment to the idea of sexual pleasure as the core of human striving, and its refusal to judge this as in any way wrong.

> The concept of 'sexuality', and at the same time of the sexual instinct, had, it is true, to be extended so as to cover many things which could not be classed under the reproductive function; and this caused no little hubbub in an austere, respectable or merely hypocritical world. (Freud, 1920, p. 51)

Freud's opposition to sexual hypocrisy was an early way in which psychoanalysis committed itself to social critique, putting it at odds with social conventions although not necessarily with the escalating interest in sexuality that marked its time.

Sexuality is thus not a procreative urge, but a summary term for pleasure, defined as a kind of ecstatic release that occurs as a result of the drive finding a means of expression. This can be understood most easily thorough a brief description of the components of the drive, which Freud lists as its 'pressure', its 'aim', its 'object' and its 'source'.

Components of the drive

Freud provides a clear account of these different components of the drive in *Instincts and their Vicissitudes* (1915a, pp. 122–3).

- *Pressure* is 'the amount of force or the measure of the demand for work' which the drive represents. This simply characterizes what a drive is like: it is a force operating on the psyche. The strength of this force is in principle a quantitative matter.
- The *aim* of a drive 'is in every instance satisfaction, which can only be obtained by removing the state of stimulation at the source of the instinct.' Basically, this means that 'satisfaction' occurs when the raised tension in the organism is reduced. This idea fits the sexual model very well, but is maybe not as convincing when applied to some other aspects of life such as curiosity or the excitement-seeking behaviour that is characteristic of sport or many cultural activities. Here it seems that *raising* 'tension' might itself be pleasurable. In Freud's scheme, there is also space for what he termed 'aim-inhibited' versions of the drive, 'in the case of processes which are allowed to make some advance towards instinctual satisfaction but are then inhibited or deflected.' What this means is that reduction of tension is not complete, but is nevertheless sufficient to allow some degree of satisfaction. Friendship, for instance, might be such an aim-inhibited version of the sexual drive. It is motivated by the sexual drive, but it does not necessarily culminate in sexual acts. This means that the satisfaction involved is only partial because the 'aim' of the drive has been 'inhibited' for social or psychological reasons.
- The *object* of the drive has become increasingly central in post-Freudian psychoanalytic theory. It is that component of the drive that is linked to the outside world and therefore is most likely to be called into play when considering the relationships that a person forms – which are usually most of what they talk about in psychoanalysis. The object, according to Freud (1915a, p. 122), 'is the thing in regard to which or through which the instinct is able to achieve its aim. It is what is most variable about an instinct and is not originally connected with it, but becomes assigned to it only in consequence of being peculiarly fitted to make satisfaction possible.' This definition is deliberately abstract. The object is not necessarily

another person or part of the person; it might not even be external to the person at all, but could easily be (and often is) 'a part of the subject's own body.' The object is *contingent*, in the sense that it just happens to be what eases the tension produced by the drive; and over the course of a lifetime, the object will therefore shift and vary. Too strong an attachment of a drive to an object becomes a 'fixation'; and continually returning to the satisfaction produced by an object more appropriate to an earlier stage of development might be a 'regression'. But still, some objects – for instance the mother or the mother's breast – are likely to be of overwhelming importance. The psychoanalytic assumption is that when these objects are in some way unreliable, perhaps sometimes gratifying and at other times not, psychopathology is likely to arise. For example, a mother suffering from postnatal depression may not be able to give her infant the experience of a lively, fulfilling presence (a 'gratifying breast') leaving the child feeling neglected or unloved, or perhaps as if it is the child's job to enliven the mother – to wake her up by being interesting, rewarding or compliant. If this situation extends over a significant period of time, this could lay the basis for the child to become someone who never feels loved for her or himself, and fears that intimate relationships will always fall apart.

- The final component, the *source*, relates the drive to its biological origins. Freud (1915a, p. 123) states that 'The study of the sources of instincts lies outside the scope of psychology.' By this he means that the source is a physiological feature of the drive (he speculates on whether it is 'invariably of a chemical nature'). He differentiates between this and what is properly psychological on the basis of what enters mental life as an idea. Only the latter can be known. Nevertheless, the bodily location or focus of the drive is important, and in Freudian developmental theory it gives rise to an account of the different ways in which the sexual drive is organized. So the first stage is the *oral* one, in which sexuality is connected with sucking and biting; the second stage is *anal*, where enjoyment is located around the excretory function; and the later stages are *phallic* and *genital* as those sexual organs come more to be the foci of sexual life. The drive in each case is the same – the sexual drive – and no doubt its source in specific chemical changes is also consistent; what varies is the physical location of sexuality and the social form it takes.

The other drive

This account of the nature and components of drives is very focused on sexuality, but Freud was at pains to argue that there is always an opposing force at work. This was partly because he assumed there is something threatening about the free expression of sexual urges that could lead to the destruction of the individual rather than to pleasure. He therefore proposed the existence of a group of what he called 'ego-preservative' drives, including hunger and thirst, which ensures the continuing survival of the person. This group of drives acts against the sexual drive to prevent the ego being overwhelmed by anxiety or being placed in a dangerous situation of social rejection. The conflict between sexual and ego-preservative drives is what then produces repression and the location of certain wishes 'in' the unconscious. This is why, for example, dreams occur: they protect sleep (necessary for ego preservation) by allowing unconscious wishes to be expressed in disguised forms and without the normal consequences attached to them. Neurotic symptoms are similar: they are compromises between the two drives, whereby a sexual wish is partially fulfilled – although, unfortunately, this is to the satisfaction of neither class of drive. And various creative activities, such as the production of art objects, derive from the expression of the sexual impulse in a disguised form, more socially acceptable than, say, masturbating in public.

Although there is a clear and simple logic to the opposition between sexual and ego-preservative drives, problems arose as Freud developed his theory in the period around 1914. The first major difficulty was due to the development of his ideas about *narcissism*. This arose from a set of observations suggesting that the ego, which was supposedly the *opponent* of the sexual drive, was itself full of sexual urges and could become the object of sexual desires. We might say that the ego 'loves itself', which is why the label 'narcissistic' applies. If this is so, it suggests that 'libido' (sexual energy) fuels the ego, which therefore could not be seen as opposing sexuality. The distinction between sexual and ego-preservative drives consequently threatened to disappear, and with it Freud's whole dualistic model.

This was compounded by Freud's reflections on the traumatic neuroses shown by soldiers in the First World War (which were sometimes treated remarkably successfully by versions of psychoanalysis) and indeed by the general devastation wrought by that war. It is worth recalling here that Freud bought into the view that science and rationalism would triumph over infantilism and mythological irrationalism. The extraordinary outpouring of irrational destructiveness in the heart of western civilization during the war was a considerable blow to his hopes and in some ways to his theory. In other respects, however, the outpouring of irrationalism might be exactly what a theory of the unconscious could explain.

War trauma pointed Freud in a different direction from his initial theory because it showed how some things are not pursued because they bring pleasure, but precisely for the opposite reason. Sometimes it seems that people hold onto and repeat the worst experiences they have, either in their dreams or in waking life. This might be because they are trying to master them or make sense of them, but whatever the case, it does not seem to be because they are finding pleasure in them. Putting these observations together, Freud came up in 1920 with a new theory proposing that the two classes of drive are not sexual and ego-preservative, but rather life (which includes *both* the sexual *and* the ego-preservative drives) and death. On the one side, that is, there is a force for elaboration and embellishment of life, for creating new and complex things; on the other side, a tendency towards destruction and dissolution, to the disappearance of the person in a kind of 'nirvana'.

The death drive

The new theory of the drives was born in Freud's (1920) book *Beyond the Pleasure Principle*. Psychoanalysis had proposed that the aim of the drives was satisfaction experienced in the form of pleasure. Yet, in neurotic behaviour and dreams the re-emergence of disturbing material could be observed again and again. Freud gives an example here from the play of his own young grandson. This example is much referenced and is one source for the later interest of psychoanalysts and psychotherapists in *infant observation* as a way of learning about child development.

Freud notes that the child, aged one and a half, was a good boy closely attached to his mother, but he had 'an occasional disturbing habit of taking any small objects he could get hold of and throwing them away from him into a corner, under the bed, and so on, so that hunting for his toys and picking them up was often quite a business. As he did this he gave vent to a loud, long-drawn-out "o-o-o-o", accompanied by an expression of interest and satisfaction.' Freud and the child's mother (Freud's daughter Sophie) agreed that this 'o-o-o-o' was a version of the German 'fort', meaning 'gone'. Then Freud makes an observation that confirms this hypothesis.

> The child had a wooden reel with a piece of string tied round it. It never occurred to him to pull it along the floor behind him, for instance, and play at its being a carriage. What he did was to hold the reel by the string and very skillfully throw it over the edge of his curtained cot, so that it disappeared into it, at the same time uttering his expressive 'o-o-o-o'. He then pulled the reel out of the cot again by the string and hailed its reappearance with a joyful 'da' ['there']. This, then, was the complete game – disappearance and return. As a rule one only witnessed its first act, which was repeated untiringly as a game in itself, though there is no doubt that the greater pleasure was attached to the second act. (p. 15)

Freud asks various questions about this game, but is most interested in the issue of how the repetition of the mother's departure can be understood given that it is very unlikely to be pleasurable. Freud was not satisfied with the first plausible explanation, which was that the child might be staging something he had no control over (his mother leaving) in order to fantasize that he could manage it (by bringing the cotton reel under control). There is in any case a considerable amount of other evidence that people plague themselves with unpleasant things. For instance, traumatic dreams are surprisingly common and apparently contradict Freud's well-known formulation that dreams are wish-fulfilments. What wish is being fulfilled when someone is subjected to deeply disturbing dreams night after night? What Freud calls the *compulsion to repeat* often brings up material which can never have been pleasurable, and which 'can never, even long ago, have brought satisfaction even to instinctual impulses which have since been repressed' (Freud, 1920, p. 20).

In the light of all this, Freud suggests that it is necessary to consider whether there may be another force at work other than the achievement of happiness. Surveying the wartime legacy of death all around, this would not contradict the idea of a drive achieving satisfaction by restoring the organism to rest, but would exaggerate it, or follow it through to its logical conclusion. Observation of the sexual life of humans had revealed that there exists a drive which aims at preserving living substances and joining them together into larger units. Now it was also clear that there must be 'another, contrary instinct seeking to dissolve those units and to bring them back to their primaeval, inorganic state' (Freud, 1930, p. 118). This would be a state of perfect rest and nothingness, a relief from all tension and unwanted stimulation – a state of death.

This idea of the death drive is very controversial as it seems to imply a kind of in-built destructiveness or 'original sin' in which people are intrinsically 'bad'. While some psychoanalysts have embraced this notion (for instance, Melanie Klein's reading of early development is largely based on it), others have baulked at the idea that there is inherent destructiveness and instead have wanted to understand it as the consequence of frustration and disappointment in life, particularly early life. There is also another issue to resolve. Freud introduced the death drive as a way to preserve the theory that there are two opposing drives at work in psychology. However, when one looks at it closely it is not clear that he succeeded in this. Both the life drive and the death drive pursue satisfaction through reduction of energy. In the former case it is by seeking an object that will achieve the aim of the drive; in the latter it is by reducing tension to zero through a return to an inactive state. This means that the basic functioning of the drive remains as it always was in Freud: the search for reduction of tension. It also suggests that the death drive is primary. 'The aim of all life is death,' writes Freud (1920, p. 38), and life is a big detour to enable the organism to die in a manner of its own choosing. So there are not really two opposed drives, but one drive towards destruction and a pull away from it into life.

Whatever one thinks of the idea of a death drive and whether it matters if there are two drives or only one, Freud's theory perhaps does describe a particular kind of phenomenon that is much in evidence in psychology: that people struggle to make something of themselves in the face of a very strong tendency to destroy everything around them. This makes the notion of the death drive an important one for dealing with individuals and with what are often intractable social conflicts. It also highlights another set of issues that Freudian theory had to deal with: if the mind is subjected to such powerful pressures as those embodied in the drives, how does it stay stable? What strategies do people use to fend off the unconscious impulses that constantly threaten to destroy their peace? This leads us to the next topic, the psychoanalytic account of mechanisms of defence.

Summary

- Drives are thought of as biological forces that are manifested psychologically through the emergence of certain ideas and behaviours.
- The components of drives are pressure, aim, object and source. The most important of these are the aim of the drive, which is satisfaction through release of tension, and the object, which is the entity that allows that release to occur.
- Freud always argued that there were two groups of drives in opposition with one another, although he changed his theory of what these two groups are.
- His first idea was of a conflict between sexual and ego-preservative drives, with the former being aimed at pleasure and the latter at protecting the individual from harm.
- Because of problems caused by theoretical developments around narcissism and observations of the recurrence of trauma, Freud changed his theory and proposed an opposition between a life drive and death drive.
- There are questions about how satisfactory this is, but the notion of a death drive does speak to the many instances of self- and other-destructiveness with which psychoanalysts and social theorists have to contend.

6

Repression and other defences

Protecting against threats

The previous chapter raised the issue of how people manage themselves in such a way as to achieve a certain degree of satisfaction while also protecting themselves against the full force of their unconscious impulses. This chapter describes the mechanisms that psychoanalysis proposes for doing this. These go under the title of 'defence mechanisms' and include a wide range of psychological strategies that are of central importance in making life liveable.

Self-protection is usually thought of as a basic and automatic response of the organism, human or otherwise, to threat. How is protection achieved? Often by taking some kind of evasive action, so that the threat is warded off or avoided altogether. Evasive action of this kind can work well, but it is also dangerous, because it involves waiting for the threat to materialize. There is thus a risk that the threat (the attack) will have an effect before it can be escaped from. A better idea is to have defences in place before the attack materializes. This still involves identifying a threat, but now well in advance of its actually making itself felt. Once one has built these defences, they tend to be permanent. This has advantages: one is always prepared in case of attack, and the defences can act to deter a potential aggressor. But permanent defences also have disadvantages. They need to be maintained in good order, which is costly and demands an expenditure of energy and (in the case of military and other physical defences) money. They can also become rigid and outdated, consuming resources that could be better used elsewhere (for instance on more appropriate defences). In particular, defences can preserve rather than resolve conflicts, by signalling continuing fear. They can also make it very hard to move forwards creatively.

In psychoanalysis, a defence is a mental action that blocks a perceived threat. This threat might come from outside, but commonly it is an *internal* threat. Effectively, some idea (a fantasy, wish or traumatic memory, for example) is experienced as dangerous to the ego and because of this it is defended against. One peculiarity of the system is that while the defences are real, it may be very hard for the person concerned to recognize that they are operating. This is because, psychologically speaking, if one acknowledges the threat it means it has already entered consciousness, and this is precisely what is unsettling and disturbing. If the threat comes from an unconscious idea it can only be managed if that idea remains unconscious. Once one recognizes it, or even recognizes that a defence has been activated against it, the idea will already have had its effect. The reasoning here, it might be noted, is exactly like that of security services dealing with threats to national security. From the point of view of the people of a country, once a threat becomes widely perceived, morale can be damaged and panic can set in. So not only do the security services try to block the threat, they do so secretly, not letting anyone know what they are dong. Similarly, psychological defence mechanisms are secret (unconscious) from the point of view of the observing ego so that the threats themselves remain unconscious. Only in this way can the ego stay calm.

Just as with military defences, psychological defences can go awry, especially if they become too inflexible. The issue here is how to deal with new circumstances, either 'external' ones such as new relationships or demands, or 'internal' ones such as growing older, becoming dependent, or getting ill. Defences might work very well in some circumstances or for a considerable length of time, but become outdated and inappropriately rigid when new situations arise. For instance, a defence against anger could be helpful when growing up with a psychologically fragile parent if the child fantasizes that expressing rage could damage that parent, on whom she or he is also dependent. But later on, the defence could be counterproductive, making it difficult to deal with events that stir up strong feelings. While any specific instance will have many subtleties and complexities, a very schematic 'case example' based on such a scenario could look like this.

A child of depressed parents feels herself to be unwanted and a burden. This generates anger in her that she can neither express nor even fully acknowledge to herself. The reason for this is an unconscious (but not necessarily unfounded) belief that if she showed her rage, her parents really would fall apart and abandon her.

Later on, this child – now an adult – is in an intimate relationship that turns sour and results in her being left. Her loss is acute and results in angry feelings similar to those that she harboured against her parents. Her long-held unconscious refusal to permit herself such anger means that she hides it from herself; but as such a process can never be fully successful (after all, the anger 'belongs' to her), she starts to feel guilty. Angry feelings are, in her mind, unacceptable and destructive, so her dim awareness that she harbours them means that she must be a bad person.

The result is that the anger that might have been unleashed towards the lost person is now turned inwards, as a punishment. This unconscious 'hostility turned against the self' is depression. The defence is therefore still operating effectively – she does not feel rage towards the other – but it is clearly self-destructive.

More generally, while defences remain necessary for survival, when they become rigid and severe they can produce symptoms and prevent psychological growth from occurring. The particular symptoms in question will relate to the specific defence used, a point which will be returned to below.

Repression

Defences can be defined as *unconscious psychological processes that ward off threatening unconscious ideas so that they leave as little trace as possible in consciousness*. It is worth noting in passing that while this is an accurate statement of the relationship between defences and consciousness, it is not quite the same as saying that defences protect the ego from unconscious ideas, because the defences themselves are (1) unconscious and are yet (2) properties of the ego. This is an issue that became clearer when Freud introduced, in 1923, his 'structural' division between ego, id and superego and proposed that the ego protects itself by mobilizing unconscious defences (the security apparatus, using the analogy of national security) against the unconscious elements of id and superego. The unconscious is thus set against itself, roughly following the lines of Freud's drive theory: sexual urges against ego-preservative ones; death drives against those dedicated to life.

The task of all defences is somehow to enable the person *not to know* what is happening 'unconsciously'. This can be achieved in various ways, but for Freud, the principle one was *repression*. This is both the most general and the most pervasive of defences, and can even be understood as a broad term for all the defensive activities that prevent an unconscious impulse from being acknowledged. Indeed, Freud defined much of psychoanalysis in terms of the action of repression and of repressed material. 'We obtain our concept of the unconscious from the theory of repression,' he wrote (Freud, 1923, p. 15). 'The repressed is the prototype of the unconscious for us.' Repression distinguished between the properly *un*conscious and the merely *pre*conscious (see Chapter 4). 'We see,' he wrote (ibid.), 'that we have two kinds of unconscious – the one which is latent but capable of becoming conscious, and the one which is repressed and which is not, in itself and without more ado, capable of becoming conscious.'

So if the repressed is so vital, what exactly is it? The first thing to note is that there is quite a lot of confusion in Freud's use of the term. One problem is that the term refers both to an *entity* – an unconscious idea kept out of consciousness – and to the *process* that keeps it there. The difficulty here is not linguistic (repression gives rise to a repressed idea), but rather conceptual, or at least a matter of emphasis. In implying the thing-like nature of the repressed, attention is drawn away from an essential characteristic of repression itself: that it is a *dynamic process*, constantly at work. Just as a nation's defences have to be rigorously maintained and patrolled in order for them to retain their effectiveness, so repression is a continually active process. If it lets up for a moment, the unconscious (repressed) idea, which is also dynamic and active, forces its way through. To reiterate: psychoanalysis assumes that unconscious mental processes are dynamic, and this applies both to the repressed and to the repressive agency itself.

A second cause of confusion around the term 'repression' is that Freud uses it in two distinct ways:

1. As a general term for the mental processes that create and maintain the unconscious. This means that repression sometimes is

used interchangeably with the term 'defence', as if all defence mechanisms have the same structure, producing repressed ideas. In some ways this is reasonable, as all defences protect the ego against awareness of disturbing unconscious ideas; but it fails to distinguish between the different ways in which this is achieved.

2. As a specific type of defence with the function of 'turning something away, and keeping it at a distance from the conscious' (Freud, 1915b, p. 147). This makes it different from some of the other defences, which for example might convert an idea into its opposite. Rather, repression is a form of 'motivated forgetting', in which something that was once known is known no longer, but kept 'under' and out of sight. The famous classification system used by US Secretary of Defense Donald Rumsfeld in 2002 referred to 'known knowns, known unknowns, and unknown unknowns'. Psychoanalysis adds another one: 'unknown knowns', and this is precisely what repression refers to. We actually 'know' something unconsciously, but defend ourselves against that knowledge. A political instance of this that relates directly to Rumsfeld's statement is the way Americans repressed knowledge of their own capacity for violence in going to war in Iraq. As Slavoj Žižek (2006a, p. 137) points out, the shock at the Abu Ghraib scandal 'shows where the main dangers are: in the "unknown knowns," the disavowed beliefs, suppositions, and obscene practices we pretend not to know about, although they form the background of our public values.' A clinical example of repression might be how some people forget having been sexually abused many years previously, and even when they are told about it they may not believe it because the memory of the experience has become so deeply hidden from consciousness. Repression of the memory might have felt like the only way to survive; bringing it into the open is therefore likely to be a complex and difficult task.

Primary and secondary repression

Freud distinguishes between primary and secondary repression. The former acts on the basic drives, or rather on their mental representations. What this means is that the ideas attached to the drives are so troubling that they are repressed *before they are ever known*. That is, according to Freud there is an area of the mind which is *always* unconscious, with repression operating upon it from the start. In addition, just as a stringent security apparatus will act against those who are in some way thought to be connected with the core 'enemy', so repression attacks ideas linked to the primary repressed. The primal repressed draws to itself ideas that are associated with it, and these too become repressed.

Secondary repression is 'repression proper', which Freud refers to as an 'after-pressure', in which material that is available to consciousness *becomes* repressed because of the threat it poses to the personality. This is what is more usually understood to be repression: something happens, and this is so disturbing that all memory of it is lost. This is because the ego's defences are alerted to the danger, and repression sets in, forcing the memory into an unconscious state, hidden from view. But some representation of this disturbing event remains 'in' the unconscious, pushing at the boundaries of perception, troubling dreams and sometimes ending up as the symptoms of psychological disorder.

Both these types of repression raise the question of what it is that the ego is being defended *against*. Freud's views on this shifted, but for most of his career he believed that it is primarily sexual desire that is the disturbing element in mental life; and that as it is dammed up (repressed), so psychic tension increases and more and more anxiety will be produced. Repression, therefore, causes anxiety, which means that more repression is needed, unless psychoanalytic therapy can be effectively used to deal with the basic unconscious conflict. Later on (in his 1926 book, *Inhibitions, Symptoms and Anxiety*) Freud reversed this to suggest that some ideas are intolerable because they threaten to overwhelm the ego through the urgency of their fantastic demands; this creates anxiety in the ego and makes repression necessary. Thus, instead of anxiety being the *result* of repression, it is now revealed to be its *source*: 'It was anxiety which produced repression and not, as I formerly believed, repression which produced anxiety' (Freud, 1926, p. 108). In this account, anxiety no longer is thought to arise from repressed sexual energy. Instead, the ego's anxiety about disintegration sets repression going.

When repression breaks down

Repression is not always a smooth process and because the pressure has to be kept up all the time, it is not always successful in preventing rebellion. Freud calls this 'the return of the repressed'. The exiled material seeps through at times, perhaps when the power of the censorship exercised by the ego is reduced during sleep, or when the disturbance to which the ego is subjected is too great. Sometimes the impact of this is relatively insignificant. There is, for example, sufficient censorship remaining in dreams to mean that little damage is usually done by them. Similarly, jokes activate repressed unconscious ideas without usually doing much harm – although they can be profoundly irritating to oppressive regimes, and knowledge of Freudian psychology is also sufficiently widespread for people to be suspicious of the motives of someone telling a particularly aggressive joke against someone else.

Sometimes a crisis occurs, for example when the only way in which the tumultuous energy of unconscious life can be contained is to allow some of it expression in the form of neurotic symptoms. This can relieve the tension a bit, but it also means that the ego is now fighting on two fronts:

- As before, it is trying to deal with the demands of the drives and their associated material.
- Now, with the formation of the symptom, some of these demands are being expressed in a distorted but still disturbing fashion and the ego has to battle against these too.

The way the ego attempts to manage this is by *adapting to the symptom*. This means that it tries to come to terms with its neurotic elements and to keep them under control, without allowing the drives too much extra room to express themselves. The result can be a degree of 'normal' neurosis, but it might also mean that people who are very troubled by their symptoms are also highly resistant to change, for fear of something worse taking their place. The situation would only be eased by total success at repression, or by complete and uninhibited absorption in the unrealistic demands of the id. These states, however, are not alternative means to mental health, but are characteristic of either neurosis (ego sides with reality at the expense of the drives) or psychosis (ego sides with the drives and ignores reality) respectively.

Imagine a highly religious adolescent who finds his growing sexual im-pulses too difficult to bear. He feels contaminated by them and repudiates them absolutely, defending himself against them by repression. However, they still exist and this leaves him with the feelings of contamination, so he prays more devoutly and washes himself more and more frequently. Eventually, the extent of his praying and washing becomes almost un-manageable. Before and after eating anything he washes his hands raw; similarly, when he has been to the toilet he has to spend the best part of an hour getting clean. His prayers never satisfy him and he has to keep starting again in order to ensure he has concentred properly. His whole day is therefore taken up in this way.

Psychotherapeutic treatment aims at lessening the defences sufficiently to enable him to become aware of, and start to make sense of, his sexual urges. However, even though his current life is awful, every time it gets slightly better and his obsessional symptoms relent, he backs away from the therapy. He prefers the compromise of just-about-manageable symptoms to the very disturbing challenge of dealing with his underlying sexual conflict.

For Freud, repression is a necessary process that makes it possible to live in a social environment that could never cope with the free expression of unconscious impulses, and also to tolerate ideas that are experienced by the person as anxiety-producing. A balanced personality would be one in which the demands of unconscious life are sufficiently managed so that they can be expressed in socially acceptable ways (this is the defence of 'sublimation') leading a person to feel content enough to enjoy life. However, this balance will always be precarious. Some people, because of constitutional factors as well as benevolent conditions in childhood, will be resilient and able to manage; others will find their mental life strained by repression and its debilitating effects.

Other defence mechanisms

Although the terms repression and defence are sometimes used interchangeably, differentiating between defence mechanisms has been quite a favourite occupation of many psychoanalysts. More to the point, people tend to have preferred defences that characterize them, at times literally hardening into their 'character'. Different psychological disorders are rooted in different types of defence. For instance, repression may be at the source of neurotic disorders in which there is a relatively realistic appreciation of reality but a problem in managing sexual and aggressive impulses. Psychosis, on the other hand, might be linked to forms of absolute denial that refuse to recognize reality, or to projection in which impulses and ideas that are 'internal' are experienced as if they actually exist in the external world.

It was Anna Freud (1936) who most influentially categorized the defences. Her thinking emphasized the importance of dealing with ego mechanisms, the key issue being the adaptation of the individual to the social world without too much disruption from wayward unconscious processes. She was interested in the developmental unfolding of ego functions in relation to drive stages and the many different ways in which drives and their derivatives could be kept in their place. Some common defences described by Anna Freud and others are briefly listed below:

- *Regression:* this describes a return to a way of functioning that would have been characteristic of an earlier stage of development. States of extreme dependency can often be 'regressive' in form. They are defensive because they enable the individual to avoid facing something disturbing by taking refuge in – or fixating upon – a way of dealing with anxiety that was successful in the distant past.
- *Reaction-formation:* this is a very familiar mechanism in which someone defends against an unconscious idea by asserting its opposite. Extreme politeness as a defence against envious hostility might be a common example of this; also risk taking as a way of dealing with timidity and hyperanxiety, or bullying as a defence against feelings of inferiority.
- *Denial:* Moore and Fine (1990) define this as a 'primitive or early defense mechanism by which an individual unconsciously repudiates some or all of the meanings of an event.' Denial is a defence that has been described in some detail by sociologists and social psychologists interested in processes by which people refuse to see the implications of their actions (for example Cohen, 2001). Denial can sometimes be a way of refusing to allow an idea access to consciousness at all ('it did not happen'), which means it merges

with other defences such as repression. But it can also signify apparent acceptance of something ('yes, I did do it') while refusing to acknowledge the significance or meaning of the event ('it was only a slight nudge'; 'it was an accident and does not mean I wanted to kill him').

- *Projection:* this is defined by Laplanche and Pontalis (1973, p. 349) as an 'operation whereby qualities, feelings, wishes or even "objects", which the subject refuses to recognize or rejects in himself, are expelled from the self and located in another person or thing. Projection so understood is a defence of very primitive origin which may be seen at work especially in paranoia, but also in "normal" modes of thought such as superstition.' The husband who sees his wife as being aggressive towards him when he is full of anger towards her is an example here; the psychotic patient who hears voices coming from outside, which are really articulations of her inward thoughts, is another. Projection is very common and forms a basis of Melanie Klein's developmental theory. It is often easily recognizable when one realizes one has been 'made to feel' something (for instance anxiety) by a person one is with.

- *Displacement:* this occurs when the emotional charge attached to one idea or object is shifted to another, more easily acceptable one. 'Kicking the cat' is a familiar example: people who cannot acknowledge the rage they feel towards their intimates or perhaps people they are dependent on (parents, employers and so on), may commonly 'take out' their feelings on others. Freud sees this as a fundamental way in which the unconscious operates, particularly visible in dreams. It also occurs in psychoanalytic therapy where a patient may treat the therapist 'as if' the therapist were a parent.

- *Sublimation:* this is a very important defence, and according to Freud it is also the basis for creativity. The idea here is that many activities that seem 'sublime' or uplifting are in fact fuelled by sexual impulses that cannot be expressed directly. Basically, energy from the drives is channelled in socially acceptable ways, which brings partial satisfaction to the person concerned and also advances culture. Art is such a socially sanctioned way of expressing the drive. Sublimation is crucial for the development of culture, while also defending society and the individuals within it from direct exposure to the drive.

- *Identification with the aggressor:* this refers to the situation in which someone has been subjected to aggression. A way of dealing with the anxiety this produces is to unconsciously take on the propensities of the aggressors – to 'identify' with them. This can be done by idealizing the aggressor, or by becoming like the aggressor. For instance, people who are consistently tyrannized may act in the same way towards others who are less powerful than them. Identification with the aggressor is a useful way of understanding why suffering individuals sometimes admire their torturers and make others suffer, and it has been used to make sense of the behaviour of delinquents and criminals as well as the military and police.

There are many other defence mechanisms that could be mentioned. What they all have in common is that they represent ways in which unconscious material is either kept solidly out of sight (for example repression) or allowed through while remaining compatible with the demands of the social order (for example sublimation). They are functional in keeping the ego protected from damage, but can become dysfunctional if they are too strong, or too widespread, or too rigidly adhered to. Because the defences are themselves largely unconscious, they often share the compulsive, intense character of other unconscious ideas; that is, one can be possessed by one's defences as much as by one's desires. For example, obsessional patients are often characterized by an absolute refusal to compromise. This is likely to be part of their defence against troubling aggressive or sexual impulses, but it is the defensive commitment to *rigidity* that actually dominates their lives. A person whose 'inner world' feels too fragile to sustain intimacy might defend against this through reaction-formation, taking the form of relentless philandering. Again, it will then be the compulsive sexual activity that becomes the 'problem', rather than the underlying vulnerability. In such cases, the task of the psychoanalyst is often to identify what defences are operating and to help the person concerned relinquish them so that the conflict that is producing the anxiety can be faced. Some analysts say this has to be done slowly; others are keen on naming the underlying anxiety as quickly as possible, showing the patient that it need not be feared. In either case, if an unconscious conflict is to be dealt with, the defence has to be tackled without destroying the ego along the way.

Summary

- The ego experiences threats from unconscious ideas, which give rise to anxiety, and it survives by defending itself against these threats.
- The way in which it does this is through use of defence mechanisms, which are themselves unconscious.
- The function of the defence mechanisms is to keep unconscious ideas out of consciousness.
- Defences are protective of the ego, but they can also be rigid and restrictive, causing psychological problems.
- Repression was for Freud the primary defence. He often used the term to refer to defences generally, but it also has the specific meaning of 'motivated forgetting'.
- There are many types of defence mechanism. Different people are characterized by their use of different defences, and certain defences are particularly visible in certain psychological disturbances.
- Psychoanalysis often aims to help people lift their defences so that the unconscious conflicts behind them can become available for analysis.

7

The structure of the mind: Id, ego, superego

Models of the mind

Having discussed in the previous chapters how the mind works as a tense series of transactions between unconscious impulses and defences, we now turn to the way in which it is structured. Freud's understanding of the mind was complex and continually developing. Sometimes these developments led to quite radical changes, but Freud's tendency was to preserve earlier versions of his theory even when later ones came along – perhaps rather as the unconscious preserves earlier ideas and fantasies long after they have ceased to reflect reality. In the case of Freud's theory, this created problems where later formulations (such as the relationship between anxiety and repression) contradicted earlier ones, while some revisions were so extensive as to call into question previous work. An example here is drive theory. In his 1920 book *Beyond the Pleasure Principle*, as described in Chapter 5, Freud drew together supposedly opposed sexual and ego-preservative drives under the heading of the 'life drives', while a new drive (death) was proposed as their antagonist – a violently different account from the earlier one. Despite this, aspects of Freudian theory continued as if nothing had been changed, sowing some confusion and allowing plenty of space for later contention. Many psychoanalysts (for example Guntrip, 1973) have ignored the death drive completely, seeing it as an aberration, while others (in particular followers of Melanie Klein) have adopted it as a cornerstone of their work.

An advantage of Freud's method, however, was that if we are not too worried about tying up all loose ends, we find ourselves faced with an overlapping set of ideas that do not always fit together neatly, but nevertheless say something important about the complicated and contradictory terrain of human psychology. We might even argue that the contradictions in Freud's account signal the healthy state of his mind. He may often have been irascible and dogmatic, but he was also able to live in doubt, to refine and shift his theories in the face of his observations, and to rise to the challenge of offering imaginative speculations when he could not be sure of the truth. This produces problems for those who prefer their theories conservative, cautious and completely logical; but it is a source of some inspiration for those who harbour doubts about the possibility of ever creating a totally sealed theory of everything.

One conventional way to understand the different accounts Freud gives of the mind is to see them as separate but overlapping perspectives or 'models' that address somewhat distinct questions about human functioning. It is usually argued that there were five or six such models to be found in Freud's work (Jahoda, 1977). The question 'what fuels the psychic system?' is dealt with in the *economic* model, where the ebbs and flows of psychic energy are traced. The workings of the drives and the conflicts to which they give rise are discussed under the general heading of the *dynamic* model, while the descriptive account of a child's journey through the various stages of sexual development is, not surprisingly, encompassed in the *developmental* model. These models often address similar issues but from different points of view. Thus, the dynamic model offers a way to trace the conflicts between the sexual and ego-preservative drives, while the developmental model shows how this is played out in practice as a sequence of stages through which a child might pass.

Two of the most interesting models are called the *topographical* and the *structural* models. The 'topography' of the mind has to do with the type of idea one is dealing with – most importantly, whether or not it is conscious. The 'structure' of the mind relates to the question of 'where' this material is held. Loosely speaking, Freud hoped that the structure would map onto actual neuroanatomical features of the brain. He was not overly worried about the precision of this mapping at the time he was writing, although he was interested in how brain science might develop and what revisions to theory that might require. As will briefly be described in Chapter 11, this interest of Freud's has been taken up in recent links between neuroscience and psychoanalysis and the invention of a subdisciplinary area called 'neuropsychoanalysis' (for example Solms and Turnbull, 2002). But Freud's main concern in developing the structural model was to consider how best to theorize a growing distinction between an idea and the 'agency' of the mind that contains and manages that idea. Specifically, what we can see emerging here is an ever more complex model of the self, which aims both to encompass important distinctions around consciousness and also to provide a way to describe the 'sense' of oneself that each person gains. In important ways, this structural model is therefore 'phenomenological', if we understand this term loosely to refer to accounts of how people experience themselves. As will be seen, it also opens the way to a more relational approach in psychoanalysis, based on a set of ideas about 'internalization' and identification with others, which was later developed particularly by 'British School' psychoanalysts such as Klein, Winnicott and Bion.

The system Ucs and its friends

Freud always distinguished between the state in which an idea might be maintained and the way in which these states might be organized – the structure of the mind. His first main version of this was a differentiation between ideas, which could be conscious, preconscious or unconscious, and what he called the 'systems Cs., Pcs. and Ucs.', which referred to the way these ideas worked (and which we first came across in Chapter 4). Conscious ideas are those being thought at any time; preconscious ideas are available, even if they are stored away (for example the words a person knows but is not using at the moment, or a straightforward memory) and unconscious ideas are repressed. Each of these states is organized in a different way. In his major paper called *The Unconscious* (1915c), Freud placed a lot of emphasis on the system Pcs, describing how it contains the important functions of conscious memory, language, reality testing and what he termed the 'reality principle'. He also emphasized how the system Pcs mediates between the other two systems, enabling communication to occur and being the locus of censorship between them. That is, the main 'place' from which repression and the other defences operate is the system Pcs. Derivatives of the system Ucs may circumvent the earlier stage of repression to reach a certain 'intensity' in the Pcs, but they may still find themselves blocked from consciousness. Repression is not, therefore, located only between the unconscious and consciousness; it happens both between the systems governing the unconscious and the preconscious and again between the preconscious and the conscious.

The Unconscious also contains another vital recognition, which at first sight seems to be at odds with the whole thrust of psychoanalytic investigation but which began the process that resulted in Freud's reconsideration of the structural model several years later. This has to do with a rather surprising statement that Freud makes, in which he argues that whether something is conscious or unconscious is not the most important factor in drawing up an account of how the mind is organized. 'Consciousness,' he writes (Freud, 1915c, p. 192), 'stands in no simple relation either to the different systems or to repression. The truth is that it is not only the psychically repressed that remains alien to consciousness, but also some of the impulses which dominate our ego.' The point he is making here is that unconscious elements can be found in all the mental structures, so simply dividing the mind up according to where conscious or unconscious material is 'stored' will not work.

In practice, what matters in the way Freud developed his structural model is the degree to which it enables us to consider *what it is that is acting to defend what bits of the mind against what particular impulses*. However, before describing Freud's formal structural model, it might be useful to have a reminder of the relevant elements that have to be taken into account.

> **The ego:** this is the central structure containing the system Cs – consciousness – and therefore is what requires protection from disturbing unconscious impulses.
>
> **Defence mechanisms:** these are the strategies for defending the ego and they are unconscious. In Freud's earlier model they operate within the system Pcs; later on he proposed that they are part of the ego.
>
> **The repressed:** these are unconscious derivatives of the drives or secondarily repressed ideas (for example memories of trauma) that are kept away from consciousness and from the ego.

Perhaps the most important point here is that defence mechanisms belong to the ego (or, in Freud's other terminology, the system Pcs) but are unconscious. This means that there has to be a framework that can explain how the unconscious can be set against itself in the form of defences (unconscious) versus wishes (unconscious). The particular framework that Freud devised was to have far-reaching implications for our everyday language and ways of thinking about ourselves.

The ego and the id

As a preliminary point here, it is worth noting the difference between the associations of Freud's German-language terminology and the effects of the work of his English translators from the 1920s until the 1950s. To describe the conscious self, Freud referred to 'das Ich', the 'I'. What he was evoking was the sense each one of us has of being a centre of consciousness, from which thoughts and feelings proceed. The decision of the translators to render this homely notion as 'the ego' deliberately distanced psychoanalysis from this everyday mode and made it more seemingly 'scientific', but also more alien. The ego became a formal system rather than an experience. Similarly, 'das Es', translated (into Latin!) as the 'id', actually means the 'it'. This conveys very well the experience of having something within ourselves that feels alien and threatens to take us over, and this seems to have been exactly Freud's intention. The id is full of primeval and repressed unconscious impulses, which are both part of 'us' yet somehow not owned; we are constituted in large part by something over which we have limited knowledge and control. The third structural agency is similarly alienated in the translation. The 'superego' is in fact the 'over-I' (das Über-Ich), an internal entity that watches over us, judging and condemning us and originating feelings of guilt.

In his earlier writing, Freud mainly used the term 'the ego' to refer to the conscious self. His notion was that the ego was an active part of the mind, present from the beginning of life in some form and containing the energy of the ego-preservative drives. Even after the development of his theory of narcissism, he still thought of the ego as the main source of psychic energy: 'the ego is the true and original reservoir of libido, and … it is only from that reservoir that libido is extended onto objects,' he wrote (Freud, 1920, pp. 51–2). But in his 1923 text *The*

Ego and the Id, Freud revised his views. Interestingly, his source for his new way of formulating things was at least as much philosophical and literary as it was 'scientific'. He seems to have been searching for a way of expressing the insight that we are often 'lived' by forces beyond us.

> Now I think we shall gain a great deal by following the suggestion of a writer who, from personal motives, vainly asserts that he has nothing to do with the rigours of pure science. I am speaking of Georg Groddeck, who is never tired of insisting that what we call our ego behaves essentially passively in life, and that, as he expresses it, we are 'lived' by unknown and uncontrollable forces. (Freud, 1923, p. 362)

This is the introduction to the 'id', the 'it' as the home of the repressed and of fundamental drives. It is the original source of energy, out of which unconscious drive impulses flow. It compels us to act in ways we do not necessarily think we choose, and its contents are unconscious, so hidden away. It is therefore the incarnation of alienation, something we are each haunted by, an 'other' within us. But although all that is in the id is unconscious, not all that is unconscious is in the id: as noted above, consciousness and structure do not go together. Both the ego and the second new invention in *The Ego and the Id*, the superego (which I will go on to discuss shortly), can hold unconscious material inside them.

With the creation of the id, Freud's notion of the ego changed quite dramatically. The ego was now seen as arising out of the id, developing in two main ways.

- The ego is the site of perception and consciousness. It gradually becomes more complex as a result of its experiences of reality. This enables it to mediate between the demands of the unconscious and what is allowable and appropriate in the world.

- The ego also develops by 'taking in' experiences of objects. This process goes by the generic name of *internalization*. Internalization is modelled on the physical events with which the infant is familiar. What this means is that the ego takes as its paradigm the experiences, fundamental to early life, of taking things in to build itself (just as the body is built by feeding) and getting rid of things in order to free itself of discomfort (just as the body excretes waste).

The ego is thus a perceptual and a *bodily* ego. As home to the perceptual apparatus, it negotiates the relationship of the person to her or his physical surroundings, testing the wishes of the unconscious against material reality. To the extent that psychoanalysis is a general psychology, it is the ego that is the seat of cognition and conscious understanding of the world. In addition, Freud's view of the ego as developing through internalization means that there is something *social* built into the ego from the start. In particular, faced with the unavoidable losses that all humans experience (for example separation from the mother), the ego takes in a representation of the lost object and makes it part of itself. The ego thus comes to be a home for lost desires and forsaken objects, which are absorbed along with the id-originated psychic energy invested in them. This, writes Freud (1923, p. 29), 'makes it possible to suppose that the character of the ego is a precipitate of abandoned object cathexes and that it contains the history of those object choices.' What this means is that the ego is developed largely through identification with things it values and loves in the outside world ('cathexes' can be understood as 'emotional investments'), taken in and made the template for structural development of the personality.

The superego

The third element of the structural model, the superego, also develops through the internalization of certain experiences along with the fantasies to which they give rise. In part, all that happens is that some important objects are set up as 'ego ideals'. The process here depends on the outcome of the Oedipus complex (to be described in the next chapter), but the main idea is that the child takes in the prohibitions placed on it by the father, developing an 'internal agency' that judges thoughts as well as behaviours, setting up a moral conscience but also an unconscious set of ideals. This is the superego, the 'over-I', the contents of which are unconscious, and it operates as a carrot and a stick, an ideal and a punishment. Perhaps showing the origins of this idea in nineteenth-century assumptions about patriarchy and child-rearing, the superego is thought of as compelling obedience to an internal authority in the same way that the child once was forced to obey an external one.

The ego strives to appease it and to be loved by it, but it cannot escape the sense of guilt that arises from the demands and criticisms of the superego, which (in contrast to the id's immorality) is 'super-moral' and cruel. The ego therefore suffers in its role as responsible for keeping the person sane and well adjusted.

> We see this same ego as a poor creature owing service to three masters and consequently menaced by three dangers: from the external world, from the libido of the id, and from the severity of the super-ego. (Freud, 1923, p. 56)

The superego is a major source of suffering, although it also acts as a guarantor of morality and hence helps preserve the individual in safety. But it is usually too strong, out of kilter with the requirements of the real world, a continually judgemental entity that punishes people not just for what they have done, but also for what they might wish – even when they are not aware of what those wishes are. The contents of the superego are unconscious, after all, yet they plague and prod us throughout our lives.

As can perhaps be seen, Freud's model of ego–id–superego is a useful one in that it allows us to picture what a mind might have to do in order to cope with the complexities of unconscious ideas as they make themselves felt in the real world. Unconscious ideas pump away, demanding things, and the ego has to mediate between them and reality so that the individual does not suffer too much. They are amoral and potentially dissolute, and it is the task of the superego to maintain standards, even if by doing so the individual becomes overly constrained. This explains why people so often feel at odds with themselves, and why it is so common to see good people wracked by guilt: they are 'good' because of the severity of their superego, which in turn explains why all their goodness does not stop them feeling bad. The structural model also offers a language in which one might describe some very complicated issues, such as how mourning takes place, why some people seem to have no conscience at all, and how it can be that in our essence, we might feel that we are 'other' to ourselves. But before we can get to some of these issues, we need to deal with the most famous developmental claim of Freudian theory: that each of us has gone through an Oedipus complex.

Summary

- Freud used a number of perspectives or 'models' to make sense of mental activity.
- Two of these are described here – the 'topographical' model, which deals with the state of an idea as conscious, preconscious or unconscious, and the 'structural' model, which describes the psychological (and possibly neuroanatomical) systems in which these ideas are embedded.
- The structural model began as a distinction between the 'systems Cs., Pcs. and Ucs.' and developed later into the famous tripartite organization of ego, id and superego.
- Structure and topography do not fully overlap. Everything in the id is unconscious, as the id is where one finds the material associated with the drives or repressed as a response to experiences. The superego is also largely unconscious, although some elements of conscience are conscious. The ego has within it the perceptual apparatus and is the site of consciousness, but it also contains the defence mechanisms, which are unconscious and which protect it against other unconscious ideas.
- The ego is formed from exchanges with reality and also by the internalization of lost objects. The superego is formed out of identifications consequent upon the Oedipus complex. It is the source of conscience and guilt.

8
Oedipus, masculinity, femininity

Why Oedipus?

Freud probably did more than anyone to repopularize the story of Oedipus Rex for a modern audience. In fact he did more than that: he made it the basis of the most significant psychological 'complex', the foundation of individual development and the core of what he termed 'civilization', meaning the structured order of society. He thought that the continuing emotional impact of Sophocles' ancient play *Oedipus Rex* was due to the way it resonated with a universal unconscious wish, which he understood fundamentally (from the masculine perspective) to be to kill the father and sexually possess the mother. In the play, Oedipus does precisely this, with tragic consequences. Freud used this idea not only to give an account of what happens in the life of every child, but also as a model for the development of civilization as a whole. The founding act of culture, he thought, was the banding together of the sons of an original tyrannical father to kill him, leaving the band of brothers in control of all the women (mothers) who he had owned but at the same time filling them all with guilt. Incest taboos and the regulation of sexuality follow from this, creating the universal structures of society. This idea was immensely important in the development of psychoanalysis, and is still one of the most widely shared notions in the discipline. For some other analysts, the 'Oedipus complex' has been more controversial, and in recent years in particular there have been moves to displace it from the centre of psychoanalytic theory. In the social sciences more generally it has been an embarrassment that has been more often than not quoted against psychoanalysis as evidence of its wildness, although *metaphorical* uses of the idea have been fairly widespread, at least in the past. In popular culture, the Oedipus complex is at best a joke.

If this is so, why bother with the idea of the Oedipus complex now? It is not even really true to the original Oedipus story, in that Freud's version emphasizes the (boy) child's desire for the mother and antagonism towards the father, whereas the original starts with an act of intended infanticide, in which Oedipus' father, warned that his son will displace him, gives him over to be killed. One could certainly argue (many people have) that Freud's obsession with younger rivals plotting to supplant him strongly affected his understanding of the story: he was less inclined to see his own part in difficulties that arose in his relationships and more keen to place the blame for them on others.

Nevertheless, there are two major reasons for pursuing some understanding of the Oedipus complex. One is simply that it has been foundational for a lot of psychoanalytic thought, which cannot be followed without knowledge of what the Oedipus complex is about. The other, more controversially, is that there are grounds for thinking that it really does say something important about psychology, society and culture. Perhaps it should not be taken too literally as a set of claims about what happens to all people in their relationships with their parents. But whether seen as a metaphor or as an abstract account of how culture and society affect individuals, it may yet offer, in a condensed way, a powerful account of what happens when each of us comes up against the limitations forced on us by others. It also says something about how we manage the need to maintain loving relationships with those who we would also like to displace.

The Oedipus complex

The Oedipus complex is best described first from the perspective of the boy child. This is because it is clearly conceptualized that way by Freud, with his understanding of feminine development lagging behind and being made to fit the model later, always clumsily and less than satisfactorily, as many generations of female analysts have pointed out. The very choice of *Oedipus Rex* as the Greek tragedy to be the model for human socialization is highly revelatory of this. It is a story of murderous father–son rivalry, with the woman (mother) as the prize, and with issues about authority and potency at their core. There are other Greek stories that deal with issues of trust, loyalty and integrity and that have women as their main protagonist. Most powerfully, Antigone, who features in one of Sophocles' sequels to *Oedipus Rex*, has been used as a core figure for many recent explorations of ethics, including several based on psychoanalytic ideas. But Freud was not so interested in this; for him it was the male sequence that set the paradigm, and the female course of development could only be understood as a divergence from it.

As described in Chapter 5, Freud's understanding of human psychology was that it was underpinned by biological drives. The most important of these was always the sexual drive, which operates from birth but can be seen in action in different ways as the child matures. Early sexuality, understood as the search for pleasurable release of the tension created by the drive, is expressed through oral impulses. These gradually are joined by, and partly give way to, anal impulses and then phallic and genital ones. What this means psychologically is not only that different parts of the body give pleasure, but also that different aspects of sexuality come to the fore as 'characteristics'. For example, the oral phase of biting and sucking has a great deal of aggression in it that can become preserved across life as an inclination to sarcasm and bitterness. The anal phase is more focused on the dynamic between giving and hoarding, although it has its own aggressive elements too. Phallic sexuality is thrusting and also possessive, but it has another characteristic that is even more important. In the oral and anal stages, the infant is understood to direct his impulses towards 'part objects', basically fantasies of the breast and penis as he encounters them in his early engagements with the outside environment. By the time the phallic stage is entered, at around three years of age (though other analysts, notably Kleinians, date it much earlier), the child is more cognitively capable of integrating his objects into gradually emerging 'whole objects' – the mother and the father. The breast remains an object of desire, but it is now experienced as part of the mother; the phallus may be a threat that is bound up with the father. This leads to the famous Oedipal situation. The boy's desire is clearly for the mother, but he is also aware of the fact that the father stands in the way of his passion, and that the father is far more powerful than he is. This is an instance in which the 'pleasure principle' is opposed by the 'reality principle', forcing a compromise on the part of the child. Freud argues that there is no ingrained reason why the child should not desire the mother – she is after all the main source of his sexual satisfaction (oral and anal) to date. He is, therefore, 'naturally' incestuous in his desires. From the point of view of the social world, however, epitomized in the family relationships in which the boy is embedded ('mummy–daddy–me') this desire is untenable and immoral. For what is effectively the first time, the social world, represented by the father, consequently says, 'No: this far and no further you may go; this wish cannot be fulfilled.' The child's 'natural' incestuous desire, operating without consideration of the conventions that determine what is or is not an acceptable sexual object, is opposed by a 'non-natural' but universal incest taboo, which structures this desire into a socialized form.

The psychological *mechanisms* at the heart of this prohibition and the effect that it has are crucial for the child's development. These are best summarized as *the castration complex, repression* and *identification*.

The castration complex

The boy's desire for the mother and consequent antagonism towards his father result in the boy's mind in a fantasy of a threat coming from the father, who is now his rival. This threat is experienced as a potential attack by a much more powerful person on that aspect of the child that is motivating his revolt. What is this aspect? Clearly it is his sexuality, now focused on his penis. Hence the boy experiences a threat to his sexual potency, and this is known as the 'castration complex'. The boy is overwhelmed by this, and matters are made worse by the way his own aggression towards the father (who he also loves) is defended against by use of projection – that is, it is pushed out of the child, who cannot bear it, and into the father. In this way, the father becomes even more threatening. Not only is he believed by the child to be hostile towards him because of the child's rivalrous desire for the mother, but he also contains the child's own projected hostile fantasies. There is no way that the feeble boy can stand up to this level of aggression from the powerful adult man, so instead he uses a strategy of appeasement to make things all right.

Repression and identification

Psychodynamically, this appeasement works in two ways. First the child's desire for his mother becomes *repressed*, which of course means that the child does not give it up but it is 'relegated' to unconscious status, and denied access to awareness. Secondly, the boy *identifies* with his father. This puts them on the 'same side' and also means that the boy can hold onto the idea that he can eventually take his father's place in a more orderly, acceptable way, for instance by finding a wife who can be the equivalent to him of his mother in relation to the father. He thus has some compensation for giving up his desire: at some point sexual power and authority will be his. All this is policed by the new structure described in the previous chapter, the superego, from which emerges an unconscious but continuing scrutiny of a person's wishes, ensuring not only that there is no forbidden *activity*, but even that illicit *ideas* are kept out of awareness. Freud (1930, p. 124) says about this, 'Civilization ... obtains mastery over the individual's dangerous desire for aggression by disarming it and by setting up an agency within him to watch over it, like a garrison in a conquered city.' This is, in essence, the model for all the individual's encounters with society: desire opposed by authority, authority internalized and made one's own.

Positive and negative complexes

One complication to the classical model of the Oedipus complex is that Freud suggests there are two forms of it, which he calls 'positive' and 'negative'. The positive Oedipus complex is the one just described, while the negative one is characterized by love for the parent of the *same* sex, and jealous hatred for the parent of the opposite sex. The complete arrangement of the actual Oedipus complex as found in any individual involves a mix of both positive and negative complexes, laying down a rich tapestry of possibilities for homosexual as well as heterosexual love. Laplanche and Pontalis (1973, p. 284) comment, 'The description of the complex in its complete form allows Freud to elucidate ambivalence towards the father (in the case of the little boy) in terms of the play of heterosexual and homosexual components, instead of making it simply the result of a situation of rivalry.' This complexity is a very useful counterweight to the tendency to reduce developmental stories to a simple 'loves mummy hates daddy' scenario, and it also normalizes homosexual love in a way quite characteristic of much of Freud's thought, if not always of that of his followers.

A psychosocial model?

It is interesting to think about this model both psychologically and socially, or perhaps to integrate these two perspectives into a 'psychosocial' viewpoint. As a psychological theory, it has many disadvantages, not least that it has proved very difficult to demonstrate the universality of the patterns of desire and rivalry that the theory proposes. However, it also communicates the emotional intensity of early childhood in a way that is often lost in the more anodyne accounts of cognitive and affective development given in, for example, cognitive or even attachment theories. Through the idea of the Oedipus complex, psychoanalysis engages seriously with the way children show immense passion and despair, excitement, sexual liveliness and aggression, all at the same time and usually towards the people who are most central to their lives, and upon whom they are most dependent. Socially, the structure of the Oedipus complex reflects the constraining force of a society which is in essence opposed to the expression of the child's omnipotent, unbridled desires: for society to function, laws and regulations have to be imposed. Desire has to be channelled into a productive form, and some outside structure that is greater than the individual always makes this so. The Oedipal father is a representation of what society allows in terms of the expression of desire and through this also of sexual difference, of what is male and female: one pattern of identifications is promoted in the boy, and as we shall see, another in the girl.

Psychosocially, if we can understand this as a perspective that brings together social and psychological elements, the contribution of the Oedipus complex is to show something about how what is 'out there' (the structures of law and society) is also 'in here' (the psychological structures of the mind). There is no one without the other: the superego comes from and feeds back into the relational and social structures in which the child finds itself, affecting the kind of 'social subject' the person turns out to be. Perhaps the clearest way of explaining this is through thinking for a moment about how *language* works, something that has become central in particular to Lacanian psychoanalysis. Language exists outside the individual, as a structure of communication with its own rules that simply have to be bought into by every individual person if they are to become part of human society. One cannot just invent one's own language, or make words mean whatever one wants them to mean, without risking psychosis. Language is therefore something social that no individual can wholly possess. On the other hand, people are language users, whose experiences refine the language dramatically, so that over relatively small periods of time (a generation or less in the case of technology and slang) a language changes. Language is also used expressively, poetically and in nuanced ways to carry the intentions and meanings of individual speakers. Thus, people are subjects or agents in language just as they are subjected *to* it; language is both cultural and personal, both social and psychological. For Lacanians, but also for other psychoanalysts, the Oedipus complex might just be the moment at which this complicated psychosocial arrangement comes fully into play, when we discover that we can do things, but we cannot have it all our way.

Feminine Oedipus

It will be very obvious that a major difficulty with Freud's account is his neglect of feminine sexual development, a point that was forcefully made by his critics from the 1920s onwards, and more or less acknowledged by Freud himself. At the end of his *New Introductory Lecture* on femininity (1933), he comments, 'That is all I had to say to you about femininity. It is certainly incomplete and fragmentary and does not always sound friendly.' He was right.

Although many people use the term 'Electra complex' (coined by Jung) to parallel the Oedipus complex, assuming it means a girl who desires her father and is rivalrous with her mother, Freud preferred to retain the term Oedipus complex for both sexes. What both the boy and the girl child have to come to terms with is the structuring power of the father's authority and the relinquishment of a desire for the first object of infantile love, the mother. The way in which this works, however, is always going to be different because of anatomical differences between the sexes and the different psychological complexes this gives rise to. Note here that both boys and girls are assumed to be psychologically 'bisexual' and that according to Freud the distinction between masculinity and femininity is not absolute, but is grounded mainly in the division between active and passive sexual aims. Active aims are masculine, passive ones feminine – a dichotomy that has given rise to a lot of confusion in theories about sexuality, sexual identity and gender identity, but which at least frees psychoanalysis to allow for a differentiation between one's biological sex and one's identity as 'masculine' or 'feminine'.

In any event, while there are ways of reading psychoanalysis as productively decoupling gender from sex, Freud's emphasis on how the girl's visual perception of the boy's preferential sexual apparatus (the penis as larger and more visible than her own phallic centre of gravity, the clitoris) rather belies this differentiation and makes sexual difference seem overly determined. Some later psychoanalysts argue that it is the boy who has more trouble reaching his gendered identity, because he must 'dis-identify' with the powerful object he knows (the mother) and instead base his masculinity on a father who is mysterious, threatening and often absent. However, Freud assumes that it is the girl child who must deal with the more difficult developmental process. This is because she must cope with two emotional moves not required of the boy and both involving painful loss: first, giving up her phallic, male focus on her own 'penis', the clitoris, and, secondly, transferring her desire from the mother to the father.

Both genders are active in their initial sexual activity, according to Freud, so that 'We are now obliged to recognize that the little girl is a little man' (Freud, 1933, p. 118). But when it comes to the phallic stage of development, the boy centres his sexual life on the penis while the girl's leading erotic zone is the clitoris. However, according to Freud (ibid.), it cannot remain so: 'With the change to femininity the clitoris should wholly or in part hand over its sensitivity, and at the same time its importance, to the vagina.' The little girl, dependent on her clitoris for sexual stimulation, becomes aware of how small it is in comparison to the boy's penis and assumes that because of this it must also be *inferior* as an organ, an assumption which does not actually seem necessary, but which Freud and many other analysts have thought must be so. This leads the girl to experience a mixture of impassioned and negative emotions. She gains a general sense of her own inferiority in the world linked with the relative ineffectiveness of her genitals in providing satisfaction for the sexual drive; she feels rage at the mother for having created her like that, in her own image; and she develops a passionate envy of the real thing, the penis possessed by father and brother alike. The little girl, just like the boy, wishes for a penis the size of the father's, and therefore wishes to become like him and to displace him. But she cannot 'have' the penis in this way, she realizes, because of the in-built difference, so she cannot model her future on an identification with the father. Instead, her identification becomes an ambivalent one: she despises the mother for being insufficient and hates her for having made her the same; but she also both identifies and competes with her in wanting the father or herself, in wanting to take her place and be desirable in a world of men.

Penis envy

One thing to notice about Freud's theory here is that it reverses the account of the boy's development, although not in a completely symmetrical fashion. The boy's castration complex emerges *as a result of* the Oedipus complex: the boy first feels desire for the mother and rivalry with the father, and then fantasizes as a consequence of this that he will be damaged by the father's aggression. The girl, however, first recognizes herself as 'already castrated', having no penis, and because of this she enters the Oedipus situation, in which her desire is to displace the mother in order to get for herself a share in the father's power. This is why, according to Freud, young girls feel strong unconscious hostility towards their mothers; it is also the source of the shift of sexual object from mother to father necessary for normative, heterosexual femininity. *Failures* of this Oedipal realignment of sexual desire can lead to lesbianism and/or neurosis. Finally, the girl's desire for the penis must itself be renounced and replaced by the desire for a baby, 'in accordance with an ancient symbolic equivalence'. With masculine fervour, Freud (1933, p. 128) suggests that the mother's happiness 'is great if later on this wish for a baby finds fulfilment in reality and quite especially so if the baby is a little boy who brings the longed-for penis with him.'

It is perhaps hardly surprising that penis envy has been one of the most contentious elements of an anyway controversial theory. Among other things, it suggests that women will have a weaker moral sense and conscience than men, because whereas the male's superego is formed as a consequence of the strong repression of desire and identification with the father's authority and prohibitions, the girl goes through no such major structural change in turning away from the father. She simply has to gradually accept that she will not get a penis, and seek for a substitute – a strategy more rather than less likely to encourage traits like jealousy and manipulativeness. The notion of penis envy feeds into this and has been taken up with umbrage by many psychoanalysts, often but not solely women, who do not think that characterizing feminine psychology as founded on an unconscious sense that something is lacking is quite the best way to think about things. As a consequence, various alternative accounts have been presented, many of them taking up the point mentioned in passing earlier: that if it is the case that the mother is the strongest early object, then it is likely that both boys and girls will identify with her, and this means it is the boy who has to give up something, not the girl.

Responses to Oedipus

The Oedipus complex and the associated tales of masculine and feminine development have produced an enormous range of elaborations and responses over the years. Some of them are listed below.

- There is very limited empirical evidence for the kinds of structures described by Freud, although there is also no doubt that aggression and rivalry towards parents are common features of early life.
- The image of the father is overly restricted in the Oedipal model, making his role (and that of the social law) solely prohibitive. In fact, just as fathers are usually loving and enabling as well as restricting and authoritarian, so society makes things possible as well as ordering individual desires into less than satisfying channels.
- The Oedipal model can be a very useful one in clinical situations, as a way of comprehending the repeated patterns of rivalry, exclusion, identification and misplaced desire that patients so frequently describe.

- The structural aspects of the Oedipus complex, with their dramatization of a conflict between fantasy and reality, have been drawn on productively in much social theory to explore how the desires of individuals are regulated and also produced by the constraints imposed on them by culture.
- The notions of a female castration complex and penis envy are commonly viewed as products of Freud's time and his conservative views on many aspects of the then-emerging gender politics. At most, they might be understood as accurate descriptions of what happens to women under patriarchy (they are denied access to the sources of power, and so on) rather than as what is determined by anatomy.
- The idea of bisexuality is an important one, as is the distinction between 'positive' and 'negative' Oedipus complexes. These ideas make it possible to decouple sex from gender, and to theorize in a more nuanced way about the interplay of unconscious urges and social identifications that produce any particular ways of sexual being.
- The notion of the castration complex communicates powerfully a widespread feeling among humans that something is always lacking, and because of this it has become a useful emblem in discussions of melancholia and loss.

Perhaps all this can be summarized by saying that the abstract form of the Oedipus complex retains its helpfulness as one is encouraged to consider how social and personal realms meet each other to produce the complicated organization of sexuality and gender. While individual children might or might not go through the mythical sequence of love and hate that Freud described, all of us have to find ways in which our desires are parcelled out, made tolerable, encouraged and refined, and we all have to deal with the resistance of our environment to them, as well as the opportunities our relationships provide to enable them to be fulfilled.

Summary

- The Oedipus complex is a central but controversial element of Freud's theory.

- It differentiates between the sexual and identity constructions of boys and girls, although this is complicated by the concept of bisexuality and by the description of 'positive' and 'negative' Oedipus complexes acting in all cases.

- The theory charts how the sexual drive is directed towards the mother but then blocked by the father, and how the feelings of threat and anxiety provoked by this (in the form of the castration complex) are resolved.

- For the boy, the resolution comes through repression and identification with the father, and the creation of the superego as an internalized structure of unconscious conscience.

- For the girl, it is less clear how the Oedipus complex is resolved. She is pushed into it by the awareness of castration (lack of a penis) and this leads to a desire to become the father's partner, as well as a repudiation of the mother as inferior. However, in competing for the father she is also identifying with her mother.

- The concept of penis envy is not a popular one, as it seems to make a socially induced gender dynamic (the oppression of women) into a natural and permanent one.

9

Psychopathology: What makes us sad (and mad)

Psychoanalysis as psychotherapy

Psychoanalysis is usually thought of as a treatment procedure aimed at easing the psychological trouble of its patients. This is clearly true, and most analysts actually make their living by working as psychotherapists, offering a service to people in distress and explicitly or implicitly claiming to be able to help them feel better. Psychoanalytic ideas have been drawn on in the development of many forms of psychotherapy, including psychoanalytic psychotherapies that are very close to psychoanalysis itself. Whether these therapies always work is another issue. The evidence on the therapeutic effects of psychoanalysis is at best rather mixed, although there is a good range of data demonstrating that interventions based on psychoanalytic principles are helpful under some circumstances, with some types of patients and problems. In particular, brief, problem-focused methods of psychoanalytic therapy and psychodynamic counselling seem to have quite good outcomes, and also to be popular with patients (Roth and Fonagy, 2005). However, the issues are very difficult to unpick, as psychoanalysis does not always present itself as a *therapeutic* procedure, but rather as a way of exploring people's unconscious lives that may or may not have therapeutic effects. While *psychotherapy* clearly sets itself up as a treatment for psychological distress, psychoanalysts will often claim that their aim is to help people deepen knowledge about themselves. If this deepening enables people to feel better, all well and good, and many psychoanalysts would claim that it should do so; but this is neither its primary justification nor its necessary end.

As noted in Chapter 4, Freud's own aspirations for psychoanalysis as a method of treatment were at best ambiguous. Sometimes he was relatively optimistic, asserting that provision of the kind of self-knowledge that psychoanalysis might offer would always bring about improvement in a person's mental state. This is because psychoanalysis assumes that the causes of psychological distress are predominantly unconscious conflicts. Consequently, if psychoanalysis can bring these conflicts to awareness so that they are no longer unconscious, their impact will be lessened and the trouble to which they give rise ameliorated. The formulation here is the familiar one of making the unconscious conscious, the idea being that this makes it easier to control the irrational urges that plague us. The state of mind to be hoped for here is that of *insight*, understood as a combination of a cognitive recognition of the reality of an unconscious conflict coupled with an emotional or 'affective' reorganization of psychic life around this recognition. Intellectual knowledge is not enough; the new, insightful awareness has to be fully experienced for it to count as psychoanalytic self-understanding. Freud had various ways of saying this. In the *Introductory Lectures* (Freud, 1917a, p. 438), the task of analysis is expressed as 'overcoming the resistances, lifting the repression and transforming the unconscious material into conscious.' The 'unconscious to conscious' theme becomes increasingly dominant in later works, with its most famous formulation, already quoted in Chapter 4, being found in the *New Introductory Lectures* (1933, p. 80) as 'where id was, there ego shall be'.

There are several versions of these statements, the key idea in each one of them being that unconscious material is not at the disposal of the person to use constructively, and that psychoanalysis, by promoting insight in the sense used above, can remedy this situation. On the other hand, as we have seen in Chapter 4, Freud was not under too many illusions that psychoanalysis would ever bring about great change. Not only does psychoanalysis sometimes only raise resistances, but even where it is relatively smooth and complete its 'total result' is only that the patient 'has rather less that is unconscious and rather more that is conscious in him than he had before' (Freud, 1917a, p. 435). But this, Freud goes on to say, is in fact really a great deal, for it represents the patient becoming what she or he might be under the best possible conditions. Similarly, Freud refuses to commit psychoanalysis to any programme of complete cure, and nor is he willing to see it as a process of adjustment producing 'normal' people. Instead, he states:

> Our aim will not be to rub off every peculiarity of human character for the sake of a schematic 'normality', nor yet to demand that the person who has been 'thoroughly analysed' shall feel no passions and develop no internal conflicts. The business of the analysis is to secure the best possible psychological conditions for the functions of the ego; with that it has discharged its task. (Freud, 1937, p. 250)

The caution of this position is striking, but it also hides a radical dimension opposed to the use of psychological treatments to control people, which has from time to time been the role of psychiatry in society. Simply, analysis tries to help in self-control, to make difficult feelings tolerable and to enable the ego to get on with the business of negotiating everyday life. It does not promise miracle cures nor even to be a panacea for unhappiness. Freud comments that psychoanalysis can never fully protect us from the trouble caused by natural processes (nature itself, as well as the sufferings of the body) and in particular by other people, our parents not excepted. So perhaps his caution was wise, given what we know about the number of things that can make us miserable, and how hard it is to have control over them all, all the time.

What makes us worried, sad and mad

That said, psychoanalysis is a practice as well as a mode of understanding, and its methods and theories have been highly influential in the development of many contemporary psychotherapies. It possesses a complex and thought-provoking set of ideas about what causes psychological distress, and of how to deal with it in clinical settings. The primary psychopathological agent, if one can put it that way, is the conflict between what is desired and what is allowed, whether that is by society itself or by internal judgements from the superego. According to Freud, it is this conflict between unconscious impulses and reality that is core for the production of all psychological disturbance, from the most familiarly neurotic, through depression and what he terms 'melancholia', to psychosis.

Freud's terminology shifted somewhat over the course of his psychoanalytic writing, but his general view on the issue of what creates psychopathology remained fairly stable. In *Neurosis and Psychosis* (Freud, 1924, p. 149), he describes what he calls a 'simple formula' to distinguish between the neuroses and psychoses. This formula (italicized by Freud) is as follows: *'neurosis is the result of a conflict between the ego and its id, whereas psychosis is the analogous outcome of a similar disturbance in the relations between the ego and the external world.'* Freud's classification system, which has remained fairly robust in the sense of still being used by psychoanalysts and to some extent by others, can be tabulated as follows.

Neurosis: primarily hysteria, phobias and obsessional-compulsive states but the category may also include some types of paranoia. Neuroses are produced by the repression of sexual urges and are divided up according to the cause of this:

* *Actual neuroses:* neuroses caused by a physical interference with sexuality.

* *Psychoneuroses:* neuroses caused by psychological factors, notably conflict between the ego and unconscious impulses.

The psychoneuroses are also termed by Freud the transference neuroses, implying that they repeat the childhood patterns that give rise to these mental states in their relationship with the therapist (Moore and Fine, 1990). This means that they are potentially amenable to treatment.

Psychosis: schizophrenia and many forms of paranoia are included here. Freud originally deployed the term 'narcissistic neuroses' to distinguish such states from the 'transference neuroses' described above. Later on, he returned to the more mainstream classification, reserving the term 'narcissistic neuroses' for manic-depressive disorder (Laplanche and Pontalis, 1973). Nevertheless, the notion of a 'narcissistic' disturbance captures the idea of turning away from reality and the relative difficulty of working with such patients.

Another way of thinking about this is to consider the main classification of syndromes employed by Freud and to think about what might be producing the symptoms that can be observed in each case. Freud had much to say about a range of neuroses, particularly hysteria, phobia and obsessive-compulsive neurosis. He also wrote one of the most penetrating and influential accounts of depression (under the title *Mourning and Melancholia*) that has ever been penned. His analyses of psychoses have been of immense importance for analysts as well as for those not convinced by psychoanalysis but still interested in the phenomenology of disturbed psychological states. Each of these conditions is understood rather differently.

- *Neuroses*

Neuroses can be understood as (failed) attempts to find a way to live in the world by controlling one's unconscious urges. In the case of *hysteria*, the underlying psychic conflict is converted into physical symptoms (this is technically termed 'conversion hysteria'). In a famous Freudian example of this, the case of the young woman he called 'Dora' (Freud, 1905), the symptoms include loss of voice and breathing difficulties that are interpreted by Freud as arising from her repressed sexual response to the advances made towards her by an older man (see the case example below). Freud tended to include *phobias* under the heading of hysteria, as 'anxiety hysterias'; in these, the anxiety generated by the unconscious conflict becomes attached to a specific external object such as an animal. The classic example of this is Freud's (1909a) 'Little Hans' case study of a child, where Hans' Oedipal wishes become the source of his fear of horses. *Obsessions* are the product of often rather desperate defences against sexual and aggressive impulses. This conflict can lead to a regressive adoption of forms of magical thinking in which wishing and fantasizing can make something happen. The result of this is often a strong feeling of guilt, suggesting that the conflict involves the superego. Ambivalence – tolerating feelings of hatred for those one loves or is dependent upon – is often central. For example, Freud's (1909b) 'Rat Man' described a very expressive example of ambivalence in an episode where he had to deal with the departure of the woman he loved. 'On the day of her departure he knocked his foot against a stone lying in the road, and was obliged to put it out of the way by the side of the road, because the idea struck him that her carriage would be driving along the same road in a few hours' time and might come to grief against this stone. But a few minutes later it occurred to him that this was absurd, and he was obliged to go back and replace the stone in its original position in the middle of the road' (p. 190).

In all these instances, what is central is that the defence mechanisms of the ego prevent the full expression of unconscious impulses, which instead find a substitute path through the creation of symptoms. This substitute is a *compromise* in the sense that it allows the unconscious element some expression. However, the problem is both that the substitutive expression is not completely satisfying, and that it causes problems of its own. Freud (1924, p. 150) notes: 'The ego finds its unity threatened and impaired by this intruder, and it continues to struggle against the symptom, just as it fended off the original instinctual impulse. All this produces the picture of a neurosis.' In shorthand, the ego has sided with reality against the id, resulting in repression and the symptoms of neurosis.

- *Melancholia*

In the case of melancholia (depression), the picture is somewhat more complicated, but Freud is clear that this is still not a psychosis. Melancholia will be returned to in more detail in Chapter 13, as it has become quite central to modern psychoanalytic thinking. In his text *Mourning and Melancholia,* Freud (1917b) describes deep depression as originating from an inability to acknowledge the reality of a loss and hence to grieve it fully, so that it continues as a kind of unconscious craving that has no outlet. Freud (1924) provides some kind of schematic explanation of why this situation might arise, seeing melancholia as the product of a conflict between the ego and the superego. The superego, which represents the prohibitions and injunctions of reality, attacks the ego (through severe criticism), producing symptoms of guilt, self-denigration and often forms of paranoid thinking ('I am responsible for all the ills of the world; everyone knows how bad I am.'). This makes it impossible to come to terms with loss, because of the self-accusations that result.

- *Psychoses*

Psychoses are 'narcissistic' in the sense that they deny the reality of the external world and are based on a kind of refusal or 'foreclosure' of otherness. They are 'narcissistic' not just because they are inward-turning, but also because they are built on a fantasy that there is no external structure to reality that marks out the boundaries of the self and regulates the way in which one can live one's life. So words really do come to mean whatever the psychotic wants them to; and whatever is in one's head (a critical voice, for example) is believed to have objective existence. Freud (1924, p. 151) explains, 'The ego creates, autocratically, a new external and internal world; and there can be no doubt of two facts – that this new world is constructed in accordance with the id's wishful impulses, and that the motive of this dissociation from the external world is some very serious frustration by reality of a wish – a frustration which seems intolerable.' An important insight of Freud's, which has stood the test of time, is that many of the symptoms of psychosis can be understood as attempts to *repair* the breach with reality, for example to make sense of things that now seem to the person concerned to be uninterpretable. A patient who invents a coherent and immutable, but utterly fictitious, account of being the victim of a conspiracy may be dealing with a relationship to reality that feels bizarre and inexplicable. The paranoid fantasy gives it order and, peculiarly, makes it easier to manage.

Some of these clinical entities and explanatory concepts have survived rather well over the past hundred years – for example the account of some forms of depression as a failure of grieving or a mode of highly punitive self-criticism, or the understanding of some psychotic symptoms as attempts to stay sane. Others are less stable: hysteria is much rarer than it was, and the Freudian conviction of a sexual origin for all psychopathology now looks very far-fetched. Psychoanalysts themselves have moved a long way in their understanding of neuroses and psychoses, and some of these developments will be addressed in Part II of this book. There have also been significant changes in thinking about how the dynamics of the various states of mind characteristic of different psychopathological states govern decisions about who is treatable through psychoanalysis and who is not. Freud, for example, was very wary about psychoanalytic therapy being carried out with psychotic patients, even though such treatments were to be found in the earliest days of psychoanalysis, in Jung's work (Makari, 2010). Since then, Kleinians and others have been very interested in psychoses and have been willing to undertake work with patients displaying 'extreme' states of mind. But perhaps what has turned out to be most productive in Freud's work is his perception that the patterns of symptom and suffering to be found in the different disorders are all to be understood as ways in which the mind tries to take care of itself. Specifically, they can be viewed as attempts to deal with unconscious conflicts that feel irresolvable (for instance between sexual desire and self-protection, or between hatred and dependency directed towards the same person), or with anxiety that threatens to overwhelm the ego and leave the person floundering and out of control.

Symptoms and defences

This last point relates to the question of how to understand symptoms and their relationship with personal defence mechanisms. In fact, it is often hard to differentiate between the concept of a defence mechanism and that of a symptom: just as defences avert danger to the ego, so too do symptoms. Both symptoms and defences take the energy attached to disturbing unconscious material and allow it some form of outlet, enabling the drive behind it to be partially satisfied without the feared consequences that would arise from its full expression. For instance, the Rat Man's compulsion to remove the stone from his lady's path and then to replace it expresses symbolically his mixture of loving and aggressive feelings towards her. Consciously, he could not fully acknowledge the latter, partly because of a magical belief that having such aggressive feelings would do her harm. The 'symptomatic act' therefore allows some of his destructive impulse to vent itself, without the actual feared consequence (harm to the lady) coming about.

More formally, symptoms are to be seen as a substitute for something that has been held back by defences. They are really instances of failed repression, a 'return of the repressed'. Certain wishes have been repressed by the ego because of anxiety, but the repression has partially failed either because it has been inappropriately applied or because of the strength of the wish. The unconscious impulse finds a way through into expression by employment of a substitute that gets round the defence; unfortunately, because this substitute is a very much reduced and inhibited version of the original impulse, it is incapable of supplying real satisfaction. Hence, the ego loses on two counts: it suffers because the unconscious impulse is achieving partial expression, and it suffers because that expression is only partial. An example might help here.

Freud's (1905) patient 'Dora' suffered from, among other things, a recurrent disturbing cough and loss of voice, with no obvious underlying physical cause. In the course of her brief analysis with Freud, she described an incident in which, when she was 14, the husband of her father's mistress, 'Herr K', attempted to sexually interfere with her. Herr K and Dora were supposed to be watching a street procession. Freud describes what happened next as follows: 'When the time for the procession approached, [Herr K] asked the girl to wait for him at the door which opened on to the staircase leading to the upper story, while he pulled down the outside shutters. He then came back, and, instead of going out by the open door, suddenly clasped the girl to him and pressed a kiss upon her lips. This was surely just the situation to call up a distinct feeling of sexual excitement in a girl of fourteen who had never before been approached. But Dora had at that moment a violent feeling of disgust, tore herself free from the man, and hurried past him to the staircase and from there to the street door. She nevertheless continued to meet Herr K. Neither of them ever mentioned the little scene; and according to her account Dora kept it a secret till her confession during the treatment' (p. 28).

Freud has been much criticized, with good reason, for his assumption that any 14-year-old girl would have been excited by this abuse. However, what he picks up on mostly is the *disgust* felt by Dora at the time. He reconstructs the situation as one in which she feels Herr K's erect penis pushing against her. This is disturbing and exciting for Dora, and she deals with it by repressing the memory and unconsciously *displacing* it from the lower part of her body to the upper. Freud suggests that the perception of the erect penis 'was revolting to her; it was dismissed from her memory, repressed, and replaced by the innocent sensation of pressure upon her thorax, which in turn derived an excessive intensity from its repressed source' (p. 30). The symptom – loss of voice and a cough – is multiply determined in this case as in others, but it serves both to partially express the sexual trauma (the kiss and the excitement it arouses in her) and to maintain the repression. It is a troubling symptom, but not as troubling as admission of the sexual event and the emotions it produced.

This example shows why it is important to try to work out the 'meaning' of the symptoms, that is, to attend to their content rather than just see them as signs that something is wrong. Symptoms, as a substitute for something that has been repressed, have meaning. Analysis of the form of the symptoms and the experiences that they are linked to will reveal this meaning, which must lie in some formulation involving conflict, loss and anxiety. It is a major strength of psychoanalytic practice that it takes seriously the content of disturb-ance in order to find clues to the underlying conflict: somewhere in a person's obsessional thought lies an indication of the precise nature of the underlying difficulty, and not just of the fact that she or he is an 'obsessional neurotic'. Psychoanalysis therefore engages with symptoms as meaningful entities that, because they are a 'compro-mise' with the unconscious impulse, reveal something important about the patient's struggle to stay sane. Unravelling this, for example discovering what investment patients might have in maintaining their symptoms, is consequently not just a way of trying to deal with resist-ance, but a way of creating psychological meaning and strengthening the ego through promoting insight.

Therapeutic work

Intervening in this struggle of ego and anxiety, conscious and uncon-scious life, is the stuff of psychoanalytic clinical work. However, it is not a straightforward intervention. Freud learnt early on that simply naming the unconscious idea at the root of a behaviour or difficulty would not be sufficient. Patients might straightforwardly deny the accuracy of the analyst's suggestion, or they might accept it, but it would never be clear what this might mean or what its effect might be. Is a patient agreeing with an analyst because of a desire to please? Is an analyst naming something that is really there (an unconscious wish that pre-exists the naming of it) or is a suggestion being made that creates a new idea and therefore produces a kind of 'false accept-ance' of the analytic interpretation? And what of the response of the patient? If a patient agrees with an analyst, is this just a form of compliance or does it attest to the accuracy of the interpretation? If a patient disagrees, does that necessarily mean the interpretation is wrong? Freud famously did not think this was the case. In *Negation,* he gives some nice examples of how the opposite might be true (Freud, 1925, p. 235).

> The manner in which our patients bring forward their associations during the work of analysis gives us an opportunity for making some interesting observations. 'Now you'll think I mean to say something insulting, but really I've no such intention.' We realize

that this is a repudiation, by projection, of an idea that has just come up. Or: 'You ask who this person in the dream can be. It's not my mother.' We emend this to: 'So it is his mother.' In our interpretation, we take the liberty of disregarding the negation and of picking out the subject-matter alone of the association.

If one's 'nay' is always potentially a 'yea' it is hard to know what evidential status to give to the patient's response when confronted with an intervention by a psychoanalyst.

The practice of psychoanalytic therapy stereotypically involves an analyst sitting quietly in a chair placed at the head of a couch on which a patient lies. This is not always the real scenario, as many psychoanalytic psychotherapists work 'face to face' and some practice occurs in other forms (for example group analysis on psychoanalytic principles, or psychoanalytic work with children who are encouraged to play as much as to talk). Nevertheless, the general principle of a *relatively* passive therapist faced with a patient who speaks is still characteristic of most practice influenced by psychoanalysis. Patients are simply encouraged to talk, even if what they have to say seems trivial. Traditionally, they are encouraged to say whatever comes into their mind – the principle known as 'free association'. The psychotherapist's task is to listen carefully, trying not to make judgements nor rush to hypothesize too quickly about what the 'meaning' of the patient's narrative might be. Every so often, although generally not frequently, the analyst will comment. Some of these comments will take the form of an interpretation, which means they will be attempts to make the patient aware of the unconscious significance of what they are saying, or perhaps of the way they are talking about it. Many of these interpretations will refer to the relationship between the patient and the analyst, as this is viewed as a kind of model of the expectations and fantasies that the patient brings to much of her or his life.

This extremely sketchy outline of the practice of psychoanalytic psychotherapy has already raised some key ideas: *free association* (the patient says whatever comes to mind); *interpretation* (the psychotherapist tries to help the patient become aware of the unconscious meaning of what they are saying); and *transference* (the relationship between the patient and the analyst becomes the object of study in the therapy). These ideas will be returned to in Chapters 17 and 18, where the historical and contemporary use of psychoanalytic theory in the practice of psychotherapy will be presented in more detail. What I want to emphasize here is how psychoanalytic psychotherapy arises from the basic Freudian idea that symptoms have meaning, and that uncovering this meaning is a way of helping people face their unconscious conflicts, and consequently is the route through to insight and therapeutic change.

Summary

- Psychoanalysis is a way of exploring the unconscious that might have therapeutic effects, but it is not solely or necessarily therapeutic in its aims.
- The assumption that psychological conflict arises from unconscious complexes suggests that if psychoanalysis brings unconscious material into consciousness, it will have the effect of lessening psychological disturbance.
- Freud was cautious about the power of psychoanalysis to make a significant difference but nevertheless believed that the movement from 'unconscious to conscious' was an important step in advancing individual well-being as well as social life.
- Psychological disturbance is caused by a complex array of phenomena, but at their core is the relationship between anxiety and repression, which produces a variety of strategies aimed at keeping troubling unconscious material out of awareness.
- The different strategies (defences) adopted by different people and in different circumstances characterize the various forms of psychological disturbance – neurosis, psychosis and so on.
- Psychoanalysis as a mode of therapy aims to produce insight. Its main methods of therapeutic activity are focused on interpretation and transference.

Part II

Developments in psychoanalytic theory

10
Psychoanalysts after Freud

Post-Freudian schools of psychoanalysis

Chapter 2 provided a brief overview of the 'family tree' of psychoanalysis, but in moving from an account of Freud's ideas to a focus on post-Freudian developments it is useful to devote space to some of the theorists who have influenced psychoanalysis most strongly. Although there are a huge number of different approaches within psychoanalysis and it is impossible to be totally comprehensive in an introductory book like this, the main 'schools' of thought are reasonably readily identified.

- Freud's own immediate legacy was propagated most clearly by his daughter *Anna Freud* and the proponents of *ego psychology* who flourished on either side of the Atlantic for several decades after the end of the Second World War. The theories of these psychoanalysts focused on the relationships of ego and defence described in some detail in Part I of this book, so this approach will be considered relatively briskly. However, it is worth noting that in terms of impact on psychoanalytic psychotherapy and a newly 'empirical' approach to psychoanalysis, Contemporary Freudianism (as this group is often termed) remains a powerful force.
- The major post-war shifts in psychoanalytic theory emerged from developments in the way in which object relationships are understood. In the somewhat differing ideas put forward by *Kleinian* psychoanalysts and *object relations theorists*, a distinctively 'British School' way of understanding the complex array of internalized ego–object (or self–other) relationships emerged. Linked with parallel developments in the USA, this has given rise to a broad 'relational' perspective that has many variants and internal

disputes, but is of undeniable centrality in contemporary psychoanalysis. The writings of *Donald Winnicott* have been especially seminal for this group and have increasingly come to the fore in recent decades as the foundations for a newly 'intersubjective' way of thinking about clinical practice and to some extent social relationships in general.

- The radically distinctive propositions put forward by *Jacques Lacan* have had an enormous impact on the psychoanalytic movement and are the basis not only of a substantial amount of clinical thinking but also of what is probably the majority of contemporary applications of psychoanalysis to art, literature and the social sciences.

It is the work of these groups that will be drawn on in the rest of this book, with this chapter offering preliminary sketches of the ideas of Anna Freud, Melanie Klein, Donald Winnicott and Jacques Lacan.

Anna Freud

- Born 1895, the youngest child of Sigmund Freud.

- Suffered from depression in her teenage years but was always especially close to her father.

- Was analysed by her father between 1918 and 1922, after which she became a member of the Vienna Psychoanalytic Society.

- One of the pioneers of child psychoanalysis.

- Gradually became her father's spokesperson as his cancer advanced during the 1920s and 1930s. (Sigmund Freud died in September 1939.)

- From 1927 to 1934 was General Secretary of the International Psychoanalytical Association. In 1935 became director of the Vienna Psychoanalytical Training Institute.

- Published her most important work, *The Ego and the Mechanisms of Defence*, in 1936. This established her as an independent thinker and as the originator of ego psychology.

- Moved to London with her parents in 1938.

- During the Second World War was involved in the 'Controversial Discussions' with the Kleinians, which led to the partition of the British Psychoanalytical Society into three main groups, one of them being the followers of Anna Freud.

- Worked with deprived and war-traumatized children, founding the Hampstead War Nursery, an interest that continued for the rest of her life.

- In 1947 established the Hampstead Child Therapy Courses, adding a children's psychotherapy clinic in 1952.

- Died in London, 1982.

As already noted, Anna Freud's main theoretical contributions to psychoanalysis include the promotion of an analysis of the ego and its defences that has had great utility in the practice of psychoanalysis as a mode of psychotherapy. In *The Ego and the Mechanisms of Defence* (1936) she states:

From the beginning analysis, as a therapeutic method, was concerned with the ego and its aberrations: the investigation of the id and of its mode of operation was always only a means to an end. And the end was invariably the same: the correction of these abnormalities and the restoration of the ego to its integrity. (p. 4)

While she does not go as far as to reject the concept of the id, she clearly regards the study of the ego as the true project of psychoanalysis, for scientific reasons (the ego is 'the medium through which we try to get a picture of the other two institutions' – p. 6) and in the interests of therapy. To a considerable extent this particular stance came from Anna Freud's interest in working psychoanalytically with children. While Melanie Klein focused on the wild fantasies of childhood, Anna Freud was more impressed with the necessity to ensure that the child could manage the demands of the social environment – school as well as family. In addition, while adults might spend much of their time in analysis dealing with memories and 'transferring' emotions linked to past relationships onto the analyst, child patients are still involved in these intense first relationships and have to negotiate them in the 'here-and-now'. For Anna Freud, the implication of this was that the priority was to create a therapeutic environment in which the child's ego could become stable and strong, and hence could show 'integrity' in the face of the anxieties produced by repressed wishes. From here to the idea that psychoanalysis might involve a process of 'adaptation' to society, which is strong particularly in American ego psychology, is not a big step and nor is it always a conformist one, although it has often been criticized as such. For example, in the famous work of Erik Erikson (1956), a secure 'identity' is forged when the needs of the individual and those of the cultural environment can be brought supportively together. This is as much a critique of harmful environments as it is of uncontrollable unconscious urges.

Another characteristic of Anna Freud's work was a reduction in the centrality of sexuality. She argued that the focus on sexual and (to a lesser degree) aggressive drives fails to encompass all the different aspects of the child's adaptation to the world. Thinking of child development in terms of 'basic interactions between id and ego' (1966, p. 59) led her to develop the concept of *developmental lines*: sequences in which particular aspects of personality gradually unfold, always from a position of relative dominance by the id to relative control by the ego. Even though numerous different developmental lines can be described (for instance from infantile sucking to organized eating, from wetting and soiling to bladder control and bowel control, or from erotic play to work), they all follow the same path. She wrote (1966, p. 60), 'In every instance they trace the child's gradual outgrowing of dependent, irrational, id- and object-determined attitudes to an increasing mastery of his internal and external world.'

The idea of developmental lines has proved to be an important addition to the psychoanalytic vocabulary. Descriptively, its assumption of continuities in development moves the theory away from the traditional Freudian concentration on fixations and regressions. This means that it is not so reliant on the idea that there is an undiluted retention of the past in everything that happens throughout life. Regressions do occur; in fact they are predictable consequences of stress. However, the thrust of development is cumulative. At every point, the child is moving forward, each step is produced by past steps and by the current state of the drives and the environment. This approach has considerable practical utility, for instance making it possible to offer guidance on children's problems in relation to what might be expected of them at a particular stage of development. This is one reason why the work of Anna Freudians on diagnostic assessments has been so important. In addition, because of its interest in the growth of the ego and hence in children's achievements, Contemporary Freudians and ego psychologists present a fuller psychological account of development than is possible from the pathology- and drive-oriented approach of Freud himself. However, the theory also has drawbacks. Characteristically for ego psychology, it contains strong normative assumptions, in that the appropriate direction for development is always towards greater ego strength and more successful adaptation to the environment. This contributes to the sequential logic of the approach, but at the price of partly neglecting the continuing irrationality of mental life.

Melanie Klein

- Born 1882 in Vienna.

- Deeply affected by the deaths of a sister (when Klein was four) and brother (when she was in her twenties).

- Planned to study medicine but became engaged in her teens, married when she was 21 and followed her husband abroad. Never gained a university degree or professional qualification.

- Moved to Budapest in 1910 and became interested in Freud's writings, possibly as a consequence of her own depression. Went into analysis with Sandor Ferenczi, who encouraged her interest in child psychoanalysis.

- Moved to Berlin in 1921 and started her own clinical practice with children and adults. Analysed her son Erich.

- Divorced in 1922.

- Entered analysis with Karl Abraham in 1924. Abraham died in 1925, removing a great source of support from Klein, who was already in dispute with the emerging work of Anna Freud.

- Invited to London in 1925 to give a series of lectures and moved to London permanently in 1926 at the invitation of Ernest Jones, whose children and wife she analysed.

- Son Hans died in a climbing accident, possibly suicide, in 1934. Klein started writing immensely influential texts on depression.

- Her ideas were dominant in the British Society in the 1930s but challenged by her own daughter Melitta Schmideberg in 1934. Arrival of Anna Freud in London in 1938 provoked dissension and led to the 'Controversial Discussions' during the war.

- Died in 1960.

As was the case with Anna Freud, Klein's theories grew out of her analytic work with children. She is often regarded as an object relations theorist, but although she employs the notion of object with considerable power, her emphasis on psychological drives (particularly the death drive) marks her out from members of the object relations school. Perhaps the most distinct contribution of Kleinian theory to psychoanalytic thinking is to make affects (emotions) the focus of attention. It is certainly one characteristic aspect of Kleinian psychoanalysis that the emphasis is on the unconscious transmission of affective states between patient and analyst, rather than (for example) the construction of a historical account of how these states arose.

It is also characteristic of Kleinianism that its interest is primarily in what has come to be known as the 'inner world' of drives and unconscious fantasies ('phantasies'). For Klein, as for Freud, drives are fundamental, biological entities. They are represented in the mind by phantasies. While Klein certainly talks in terms of both life and death drives, the momentum of her theory is towards the latter, with various forms of destructiveness being her prime concern. The death drive finds its expression psychologically in envy, understood as a destructive urge aimed at all that is good in the object. Envy is moderated by gratitude; the balance between them depends on constitutional features of the infant and also on the real conditions she or he experiences. For example, a loving, generous mother will ameliorate the infant's envy; a depressed, fragile or resentful one might aggravate it.

Where Klein differs most markedly from Freud is in her assumption that the drives are always directed towards particular objects. This means that satisfaction of the drive requires the presence of the object and the appropriate object is always known. Sometimes it seems that this knowledge is achieved through early experience, but more often Klein implies that knowledge of objects is inherent in the drives themselves, based on inherited knowledge of bodily parts. Whereas for Freud the object is contingent, in the sense that whatever satisfies the drive becomes its object, for Klein drive–object relations are to a considerable extent predetermined: the mouth seeks the breast, the penis the vagina. Klein also emphasizes defences other than repression much more than does Freud. For her, processes of projection and introjection, which are modelled on the early bodily experiences of taking in and pushing out, are vital to the development of the child's mind. They retain their power throughout life in various forms, and are highly visible in the transference relationships that arise in analysis.

Klein also revised, or at least added to, Freud's developmental theory by proposing that there are two major 'positions' taken up in the infant's mind, what she termed the paranoid-schizoid and depressive positions. The former is characterized by splitting and projection; the latter by feelings of loss and guilt. For Klein, these are both developmental phases that the infant goes through, and lifelong tendencies of mental functioning.

Klein's theory is usually seen as focused on powerful, 'primitive' emotions that unconsciously fuel mental states throughout life. The theory itself often seems powerful and primitive, and extreme in its concentration on destructiveness. It also emphasizes supposedly 'internal' processes over external ones. While it might be true that it neglects the full importance of the social environment, its strong account of destructiveness and on what can be done to ameliorate it has made it one of the most influential approaches to understanding very disturbed children and adults and also has given rise to some important analyses of social violence.

Donald Winnicott

- Born 1896 in Devon, England.

- Trained as a doctor, qualifying in 1920.

- Became a paediatrician at Paddington Green Children's Hospital in 1923, staying there for 40 years.

- Went into analysis with James Strachey in 1923, becoming a trainee analyst in 1927. Qualified as an adult analyst in 1934 and as a child analyst in 1935. Supervised by Melanie Klein. Had a second, Kleinian analysis with Joan Riviere starting in 1936.

- Became consultant psychiatrist to the evacuee programme during the Second World War. This led him to consider the importance of the mother's role and of the 'environment' in supporting the development of a child's self.

- Central to the Middle or Independent Group of psychoanalysts within the British Psychoanalytical Society. Twice president of the Society and also ran the Institute of Psychoanalysis' child department.

- Married his second wife, Claire, in 1951. Published significant texts in the 1950s and 1960s.

- Died in 1971. Several important works published after his death.

Winnicott's work emphasizes the actual relationship between infant and mother and the impact this has on the child's developing self, with the father having a much less significant role to play. It has been controversial at times, because of the apparent tendency in it to place all responsibility for a child's well-being on the mother, and to romanticize the mother's role so much that it appears ideal and impossible to fulfil adequately. However, as time has gone on the versatility and subtlety of many of Winnicott's ideas have become apparent and there has been increasing use of them not only to theorize child development, but also to provide accounts of creativity and what has come to be called 'intersubjectivity' – the development of selfhood in relation to other people's minds. Winnicott's ideas also link very well with attachment theory, which has itself become increasingly influential and which has also been taken up productively by many Contemporary Freudians as well as object relations theorists. Winnicott's writing is currently more heavily cited than that of any other psychoanalytic author save Freud.

Winnicott suggests that the mother has the role of providing a 'facilitating environment' in which the child's inner potential to develop a 'true self' can unfold. At birth, the infant is an unintegrated being, liable to fall apart, psychologically speaking. It is the mother's role to support the infant's ego by herself entering a state of 'primary maternal preoccupation' in which she has complete oneness with her baby and can provide perfect 'holding', allowing the child to gain a sense of trust in the world and of security in her or himself. This holding is a psychological as well as a physical act: it refers to the capacity to mirror back to the infant the sense that it is safe and supported and that the infant's needs are being held in mind. The ability of the mother to do this kind of thinking about her child is indeed what makes it possible for the *infant* to think – that is, we can only think properly if we have been thought about. In part, what the mother does is name the child's experiences so that they feel less fearsome, for instance communicating that the pressure a child might feel is that of hunger or anger. But it is also more than that, a way of settling the child by making it feel that nothing will be allowed to destroy it. The 'good enough mother' communicates this to her infant without taking the infant over. She is both there for the infant whenever needed, and capable of separating herself sufficiently so the infant can develop into her or his own self. The analogy of a plant growing is very applicable here: it needs tender loving care, but also not to be overwatered. The mother's ability to carry off this task is rooted in biology and is something that develops over pregnancy and is intuitive and special, qualitatively distinct from the knowledge possessed by childcare experts. It is the naturally occurring basis for all healthy human development. Conversely, psychological problems of all kinds are 'environmental deficiency diseases', stemming from early failures in mothering.

A second concept developed by Winnicott has also proved influential, even though it is also widely criticized for being too simple. This is his famous distinction between the 'true' self and 'false' or conformist self. The mother is supposed to provide her infant with the conditions under which her or his potential for selfhood can be realized. In many situations, something interferes with this process, often because the mother herself has been made anxious or depressed by situations in her life. The infant experiences this interference as an 'impingement' on the ideal relationship with the mother by something that should not be there (the stress of the external world). This means that the infant's natural emergence into a solid being is blocked and it leads to anxiety in the infant about total psychological disintegration. As a strategy for dealing with this anxiety, the infant tries to win back the mother's complete attention and love by falling into line with *her* needs rather than the infant's own. The result is that the infant begins to form a conformist 'false self'. The false self is inauthentic because it is built up on the pattern of the mother's needs, not the child's. The child is someone else's image of her or him, acting in line with the mother's expectations and wishes so as to win her love. As a consequence of all this, the child's spontaneous desires – which under the right circumstances would flower into a 'true self' capable of creativity and integrity – are hidden away and become secret and unfulfilled.

Thirdly, Winnicott's (1971) notion of transitional objects and transitional space has become very widely known. He describes for example how a growing child might use a blanket or toy to represent the mother. It is both a real object and a symbolic one, and enables the child to live in the realms of fantasy and reality at the same time. The idea of a kind of 'space in between', which is both real and fantastic, has become enormously important for contemporary theories of creativity and also for thinking about the 'third'. This refers to a space between the 'me' and the 'not-me' that is perhaps best thought of as a relational field constituted by the way we might hold each other in mind. It is an especially useful idea for conceptualizing how people who engage with each other intimately, such as an analyst and a patient, might find a way to communicate imaginatively in order to construct something new between them.

Jacques Lacan

* Born 1901 in Paris.

* Trained as a doctor focusing on psychiatry from 1927 onwards.

* Gained his doctorate for a thesis on paranoid psychosis in 1934; this thesis became influential among the surrealists. In this period Lacan attended philosophical seminars that affected him greatly, and was heavily involved in Parisian cultural life.

* Joined the Psychoanalytic Society of Paris (SPP) in 1934 and underwent personal analysis with Rudolph Loewenstein, who later became known as an ego psychologist.

* Spent the war years working at the Val-de-Grâce military hospital in Paris. After the war he rejoined the SPP and began to develop his psychoanalytic system.

* From 1953 onwards gave a regular seminar that continued for nearly three decades and was increasingly influential among intellectuals in France. Much of Lacan's published work is derived directly from these seminars.

* Left the SPP in 1953 to form the Société Française de Psychanalyse (SFP). This move mainly arose from a dispute over Lacan's practice of offering variable length (usually brief) psychoanalytic sessions. The new group applied to join the International Psychoanalytic Association, but this

Lacan's system of thought is complex and in places contradictory, and of course it developed significantly over his lifetime. One sustained theme was an emphasis on psychoanalysis as a practice of language: it is what happens in the consulting room when one person speaks to another. The speaker is made the 'subject' of this process; the consequence of this is to understand the unconscious as something that is produced in speech, rather than as a thing that is waiting to be given expression. For Lacan, language creates the human subject; language is therefore not a tool, but the medium that makes psychoanalysis possible. It even, according to Lacan, 'structures' the unconscious, partly because the unconscious is held by Lacan to be organized as a language itself (a difference from Freud's view), but also because language separates out that which can be communicated from that which cannot.

There is a great deal of complicated theoretical material attached to Lacan, which has been taken up in various ways by social and political theorists as well as by cultural critics. However, perhaps what is worth mentioning here is the division he makes between different orders of experience, which he terms the *Imaginary*, the *Symbolic* and the *Real*. These will be described in more detail in Chapter 16. The Imaginary is an order of fantasy in Lacanian thought. It is a kind of narcissistic realm in which we act as if we are whole and can find the true meaning of our lives, when in fact what we are embedded in is a fragmentary world in which there are splits and fissures, contradictions and impossibilities. The Imaginary originates in what Lacan calls the 'mirror phase', which he presented as a developmental fact but which has also been widely taken up as a metaphor for the way in which the ego operates. The specific claim here is that at about 18 months of age the infant, who up until then has experienced itself as at the mercy of its drives and struggling to hold itself together psychologically, is shown the image that it makes in the mirror. This image has a very powerful effect, because it suggests to the infant that it is really a whole and integrated being, rather than a fragmentary one. It is a kind of false 'alibi': just as the purpose of an alibi is to suggest that someone has been where in fact they have not, so the image persuades the child that its real presence is revealed there, in the mirror. The mirror phase is the origin of the ego and means that the ego is something that is 'adopted' from outside. It is not a real thing, but rather a way of relieving the sense of fragmentation, a kind of defence against falling apart. From that moment onwards, Lacan suggests, the infant uses the ego as a kind of prop, and it leads her or him to see the whole world, including the self, as potentially integrated and whole. However, this is a fantasy, and reliance on it leads to all sorts of other errors – for example the belief that one can find true and full love in another, or that someone (a teacher or psychoanalyst or political leader) has a complete answer to all one's questions about existence.

In contrast to the Imaginary, the Symbolic order acknowledges the reality of splits and divisions, most notably because it makes language central. What this means is that in order to become a member of a society, the individual has to become 'subject to' language, using it in ways that are comprehensible to others and consequently having her or his thoughts and fantasies structured by it. This is linked by Lacan with the Oedipus complex, which is the moment in development when a Symbolic 'law' operates to break up the Imaginary fantasy that the child can possess the mother – that is, that it is possible to have everything one wants. The Symbolic order is thus the province of language and sexual difference, marked by the splitting of the subject and the creation of subjectivity around lack.

The third Lacanian order is known as the Real. It is not a biological given, but refers to that which cannot be symbolized, but which nevertheless is always somehow 'there' as a possibility and as a disruption. In some ways it is close to other ideas of the unconscious, or perhaps it is a version of the death drive. The Real resides outside the registers of Imaginary and Symbolic; it is the order of the leftover, that which is under the surface, rhythmic, uncertain and disruptive.

Summary

- A brief sketch is offered of the biography and theories of four major psychoanalysts who all have significant contemporary influence.
- Some of these ideas will be returned to in more detail in later chapters.

11
Attachment and mentalization

Biologically based psychoanalytic theory

In the last chapter, I gave a brief sketch of some of the key figures in post-Freudian psychoanalysis. Here, I begin the process of describing some of the most important elements in contemporary psychoanalytic theory. In subsequent chapters I will develop the argument that contemporary psychoanalysis has veered strongly in the direction of relational thinking. This means there is an increasingly shared perspective that early social interactions are central to the development of psychic structures, and in particular that mental life is organized around important 'object relationships'. The technical language used here will be clarified in Chapter 12, but in this chapter I want to introduce a set of concerns that link the more biological tradition of Freudian theory with this relational perspective, and that also seem to provide a possible bridge between Contemporary Freudianism (derived from Anna Freud's theories) and relational thought.

There is a tendency to see Freudian drive theory as biologically based and object relations theory as attending more closely to 'environmental' events, notably the role of parenting in children's development. This has some truth to it, in that drive theory by definition ascribes causal power to biological factors. The life and death drives were certainly seen as inbuilt constitutional features of individuals, and both Freud and Klein are explicit about how important they are. Conversely, object relations theory (and relational psychoanalysis in general) is much more open to the impact of early relationships. These not only influence how the drives are played out; in important ways they also 'create the mind', so that for example people's capacity to think and feel deeply arises out of the quality of their interactions with early caregivers.

Despite this, there is also a strong tradition of relational thinking that is biologically based, and in recent years this has become more important in some new developments in psychoanalytic theory. These developments come from analysts and others working both in the Contemporary Freudian and the relational traditions. What links them is particularly an interest in ways in which psychoanalysis can be informed by new empirical work in child development and neuroscience that complements the traditional reliance on case and clinical studies. It should also be noted that many other psychoanalysts are wary or even disparaging about this work. They think it misses the point of psychoanalysis and threatens to reduce it either to a biological science or to a cognitive one.

Attachment theory

Attachment theory originated in the work of John Bowlby (1969) and became highly influential in developmental psychology and also in clinical psychological and social work practice – but not in psychoanalysis, despite Bowlby's own status as a psychoanalyst. In some ways this is surprising, as several of the basic assumptions of attachment theory seem to fall in line easily with object relations theory. Attachment is assumed to be an innate propensity, arising from evolutionary processes, for humans to seek closeness to others. They do so, it is argued, because of the dangers of the external world and the need for protection and succour. Infants seek proximity to their caretakers; young animals do so by moving towards them and clinging to them, while young humans, who are less mobile, cry and demand, eliciting responses from mothers and others who then come to them to look after them. Attachments protect children, who could not otherwise survive on their own. Attachments do not only have physical effects, however; they also fulfil emotional needs, making it possible for infants to grow into people capable of reflecting on their situation and, importantly, understanding the emotional states of others (Bowlby, 1969; Fonagy and Target, 2007). In agreement with much contemporary psychoanalysis, attachment theory takes the social orientation of the human subject as a given, and argues that the infant is 'hardwired' to pursue social connections as fully as possible. The 'aim' of life is to find fulfilling personal relationships that are founded on this biological base, which will lead not only to the perpetuation of the species but also to the successful raising of children (attachment behaviours protecting them against predators and other dangers). One implication is that the *feelings* that go along with attachment – love in all its aspects, from romance to love for a parent or child – work biologically in the service of this social orientation. Love is passionate because as a feeling it promotes the kinds of behaviours that humans need in order to survive. In later work, Bowlby (1973, 1980) developed these ideas further to examine the effects of separation on children's development and also to produce a cognitive model of the impact of loss on psychological functioning.

These ideas have spawned a huge empirical enterprise. Various ways of measuring attachments have been developed, ranging from the 'strange situation' used by Mary Ainsworth and others (for example Ainsworth and Wittig, 1969) to examine infants' responses to separations, to Mary Main's 'Adult Attachment Interview' (Main and Goldwyn, 1990), which examines the narrative style of adult interviewees to place them in different attachment categories. This work has convincingly shown that there are some predictable consequences of erratic or rejecting parenting on young children's attachments; and that these may have long-term effects on later relationships and also on cognitive and affective styles, which can in turn produce intergenerational effects. The categories of 'secure' and 'insecure' attachments have become familiar to generations of childcare professionals, while the distinctions between various types of insecurity (for instance 'avoidant', 'resistant' and 'disorganized') have become the stuff of many studies and theoretical formulations.

On the face of it, it may be unclear why this work should have been as controversial as it was among psychoanalysts, although the relative lack of interest in the vocabulary of the unconscious is a clue. Especially after Bowlby (1973) developed the idea of 'internal working models' to explain ways in which people 'carry around' inside them certain expectations about relationships derived from their early attachment experiences, it seems obvious that there might be clear overlaps with psychoanalytic thinking. Like psychoanalysis, attachment theory emphasizes the importance of early experience. While it uses a more cognitive language than does psychoanalysis, the idea that these experiences lead people to hold 'preconscious' templates that govern their later relationships does not seem impossibly far from object relationship assumptions. However, for many years there was great opposition to attachment theory, for a number of reasons. Peter Fonagy and Mary Target (2007, p. 415), who have produced perhaps the most significant body of work developing the relationship between psychoanalytic and attachment thinking, describe the limitations of the latter:

> Attachment theory is limited from a psychoanalytic perspective in that it sidesteps sexuality; sees aggression as secondary to more fundamental motivations; arguably offers mechanistic models of conflict; is mute on unconscious fantasy; is reductionistic in its focus on a handful of empirical paradigms (e.g., the Strange Situation and the Adult Attachment Interview) that provide broad classifications that lose the subtlety and detail of the original material; and offers a limited framework for clinical work. ...There is ... little attention paid by attachment theorists to the qualitative differences between conscious, preconscious, and unconscious experience, and the psychic contents that are assumed to be most formatively defended against are focused not on drives and their derivatives and ensuing conflicts but on the development of the self and the self in relation to another.

Bowlby himself seemed to waver between what he called an 'ethological' or evolutionary perspective and a cognitive one, and perhaps his rejection by his psychoanalytic colleagues also moved him to become more hostile towards the tenets of psychoanalysis. In any case, the charge is that attachment theory loses the flavour of psychoanalysis and reduces to a set of assumptions about cognitive templates for relationship-formation linked to early interactions but with little to say about the kinds of unconscious conflicts with which psychoanalysts are mostly concerned.

Attachment and psychoanalysis

While there continues to be suspicion of what many psychoanalysts see as the relative shallowness of attachment theory in conceptualizing mental states, there has also been a considerable degree of rapprochement between the two approaches. Fonagy and Target (2007, pp. 415–18) give several reasons for this, including those listed below. (Fonagy and Target's points are in italics; my commentary follows.)

- *There may be an increasing acceptance by psychoanalysts of the formative nature of the child's social environment.* This seems to be true across most psychoanalytic schools, including those derived from Anna Freud (of which Fonagy and Target are members) as well as object relations thinkers.
- *Concern with the actual social environment from psychoanalysts was also driven by an increasing interest in infant development as a legitimate way of explaining differences in adult behaviour.* It may seem surprising to see this as a new development. However, what Fonagy and Target are referring to here is that psychoanalysts who had previously relied mostly on the reconstruction of childhood experiences through adult memories have, over quite a long period of time, become increasingly open to researching observable elements of parent–infant interactions and to considering their importance for later development.
- *'A range of psychoanalytic orientations … have opted for an implicitly dialectical model of self development'* (Fonagy and Target, 2007, p. 416). This basically means that the interactional or intersubjective model, in which parent and child influence each other, is becoming more common among psychoanalysts.
- *As the object relations model moved to replace ego psychology as a dominant international psychoanalytic paradigm, so the attachment theory emphasis on an autonomous need for a relationship came to be embraced by a majority.* The almost universal adoption of the language of 'objects' among psychoanalysts is some testament to this claim (see Chapter 12).
- *The relationship context of the emergence of mental functions such as emotion regulation, the capacity for symbolization, and empathy.* Again this highlights the significance of early relationships for core aspects of development.
- *The growing interest in measures based on attachment theory among psychoanalysts who have pioneered the path of empirical research.* This is part of a trend towards more acceptance of systematic obser-

vation and empirical research among psychoanalysts, driven both by external demands for evidence and by the influence of child psychoanalysts drawing on their own long tradition of infant observation.

- *'From our point of view a less welcome change that has facilitated the increased acceptability of attachment ideas is a reduced emphasis on infantile sexuality as the predominant explanation of psychological disturbance'* (Fonagy and Target, 2007, p. 418). This is actually one of the criticisms of attachment theory and some of its derivatives, so it is interesting to see it listed here as also true of psychoanalysis. Certainly one has the impression that relational psychoanalysis is less likely to give priority to sexuality as opposed to non-sexual intimacy in its case studies and theoretical pronouncements, and perhaps Fonagy and Target are right that this means it is also less averse to the de-sexualized approach of attachment theory.

As a consequence of these and some other developments, many psychoanalysts have become more at ease with accepting the attachment theory propositions that: (1) early relationships determine the degree of security experienced by a child; (2) this leads to differences in inner 'models' of what relationships are like; (3) secure versus insecure attachment patterns are connected with differing self structures; and (4) some of these have longstanding consequences and can give rise to psychological difficulties, particularly in the form of 'character' disorders. Put like this, it can be seen that there are especially suggestive links with Winnicott's ideas (different degrees of responsive mothering determining true and false self-development, for instance) as well as with the broader relational paradigm.

Fonagy and Target have themselves produced an especially important seam of work on how attachment relationships in adulthood are related to the security or otherwise of infant attachments. The most interesting point here is that ways in which parents talk about their attachment experiences in childhood seem to predict the quality of the relationship they have with their own infants. For example, Fonagy and Target (2003, p. 239) summarize findings showing that 'dismissing AAI [Adult Attachment] interviews predict avoidant Strange Situation behaviour, while preoccupied interviews predict anxious avoidant infant attachment.' While there are some technicalities in the terms they use, the general idea is that adults' ability to reflect thoughtfully on their experiences might also affect the quality of the relationships they can manage with their own children. This again suggests that some kind of internal template is at work, inhibiting or facilitating people in forming open, loving relationships.

Mentalization

These ideas about emotional responsiveness and reflective capacity have come together recently in work on 'mentalization', defined as 'a form of mostly preconscious imaginative mental activity, namely interpreting human behaviour in terms of intentional mental states (for example needs, desires, feelings, beliefs, goals, purposes, and reasons)' (Fonagy, 2008, p. 4). Fonagy continues:

> Mentalizing is imaginative because we have to imagine what other people might be thinking or feeling; an important indicator of high quality mentalization is the awareness that we do not and cannot know absolutely what is in someone else's mind. We suggest that a similar kind of imaginative leap is required to understand one's own mental experience, particularly in relation to emotionally charged issues. ... The ability to understand the self as a mental agent grows out of interpersonal experience, particularly primary object relationships.

There is a lot to unpack in these few sentences. First, it is worth noting the reference to the intimate link between self and others. The focus is on an imaginative form of 'understanding' in which a person is able to enter into the mind of another, to work out what she or he is thinking or intending and to understand things from that other person's perspective. Not only is this seen as necessary for understanding others; it is also crucial for understanding one's own mental functioning. Interpersonal experience leads to knowledge of the self as a mental agent. Put differently: without a certain kind of early object experience, it is not possible to become a self. Fonagy (2008, p. 10) comments, 'Psychoanalysts have long assumed that the child's capacity to represent mental states symbolically is acquired within the primary object relationship. Therefore early disruption of affectional bonds will also undermine a range of capacities vital to normal social development. Understanding minds is difficult if one does not know what it is like to be understood as a person with a mind.'

The link with attachment thinking should also be clear from this quotation. It is in the context of a certain kind of secure relationship with a responsive other that the capacity to mentalize arises. This is basically assumed to be because the mother or other caretaker is used by the infant as a kind of mirror that can accept the infant's feelings and *reflect them back as thoughts*. Fonagy proposes that what happens is that infants' emotional arousal is alleviated through contact with their caregivers in two ways. First, the infant discovers that its emotions are very arresting for the adult and result in interactional sequences ('mirroring') that are themselves rewarding, helping the infant experience itself as a 'regulating agent' (2008, p. 16). Secondly, the caregiver's ability to hold onto the emotion and to make sense of it communicates to the infant that it is possible to regulate one's own affective state; that is, 'they can also be experienced as something recognizable and hence shared' (ibid.). Indeed, the main point here is that the infant learns about the 'shareability' of experience and, in the right circumstances, the trustworthiness of the context of human relationships. On the other hand, if things go wrong, the infant will have trouble in precisely this region of managing emotion: 'If the parent's affect expressions are not contingent on the infant's affect, this will undermine the appropriate labeling of internal states which may, in turn, remain confusing, experienced as unsymbolized and hard to regulate' (ibid.).

Mentalization is not conceptualized as a purely cognitive phenomenon, but there are strong links with emotional experience too. This is part of what might make it a useful notion for psychoanalysis. In addition, the process that Fonagy proposes, whereby an infant 'externalizes' emotions so that they can be managed by the parent and then taken back in a more comprehensible form, is very much like the cycles of projection and introjection described by Kleinian psychoanalysts, to be presented more fully in Chapter 15. Fonagy and Target (2003) also outline an intriguing notion that they call the 'alien self', which has very strong links (as they point out) with ideas to be found in the writings of the British psychoanalysts Winnicott and Bion. Briefly, the idea here is that insensitive caregiving is a kind of inaccurate mirroring in which instead of the child finding itself reflected back by the parent, it rather has to manage the impact of the parent's own concerns. Fonagy and Target (p. 279) describe this as resulting in the child having to 'internalize the representation of the object's state of mind as a core part of himself.' This leads to the incorporation of an 'alien self', which is experienced as disturbing instead of containing, and to increasingly desperate attempts to externalize the alien elements and a resulting disorganization of the personality. Fonagy and Target argue that everyone has some degree of an alien self as no parenting is perfectly attuned to an infant's needs. Under the kinds of conditions that Winnicott might have called 'good enough mothering' the child will develop a mentalizing capacity that will enable it to manage these 'gaps in the self'; but when such conditions do not prevail, or when profound trauma occurs, these incoherent elements of selfhood will come to the fore.

Neuropsychoanalysis

A final distinctive element of the approaches described in this chapter is that they are linked to a wider movement among some psychoanalysts to find ways of integrating their own discipline with the rapidly emerging science of the brain. 'Neuropsychoanalysis' tries to establish the brain mechanisms that might underpin psychoanalytic phenomena, and in so doing clarify what is tenable and what is not in psychoanalytic theorizing (Solms and Turnbull, 2002). The neurobiology of attachment has been especially interesting for such workers, as has how the brain works to allow or block the kinds of reflective capacities implied in the research on mentalization. In a critique of the move towards neuroscience, Blass and Carmelli (2007) list the four areas of 'trauma and memory, motivation and affect, dream theory, and theories of the mind' as having especial interest for psychoanalysts (p. 20). They sketch the claims in each of these areas as follows:

- *Trauma and memory:* 'Neuroscientific findings regarding explicit and implicit memory systems make clear that memory organization is such that many traumatic memories are not coded explicitly and thus are unrecoverable as memories per se. … This has clinical implications as one must no longer search for certain traumatic memories or convey to the patient that it is necessary or always possible to do so' (p. 21).

- *Motivation and affect:* 'Neuroscientific research reveals the existence of several motivational centers. This research supports the development of new psychoanalytic theories that view the individual in terms of a variety of motivations, and points to the inadequacy of classical theory, which limits motivation to instinctual motives' (p. 26).
- *Dream theory:* Neuroscientific findings suggest 'that somatic stimuli ... instigate a series of events ultimately leading to the dream, but that higher-level motivational processes are responsible for the appearance of the dream. The involvement of these motivational processes provides neuroscientific support for Freud's dream theory' (p. 28).
- *Theory of the mind:* 'The neuroscientific theories adequately explain the empirical data regarding the mind's functioning and have tested their models according to acceptable empirical standards. Psychoanalysis has failed in these regards. Consequently, psychoanalysis will have to adopt neuroscientific theories in order to adequately pursue its task' (p. 32).

These neuroscientific claims, among others, have begun to intrigue many psychoanalysts who see them as enabling refinement of some psychoanalytic theories while proffering support for others, such as the theory of dreams. Freud himself might have held this view, given his hopes that advances in biological science would provide evidence about the causes of psychological functioning. However, they remain highly controversial. In particular, the current fascination with the brain may itself be something in need of interpretation, in that it may represent a flight from the complexities of meaning into something that appears to be more concrete and clear. This is a variant of a familiar criticism of biologically based theories, that they are *reductionist* in the sense of being on the wrong level to explain psychological phenomena. Blass and Carmelli (2007, p. 34) comment along these lines, 'Neuroscience can tell us of the biology of the mind while dreaming, while feeling motivated, while having affective experience, but not of the meaningfulness of that biological substrate or how it can be understood and categorized meaningfully. Since psychoanalysis is a process and theory geared towards understanding the latent meanings and psychic truths that determine the human psyche, such neuroscientific findings are irrelevant to its aims and practice.' Clearly, not everyone would agree. Nevertheless, while it is apparent that any comprehensive theory of the mind must recognize the significance of discoveries about brain function, perhaps it is reasonable to ask whether neuroscience is genuinely vital to the theory and practice of psychoanalysis.

Summary

- There is continuing interest among some psychoanalysts in biologically and evolutionary based theories that might integrate with their own.
- Attachment theory, which was for a long time rejected by most psychoanalysts, has become more acceptable and is leading to some useful research on how the relational context of early infancy affects development.
- Emerging from recent attachment-based evidence on reflective functioning, the concept of mentalization has been developed as a way to theorize the knowledge that infants gain of other people's minds. Although this was initially a cognitive theory, it has become more attuned to psychoanalytic concerns such as how emotion is regulated and the effects of parents' mirroring and containing of their infants' anxieties.
- These theories are aligned with neuroscientific thinking. Neuropsychoanalysis is a controversial attempt to use brain science to inform and support psychoanalytic theory and practice.

12

The principles of object relations theory

Objects and object relationships

The previous chapter considered some recent developments in Freudian theory that link biological and social concerns. This can also act as an introduction to a major set of theoretical assumptions that underpins much contemporary psychoanalysis. These assumptions are especially strong in the British School of psychoanalysis (that is, object relations and Kleinian theory), which is the main tradition drawn on in the next four chapters. The British School is significant in providing the basis for a more 'relational' way of thinking in psychoanalysis that has heavily influenced theory and therapeutic practice and has also been important for some applications of psychoanalysis in the humanities and social sciences. The starting point is a concept that has been taken up in most psychoanalytic schools of thought and has become central to many: that of *objects* and, alongside it, *object relationships*.

In psychoanalysis, the people and parts of people towards which love and hate are directed are known as 'objects'. This might seem quite peculiar, as it suggests a process of 'objectification' that divests these people of their humanity. It appears to imply that they are somehow 'things', with 'object' being the opposite of 'subject'. To some extent this is simply a matter of the history of the term. As noted in Chapter 5, for Freud the mobilizing forces of psychic life were the drives, and these would find objects to which they were directed and which could satisfy them by allowing an outlet for pressure. As the theory developed and began to include a more subtle understanding of how the ego related to these objects, they came to be more clearly personal and relational, without the term ever being changed. The result is that 'object' has come to mean something different in psychoanalysis from its ordinary common-language use. It sometimes refers to the things themselves – parents, or the mother's breast, for instance – but its main meaning is that of the mental *representations* to which these things give rise, the 'internal', fantasized versions of people that populate the mind. This is why one can talk about a 'gratifying object' or a 'punitive object': the 'real person' concerned may or may not have these attributes, but in the mind they have become *personalized* in these ways.

In their dictionary of psychoanalytic terms, Laplanche and Pontalis (1973, p. 278) offer a helpful introduction to the idea of object relationships. They note:

> As we know, a person is described as an object in so far as the instincts are directed towards him; there is nothing pejorative in this – no particular implication that the person concerned is in any sense not a subject.

> 'Relationship' should be understood in the strong sense of the term – as an interrelationship, in fact, involving not only the way the subject constitutes his objects but also the way these objects shape his actions. An approach such as Melanie Klein's lends even more weight to this idea: objects ... actually act upon the subject – they persecute him, reassure him, etc.

The to-and-fro of object relationships is very important and conveys something else that Laplanche and Pontalis point to, and that is central to the object relations perspective. This might be described as a move from a 'closed' to an 'open' system, or more simply from a one-person psychology to a two-person one. The table below gives a brief comparison of Freudian and object relational perspectives to try to elaborate this, although it must be recognized that neither approach is completely consistent, and, for sake of clarity, the characterization of them may be more extreme than can always be fully justified.

Table 12.1 Comparison of Freudian and object relational perspectives

Freudian theory	Object relations theory
Motivation is due to biological drives, primarily of sex and aggression (sexual versus ego-preservative; life versus death).	Motivation is due to humans' 'object-seeking' tendency, meaning that they are primed for seeking out relationships.
Drives lead to object relationships as a way to achieve satisfaction.	Object relationships are intrinsically satisfying (they are what life is about).
Psychology is individual, arising from inner sources (the drives) and embracing other people only to the extent that they satisfy those drives.	Psychology is interpersonal or intersubjective, starting from the idea of a relationship (for example between the baby and mother) out of which the human subject individualizes.
Basic concepts are biological and impersonal.	Basic concepts are social and relational.
Focus is on sexuality. The sexual drive leads to object relationships.	Focus is on intimacy. Sex is an expression, and in the service, of an intimate loving relationship.
Destructiveness and aggression are inbuilt, deriving from the death drive.	Destructiveness and aggression are the product of frustration and inhibition of object relationships.
The Oedipal 'third' is understood as a prohibiting force (the father) preventing unwarrantable types of sexual intimacy (fulfilment of the child's desire for the mother).	The Oedipal 'third' is only one type of third; another one has to do with ways of pooling individual subjectivity into a place of meeting and intimacy. The third can therefore be nurturing as well as prohibiting.
Therapy focuses on developing insight into the repressed ideas that are causing psychic troubles. The relationship with the analyst is used to bring greater clarity into this process.	Therapy focuses on using the therapeutic relationship to re-experience and rework damaged object relationships.

It will be clear from this table that the key development that object relations theory embodies is a move away from a drive-based approach in which what is of interest is solely what happens 'within' the individual. In the traditional psychoanalytic view, human psychology is driven by the impulse to give expression to the drives, and it is in order to do this successfully that relationships with others are formed. In object relations theory, this order of events is reversed. Freud's sexual and aggressive drives are replaced by an assumption that humans are fundamentally relationship-seeking creatures. Consequently, while there is still a focus on the inner world (as is the case with all psychoanalysis), there is much more openness to environmental and social issues, and the primary concern is not with the control of disruptive impulses, but rather with the quality of a person's relationships. Moreover, the role of these relationships, specifically early ones, in forming the person's mind is highlighted, something which is implied in Freud's thought but is not fully elaborated.

Some sources of object relations thinking

There are various ways of thinking about how and why object relations theory has developed in the powerful way it has. One source of it is clearly in Freud's own work, in two respects. The first is his account of the development of the ego. Particularly in his later theory, Freud understood that the ego, which starts life largely as the home for perceptions, becomes strengthened and elaborated by processes of internalization. This involves representations of objects and their attributes being 'taken in' to the mind, used and often identified with. This is especially the case with desired sexual objects – objects in which the child has a libidinal 'investment'. As the growing child has to give these up, for example because the mother is not fully under the child's control but separates herself from the child or is not immediately gratifying, so the ego takes them in, internalizing them and in the process altering itself. The ego thus comes to be a home for lost desires and forsaken objects, which are absorbed, along with the psychic energy invested in them. This, writes Freud (1923, p. 29), 'makes it possible to suppose that the character of the ego is a precipitate of abandoned object cathexes and that it contains the history of those object choices.' 'Cathexis' here means 'psychic investment'; Freud is basically saying that the ego gradually becomes stronger through experience and through the way its investments in objects are transformed into ego structures. Desire for an object leads to that object being taking in until it becomes part of the ego. The mind is thus to a considerable extent constituted by internalized (fantasy) versions of actual relationships. This is also why Freud (1917b, p. 249) can say that the ego identifies with the object and, in a very famous phrase that has to do with mourning, that 'the shadow of the object fell upon the ego.' What starts 'outside', comes in.

This is also what happens with the most obvious object relational element of Freud's thinking, the Oedipus complex. As described in Chapter 8, the Oedipus complex takes the form of a relational conflict between the (boy) child and the father over the child's wish to sexually possess the mother; it is thus an object relational drama. The result of it is a pattern of identification and repression that reorganizes the child's mind, in particular by giving rise to the superego – a new agency that is defined in terms of its relationship with external figures. Laplanche and Pontalis (1973, p. 436) write that 'In classical theory, the super-ego is described as the heir of the Oedipus complex in that it is constituted through the internalization of parental prohibitions and demands.' Yet the superego is a mental *structure*; thus, the mind has been changed by the encounter with the relational world.

These Freudian sources of the idea that object relations can be formative for the individual offer legitimacy to object relations theorists, but in truth the real motivation for the move towards relational thinking comes from elsewhere. In the late nineteenth and early twentieth century, Freud's patients seemed to be struggling to manage their desires and disturbing impulses, and for them, a theory that focused on the anxiety produced in the ego by unconscious urges worked well. However, as time has gone by, the patients of psychoanalysts have become more worried about their relationships: how to form them, how to become intimate in them, how not to damage them, how to feel real in them. Typical disturbances have moved away from hysteria and phobias and towards 'narcissistic' and 'schizoid' or 'borderline' states, all of them connected with issues of security of the self and the capacity to form trusting, dependent and mutually satisfying relationships. It is as if the problems people are troubled by are now less to do with controlling impulses (though these are certainly present, as the proliferation of mechanisms of surveillance and social control testifies) and more to do with how to relate to others. The rise of group and family therapies supports this view, as does the plethora of relationship counselling techniques and institutions. It all suggests that relational psychoanalysis is part of a general movement that understands the basic issues of unconscious life rather differently than was the case for Freud.

Relational thinking

Perhaps two statements define the object relational stance most clearly. One comes from the Scottish psychoanalyst Ronald Fairbairn (1944, p. 70): 'libido is primarily object-seeking (rather than pleasure-seeking, as in the classic theory), and ... it is to disturbances in the object-relationships of the developing ego that we must look for the ultimate origin of all psychopathological conditions.' The impulse towards relationships is thus 'hardwired' into the infant, and it is frustrations and disruptions of that impulse that produce psychological difficulties. The second quote comes from Donald Winnicott, whose highly influential work was briefly described in Chapter 10. Winnicott (1975, p. 99) writes, 'There is no such thing as a baby ... if you show me a baby you certainly show me also someone caring for the baby, or at least a pram with someone's eyes and ears glued to it. One sees a "nursing couple".' While this might seem an overly concrete way of considering the earliest relationships of life, with strongly middle-class norms attached to it, it succinctly makes the point that humans are social beings, born into relationships of mutual dependency, and that the way these relationships work out is a powerful influence on the psychological make-up of everyone. It is not that people are born separate and then have to forge links with others. It is rather that we are born in the context of intimate, dependent relationships and the nature of these relationships is crucial in determining what our emotional lives will be like.

Object relations theory, and relational thinking generally, thus proposes that the human individual's basic reality is expressed in her or his relationships. These are organized to meet fundamental needs that are very different from the needs that are the stuff of Freudian drive theory, being concerned instead with the interpersonal conditions required for healthy psychological development. Greenberg and Mitchell (1983, p. 198), for example, list the basic 'needs' implicit in Winnicott's theory as including 'an initially perfectly responsive facilitation of [the infant's] needs and gestures; a nonintrusive "holding" and mirroring environment throughout quiescent states', and so on – no mention here of feeding or the gratification of any sexual impulse, the usual bases for a biological drive theory of human social development. Fairbairn thought that at the start of life a relationship-seeking ego constitutes the whole of the infant's mental structure. Consequently, it is not necessary to assume the existence of an 'id' as a separate psychic structure which contains a pool of impulses that fuel psychological functioning. Instead, the psyche is thought initially to be a unity, a total ego, which has the potential to develop into a coherent and integrated personal self. Psychic splitting is a *secondary* phenomenon, a derivative of something else, and signifies a distortion of ideal development. Fairbairn's claim is that the child is a whole being from the start of life and would naturally remain whole however much might alter during development, except that various frustrations get in the way. In Guntrip's (1973, p. 93) gloss, 'Fairbairn believed that we must be aware of the fundamental dynamic wholeness of the human being as a person, which is the most important natural human characteristic. To Fairbairn, the preservation and growth of this wholeness constitutes mental health.'

Winnicott and the mother

The emphasis on *naturalness* in object relations theory here can also be seen in Winnicott's work. Winnicott's ideas are not always formulated exactly as a set of theoretical propositions, but a few major points (in addition to those mentioned in Chapter 10) drive the relational perspective forward. These can be briefly summarized as follows.

- For Winnicott, while the death drive is not a tenable idea, there is a place for aggression. However, aggression is not destructive as such. Instead, Winnicott interprets aggression in a manner that exemplifies the tendency to see the developmental process as one of active striving with external objects in the service of an integrating relational urge. Winnicott declares aggression to be 'almost synonymous with activity' (1975, p. 204), giving it a central role in early development. Aggression and eroticism are two components of an initially unified 'life force', which splits in early development before, all being well, becoming the basis of an integrated or 'fused' self. The aggressive component has the important function of allowing the infant to establish its opposition to – or difference from – the external world, thus helping to establish the boundaries of the self.

- Related to this is an idea developed in Winnicott's remarkable short papers, 'The Capacity to be Alone' (1958) and 'The Use of an Object' (1969). The former describes how the ability to be alone and to retain the kind of curiosity that is required to reach out to the world depends on having previously internalized a sense of being *thought about* by another. This results in the conviction that we are never truly alone: we are always in the presence of someone who cares, even if that person is not actually there at that time. The 'use of an object' describes how the infant has fantasies of destroying the person ('object') she or he is attached to, because of the necessary frustrations of life and also as a product of inbuilt aggressive urges. The ability of that person to survive these 'attacks' convinces the infant that the other is a separate person, that she is not the product of the infant's own fantasies and hence has resilience and reliability, and so can be 'used' in productive ways.

- All these ideas converge on a general notion of *trust*. If the world is trustworthy, it 'holds' the child, and because of this the child's 'true self' can grow, rather than becoming hidden behind a conformist 'false self' that desperately hides its feelings because it needs to be accepted by an unreliable or needy parent. This way of thinking about things has become very important in some recent sociological theory, where attempts have been made to describe the conditions necessary for societies based on trust and mutual recognition. In writings such as those of Anthony Giddens (1991) and Axel Honneth (1996) there is a strong emphasis on developmental modes of sensitive responsiveness that produce secure selves and positive relationships that in turn can provide the foundations for a more socially progressive society.

- Winnicott's emphasis on the absorption of the mother in her infant (primary maternal preoccupation) was alluded to in Chapter 10. At first, this mother–child interaction centres on periods in which the infant is excited and the mother anticipates the object suitable to the child's desires (for example offering the breast when the baby is hungry), conjuring up a sense of omnipotence in the infant which serves as the basis for a creative sense of a powerful self. In between these periods, when the child is peaceful, the mother's role is to be a solid but nonintrusive figure, allowing the child to feel secure in the presence of someone else. Gradually, as the child begins to establish a sense of self, the mother has to learn how to 'fail', to recover in stages from the 'illness' of primary maternal preoccupation, so that the child can learn the limits of her or his power and can gain the experience of becoming a separate being in a real world.

- Throughout early development, the mother functions as a kind of mirror to her child, mediating reality gradually, at a pace appropriate to the infant's development. This is the foundation of 'good enough mothering'.

Adam Phillips (1988, p. 100) glosses this whole set of ideas as, 'Where the Id of the infant is, the mother's Ego must also be.' All this puts an enormous weight on the mother's behaviour and in particular her receptivity to her infant and her resilience in dealing with crises and difficulties. Many writers have criticized Winnicott for this, suggesting that his idealized view of the mother reflects a traditionally patriarchal set of attitudes that makes the mother responsible for everything. There is truth in this criticism, but it is also worth noting how Winnicott's ideas, like object relations theory more generally, move psychoanalysis towards a greater degree of engagement with the actual developmental context in which children grow up, and hence potentially take fuller account of their social circumstances.

Subjectivity and intersubjectivity

Winnicott's notion of transitional space, outlined in Chapter 10, has proved productive for another group of theorists, calling themselves 'intersubjectivists'. 'Intersubjectivity' is a term used to refer to the capacity to represent another person as a *subject* in the strict sense of a separate being with whom one can have a dialogue based on mutual recognition. It is thus a step forward from the usual subject–object dichotomy which dominates in much western thought, including psychoanalysis. In a highly influential paper on 'The Analytic Third', Thomas Ogden (1994, p. 3) summarizes his own stance, which would be shared by this group of analysts, as follows.

I believe that it is fair to say that contemporary psychoanalytic thinking is approaching a point where one can no longer simply speak of the analyst and the analysand as separate subjects who take one another as objects. The idea of the analyst as a neutral blank screen for the patient's projections is occupying a position of steadily diminishing importance in current conceptions of the analytic process.

Ogden conceptualizes the clinical encounter as one characterized by a dialectic in which each partner (analyst and patient, paralleling mother and infant) exists both as an individual and in relationship with one another. His point is that the relational element – the 'third' – cannot be reduced to the individuals, but nor does it take them over completely. 'In both the relationship of mother and infant and of analyst and analysand,' he writes (p. 4), 'the task is not to tease apart the elements constituting the relationship in an effort to determine which qualities belong to each individual participating in it; rather, from the point of view of the interdependence of subject and object, the analytic task involves an attempt to describe as fully as possible the specific nature of the experience of the interplay of individual subjectivity and intersubjectivity.'

I will return to some of these ideas later in the context of a discussion of therapeutic processes. However, a key point here is the way in which the relational perspective makes it possible to conceptualize a set of unconscious dynamics that go further than just the individual concerned. Psychoanalysis becomes more communicational in this model, without being reduced to an interpersonal psychology that ignores unconscious elements. The relationships with which it deals are infused with unconscious processes that make it possible to imagine different subjective worlds colliding and affecting one another; and this is seen as the most significant way in which psychoanalysis itself has its therapeutic effects.

The intersubjectivist perspective builds upon object relations theory to address social issues through the relational capacities of the human subject. Whereas traditional theory has been interested in how individuals incorporate aspects of the outside world, for example taking in maternal or paternal attributes, intersubjectivism spotlights the question of *recognition*, of appreciating, accepting and relating to others as 'subjects'. The self consequently can be seen to arise out of a process of recognizing the intentionality and agency of the loved other and identifying with this. This idea moves psychoanalytic theory away from its tendency to see social life as a struggle between individuals and towards a vision of the bridging of differences. It has been taken up very productively by psychoanalysts and social theorists (particularly feminists) interested in developing thinking on conflict resolution and in finding ways to encourage acknowledgment of social suffering (for example Benjamin, 2004; Butler, 2009). Returning to Winnicott, it also re-establishes the mother (or more general 'other') not just as a passive support for the infant, a mere reflecting mirror, but as an active agent, exploring the infant's developing self and in so doing communicating the significance and centrality of the appreciation of other people's minds.

Summary

- Object relations theory has its roots in Freud's ideas about the development of the ego through internalization of lost objects, and the way in which the Oedipus complex produces 'structural' changes in the mind.
- 'Objects' here are primarily internal representations of relationships with people or personified parts of people, such as the breast or penis.
- A major claim of all relational theorists is that 'libido is object seeking'. At its broadest, this means that relationships are primary, and that what appear to be the 'drives' of sexuality and aggression act in their service or are produced by them.
- There is a strong sense in much relational thinking that the individual has a natural propensity towards psychic growth and seeks fulfilling relationships, but that these can be blocked and frustrated, leading to the patterns of psychopathology with which psychoanalysts are familiar.
- Winnicott's ideas are particularly influential, even though they are clearly rooted in a set of normative assumptions arising from his historical context. His notion of a maturational environment draws psychoanalytic attention to the conditions within which children develop and therefore has the potential to make psychoanalysis a more socially refined theory.

- One important contemporary relational approach is intersubjectivism, which focuses on how individual subjectivity is 'pooled' when we are in intense contact with others.
- The general relational perspective makes psychoanalysis more amenable to use as an element in social theory. It has been particularly productive in supporting the development of thinking on conflict and on the necessary conditions for recognition of the rights and needs of others.

13

Mourning, melancholia, depression and loss

Mourning and melancholia

As will be clear from the discussion in the last two chapters, much contemporary psychoanalysis has reacted against classical Freudian drive theory, seeing it as mechanical or biologistic, perhaps neglecting the more 'human' elements of subjective experience. Instead, many psychoanalytic theorists share the project of bringing relationships more to the fore and developing a fuller understanding of how people's 'inner worlds' are made up from the intimate encounters that they have with others throughout their lives. In particular, relational psychoanalysis is interested not so much in the sense that people have of being 'driven' by forces that they cannot control, but rather more in how experiences of love and loss weigh on their minds.

As it happens, Freud was not blind to this more humanistic element of psychology, and produced some very rich thinking on this that still passes muster today. The idea that the ego might be built up on the basis of internalization of lost objects has already been encountered. However, it is perhaps in his very striking analysis of depression that he conveys most vividly what psychoanalysis might have to offer; and it is relevant here that this analysis, couched in terms of 'melancholia', is still very influential in clinical and in social thought.

In his very important text *Mourning and Melancholia*, Freud notes that loss is a central component of both 'normal' mourning and the excessive variety that goes by the name 'melancholia'. 'Mourning,' he writes (1917b, p. 243), 'is regularly the reaction to the loss of a loved person, or to the loss of some abstraction which has taken the place of one, such as one's country, liberty, an ideal, and so on.' It is the loss of a *person* that is central, with other kinds of loss being secondary to that – they have 'taken the place' of a person, perhaps because they are associated with one (loss of an ideal based on someone previously admired, for example) or perhaps because the emotional energy that was once attached to the person has been displaced onto something else (love for a parent transformed into love for one's 'motherland' or something similar). Freud goes on to explore the relationship between mourning as a normal reaction to these kinds of losses, understandable as sadness that might lift after a time and is proportionate to the loss involved, and melancholia as a pathological condition in which mourning cannot properly take place, and for that very reason allows the loss to poison the mind – to become what is now termed severe depression.

Freud's account of mourning and melancholia is worth presenting at length as, despite its somewhat archaic language, it is still unsurpassed in its descriptive acuity.

> The distinguishing mental features of melancholia are a profoundly painful dejection, cessation of interest in the outside world, loss of the capacity to love, inhibition of all activity, and a lowering of the self-regarding feelings to a degree that finds utterance in self-reproaches and self-revilings, and culminates in a delusional expectation of punishment. This picture becomes a little more intelligible when we consider that, with one exception, the same traits are met with in mourning. The disturbance of self-regard is absent in mourning; but otherwise the features are the same. Profound mourning, the reaction to the loss of someone who is loved, contains the same painful frame of mind, the same loss of interest in the outside world – in so far as it does not recall him – the same loss of capacity to adopt any new object of love (which would mean replacing him) and the same turning away from any activity that is not connected with thoughts of him. (Freud, 1917b, p. 244)

This passage has a number of interesting components. First, melancholia is seen as paralleling mourning, and as mourning is a response to loss then it implies that melancholia has similar causes. Secondly, as well as identifying the passivity and loss of interest in the world to be found in depression, Freud draws attention to the 'self-reproaches and self-revilings', to the way the *self* becomes the object of attack. He is pointing out here that in depression self-recrimination dominates and it often seems that the depressed person is behaving as if she or he has caused the loss, whether or not this is actually the case.

The *difference* between melancholia and mourning in this way of thinking about things is subtle but important. Psychoanalysts, following Freud (1917b, p. 246), would say that 'In mourning it is the world which has become poor and empty; in melancholia it is the ego itself.' The implications of this can perhaps be understood relatively easily, even if the division between mourning and melancholia is not necessarily as clear as Freud makes out. If it is the world that has lost meaning, then we might find ways of acting on the world to recover it; we might even accidentally find that meaning is restored through the presence of someone who cares, or who we care about, or some other positive response. In melancholia, however, because it is the ego that is depleted, there is no inner capacity to respond to such potentially rescuing moments. Whatever actually exists in the world, however benevolent it might 'objectively' be, it cannot be used. Melancholia – severe depression – feeds on itself, consuming the person until there is nothing left that can respond to the feelers put out even by those who are full of genuine concern.

Melancholia as social being

The imagery of melancholia is proving to be very useful in many ways, some of them quite surprising. Clinically, it draws attention to a number of features of depression and loss that are readily observable but not always easy to make sense of. At times, depressed patients can seem almost 'psychotic' in the degree to which they blame themselves for everything that is wrong in the world, and indeed sometimes they actually have psychotic symptoms such as the belief that other people can see right into them and know how bad they really are inside. These patients may have suffered significant losses – and in reality, everyone has suffered *some* loss that is significant to them – but their mental suffering is way out of proportion to it. The psychoanalytic idea that melancholia is a kind of distorted mourning makes the link to the loss but also offers a route towards understanding the exaggeration. The key elements in this are the self-hatred mentioned above but also how the loss is somehow kept alive in the mind, rather than properly grieved. Mourning is a process whereby we recognize the loss of an 'object' (a person or the substitute for one, as outlined above) and grieve for it. Healthy mourning results, however painfully, in coming to terms with that object's demise, and in incorporating it into the ego so that life can go on. In melancholia, however, there is no recognition of the loss of the object, which instead becomes an unconscious spur to continuing psychic trouble. It exists 'in' the unconscious as something that cannot be grieved because its loss is never acknowledged. This has some paradoxical effects. The object is not recognized so cannot be seen for what it is, and therefore cannot be let go of; it continues to trouble the person. The sense that so many people have of being 'haunted' by something that has happened, or perhaps by something they feel they have damaged, is linked to this failure to mourn. In a complicated way, this means that the object is in some sense *preserved* as an unconscious entity, kept alive so that the person can somehow believe in its continued existence – but also, like a ghost, not laid to rest.

This idea of a refusal of loss has been taken up not only in clinical work but also in social theory, for instance in the context of postcolonial thinking. This is a complex terrain, but the most important idea is that societies that have freed themselves from colonialism nevertheless embody something from the unremembered past, unacknowledged and unwanted yet having intensely ambivalent effects (Khanna, 2004). Colonialism so comprehensively destroyed the sources of value within the cultures that it conquered that, while there might be powerful sensations of loss at work in those cultures, there is little access to the actual things that were lost. At times, it is suggested, this leads to a psychic response in which the unbearable nature of this loss is denied and replaced by a manic rush towards the *colonizer's* mode of being, for example in copying the structures of the colonial nation state. It can also result in a form of melancholic subjectivity that produces a restlessness in which it becomes known, or at least felt, that something has gone missing – that something has been *stolen*. Because it is impossible to trace what this is, the society is haunted by a kind of empty rage and odd deference to those who possess things to which they can point as having value. Envy and internecine destructiveness arise from this, a mode of violence that covers over loss.

Whether it is legitimate to extend clinical accounts of melancholia to social theories applying to whole cultures is a moot point, but the metaphor of postcolonial melancholy is certainly proving to be a powerful one and helps to bring into focus questions about subjectivity that are often neglected in more conventional ways of doing history and politics. This is true generally about postcolonial uses of psychoanalysis, which have begun to offer new ways into the complex question of racialized subjectivities – of how the unconscious is affected by 'race', ethnicity and culture. For example, Kalpana Seshadri-Crooks (2000) has examined the psychoanalytic underpinnings of the 'desire for whiteness' and Rhanjana Khanna (2004) has attended to ways in which psychoanalysis has informed political and cultural explorations of colonialism – despite itself being heavily infiltrated by colonialist assumptions. In the context of melancholia, the postcolonial stance also suggests that there might be something about how loss is processed that affects the well-being of individuals and societies as wholes. This makes it worthwhile to turn now to the theory of depressive functioning derived from the work of Melanie Klein, which arguably has provided our most cogent version of how we might manage to live with loss.

The depressive position

To understand Klein's idea of the depressive position one has first to realize that her theory emphasizes the interplay of powerful drives and object relationships that give rise to intense affects and also determine the direction of development of the mind. At first, the infant is dominated by sensations of love and hate that can only be coped with by projecting them outwards onto the object; this is the characteristic defensive strategy of the 'paranoid-schizoid position' and will be described more fully in the next two chapters, when considering psychotic processes and extreme defences. Another strategy at this point (which is returned to whenever the mind is under strain) is to divide loving from destructive feelings so that the latter can be split off and contained more easily. The 'schizoid' element of the paranoid-schizoid position refers specifically to this splitting, separating tendency. However, Klein also assumes the existence in the early ego of integrative tendencies, derived from the operation of the life drives. These gradually become dominant and splitting ceases to be the mind's main mode of functioning. Instead, the infant begins to relate to her or himself and to external objects as wholes, both good and bad, containing elements of loving kindness and of destructive envy. This is a relief in many ways, as it lessens the persecutory sensations that the infant has. However, a new problem is also created. Because the mother is experienced as a whole object, not split into good and bad parts, she becomes the source of both gratification and pain, and the child's attitude to her is one of *ambivalence*. Thus, the good mother, from whom the child derives nurture and love, is no longer imagined as separate from the frustrating mother towards whom the child feels hostility. The child starts to imagine that her or his rage can damage or even destroy the mother, leading to loss of the most precious object, on whom the child depends. This gives rise to feelings of grief over the lost good object, and guilt over the way it has been destroyed (in fantasy) by the child's own aggression. The mind itself becomes an arena for destructiveness that is no longer experienced as only 'out there' in the world of external objects, but rather as 'in here', *owned* by the child. Put crudely, once we are exposed to ambivalence we discover that it is possible to do damage to the things (and people) we love. With this discovery comes the realization of loss, leaving the person feeling wasted and empty. The mixture of feelings experienced at this point – love and hate, guilt and loss – constitutes what is known as the 'depressive position'.

To summarize, the depressive position has the following components:

- Growing integration of the life and death drives.
- Growing integration of the object.
- As a consequence, the emergence of ambivalent feelings.
- Recognition that one can love and hate the same object and that one's destructive urges can do damage.
- Resulting sensations of loss, grief and guilt, which constitute a 'normal' depression in early life and also become the paradigm for depression whenever it occurs.

A brief clinical example might help flesh out this abstract account.

A patient in psychotherapy describes intense anger directed at people she perceives as being critical of her husband, who has recently died. The criticism is over his failure to look after himself properly when he knew he had a potentially serious illness, and more generally his inability to share his health worries with anyone, which resulted in his taking action too late to receive effective treatment. The patient believes that her husband was actually a very brave man who protected her and their children from the knowledge of how sick he was, so as to prevent their worrying too much. The people who criticize him not only fail to understand this, but also, by their attitude, spoil her memory of a wonderful person.

Over the course of several psychotherapy sessions, it becomes clear both to the therapist and to the patient that there are actually very few instances in which people express the critical views she is ascribing to them. In fact, people are very supportive and seem willing to listen to her talk about her husband's qualities without demur. She gradually becomes clearer in her mind that while some people do have a negative view of how her husband handled his illness, what actually happens is that she listens out for the slightest indication that this idea is around and then reacts strongly to it. A friend need only ask about the treatment he received, or comment on how well he had looked shortly before he died, for her to feel this to be a criticism and to react quite explosively. She begins to wonder if in fact she is on the lookout for criticisms because they raise something that she thinks herself, but feels is disloyal and wrong to express.

Gradually, the patient starts to talk about how much she loved her husband but how infuriatingly secretive he could be about what was going on for him, especially when he had any anxieties. She wishes he could have spoken more openly to her and that they could have created a more 'sharing' marriage. She acknowledges that the critical ideas she ascribes to others are in many ways her own – that if he had been more open he might have got better treatment, and in any case she would have been able to support him more. She would also not have had such a terrible shock when he suddenly entered the final stage of his illness, but could have prepared herself and her family better. She feels angry with him over this, but also sad. As she starts to realize that this mix of feelings is her own, she becomes less persecuted by other people's comments.

Very schematically, we might say that the patient has moved from an earlier paranoid-schizoid mode of thinking in which all the 'badness' is located outside herself, to a more depressive mode in which she can 'own' her mixed feelings and recognize her anger as well as her sadness and love.

Reparation

The suggestion that depression is the best one can hope for might seem unduly pessimistic. However, what is being worked out here is a way to conceptualize the gradual deepening of the capacity to feel and to think about one's feelings. If a person feels little, they are to some extent protected against depression; but they are also unable to manage the challenges of intimacy and love. Once a person takes the psychological risk of allowing that it is possible to feel strongly about those on whom we depend – that relationships are complicated and messy and that each of us contributes to this situation – then meaningful links with others arise, which might cause pain but also bring rewards. Put slightly more psychoanalytically, one could say that in the depressive position the person is exposed to feelings of loss and guilt, but the realization of the integrated nature of the object produces a sense of optimism which can carry her or him to a triumphant working through of these difficult feelings. This is because the badness of the object and the destructiveness of the internal world are now experienced as ameliorated by the goodness of the same object and the loving, constructive manifestations of the life drive. In its integrated form, destructiveness is less threatening than in its split, pure form, and the person is more able to overcome it and become engaged in a benevolent cycle of depression and reintegration.

Perhaps the most important new development in the depressive position is that of *reparation*. The idea is a simple one: reparation includes 'the variety of processes by which the ego feels it undoes harm done in phantasy, restores, preserves and revives objects' (Klein, 1955, p. 133). The concept of reparation transforms the idea of aggression from a purely destructive principle to a *complex* containing positive possibilities: the formation of loving personal relationships out of a desire to make good out of what is potentially damaged. Hanna Segal (1973, p. 95) emphasizes how central reparative processes are to healthy mental functioning, stating: 'Reparation proper can hardly be considered a defence, since it is based on the recognition of psychic reality, the experiencing of the pain that this reality causes and the taking of appropriate action to relieve it in phantasy and reality.'

Reparation derives from the depressive position because it depends on the acknowledgement of the integrity of the good-and-bad object and the ambivalent drives. Something only needs to be made good if it is valued as well as hated; reparation is only possible if the ego contains good impulses as well as bad. The love immanent in reparation thus supports the integrating tendencies present in the ego. Eventually, the experience of reparation allows the depressive position to be transcended, as the child discovers within her or himself the resources to mitigate destructiveness, becoming more stable and also more psychologically realistic. Reparation is also the basis of the Kleinian theory of creativity, which assumes that the drive to 'make good' that which is experienced as damaged is the source of the artistic impulse and the explanation of the relationship between cultural forms and the psychological processes of the artists who produce them. This idea has proved especially fruitful in explorations of modernism, notably studies of authors like Virginia Woolf, for whom issues of fragmentation, regeneration and destructiveness were central (for example Stonebridge, 1998).

Depressive phenomena in the world

Just as Freud's ideas on melancholia are proving helpful for thinking about some social issues in relation to postcolonial states, so the Kleinian idea of the depressive position has directed sociological attention to ways in which societies might strive to overcome destructiveness and create the conditions under which reparative urges might predominate. The general argument is that the 'depressive' tendency to brood on feelings of loss and responsibility can be enlisted in the service of social arrangements that offer stability and resilient love in the face of aggression and in particular that recognize that the capacity for care depends on these kinds of mechanisms (for example Rustin, 1991). We cannot deny negative feelings; but the existence of such feelings should be a spur to working them through rather than to punitive responses. These ideas can be applied, for example, to attempts to introduce 'acknowledgement' and conflict resolution work into political situations in which destructive hatred is evident. They are particularly apposite to the work of post-conflict 'truth and reconciliation commissions' (for example Potter, 2006), which often have religious overtones but also draw explicitly on a language of forgiveness and reparation that can be problematic (Rose, 2003) but nevertheless has strong psychoanalytic resonance.

There is a tendency here to move quite quickly from a psychoanalytic framework to a moral one, in which finding ways to take responsibility for one's destructive feelings is seen as a primary task in life; and it is arguable whether psychoanalysts should go exactly down that route. On the other hand, it might be suggested that this is precisely the arena in which psychoanalysis travels – it is a discipline of 'practical ethics' as much as it is a technology for treatment or a theory of the mind.

Summary

- Freud developed a theory of 'melancholia' that sees it as parallel to mourning, but characterized by self-reproaches and a depletion of the ego.
- Freud's ideas have been taken up in contemporary psychoanalytic theory and linked with the suggestion that in melancholia/depression the grieving required for healthy mourning does not occur because the loss of the treasured object has never been fully accepted.
- This has the paradoxical effect of 'preserving' the object in the psyche in an unrecognized (unconscious) way, so that it continues to have an impact on the person. This gives rise to a sense of being haunted by the object.
- Links have been made between this set of ideas and various social situations, notably that of 'postcolonial melancholy'.
- A further highly influential psychoanalytic account of depression comes from the work of Kleinian psychoanalysts and their idea of the 'depressive position'.
- The depressive position is a normal developmental phase characterized by increasing integration of loving and destructive impulses and a growing appreciation of the integrity of the external object.
- This results in ambivalence, with the consequence that the child can feel sadness, guilt and loss as a consequence of her or his own destructive urges.
- The intensity of ambivalence is a sign of deepening capacity for feeling but can also be painful and is the foundation of depression.
- Working through the depressive position, particularly through making reparation, is a developmental, psychotherapeutic and cultural task.

14

The paranoid-schizoid position and other extremes

Neurotic children, psychotic infants

In the last chapter, the focus of attention was on how contemporary psychoanalysis, especially Kleinian theory, makes sense of experiences of depression and loss. Some of the states of mind described there could be seen as 'normal', for example the sadness a person might feel on being bereaved. Other states, termed by Freud 'melancholia' but nowadays seen as severe depression, are clearly more severe. In this chapter, I turn to yet more extreme ways in which the mind might operate and in which what are commonly called 'psychotic' breakdowns might occur. As described in Chapter 9, these are states of mind in which the relationship with reality is called into question. In the classification system of psychiatry, they relate to 'schizophrenia' and various forms of paranoia. For psychoanalysis, the key issue is that they can be conceptualized as attacks on thinking itself – as ways in which the ego tries to protect itself against collapse by forcefully repudiating the unconscious impulses that rise up against it.

Freud seems to have believed that psychoanalysis was unlikely to be very effective with psychotic patients. This was primarily because of the fragmented nature of psychotic relationships with the world or, to use Freud's own formulation, the *narcissistic* characteristics of psychosis itself. At its simplest, this means that the patient's libidinal interests are turned inwards rather than outwards, with the effect that she or he has only a very limited capacity to form the kind of relationship with an analyst that is necessary for therapeutic change to occur. Put crudely, psychotic patients are seen as less likely to form 'whole object' relationships in which the other is seen as a person with an objective existence of her or his own, who can be 'used' as a source of insight and growth (Winnicott, 1969; see Chapter 12). Neurotics might struggle to manage their unconscious urges or to deal with ambivalence, but at least they can conceptualize that other people exist in their own right and might in principle have something to offer them. Psychotic patients, embedded in a world of 'part objects', of a mind that consists of bits and pieces not properly linked with each other, cannot do this. They are more likely instead to feel that there is no proper boundary between self and other, and no clear organization of their mental space. This has consequences for the kinds of defences that predominate. Neurotics are especially addicted to repression and other defences that hide unconscious wishes from consciousness. Psychotics are bedevilled by, and dependent on, splitting and projection, in which parts of the mind are separated from each other, with disturbing material and, at the extreme, pathological mental structures (a highly punitive superego, for example) experienced as if they belong to the *external* world. This is one source of hallucinations: the person's disowned thoughts are 'speaking' as if they come from elsewhere.

In very loose developmental terms, the contrast between neurosis and psychosis parallels that between childhood and infancy. The idea here is that the integration of the psyche and of the object world is a developmental achievement, not fully attained until the Oedipus complex is worked through. Prior to that, the infant is in a kind of primeval state of confusion, governed by powerful impulses derived from biological sources, and lacking the mental capacity to make sense of them or to integrate them into some kind of whole. Both inner and outer worlds feel like they are fragmentary. Some of this experience can be translated into terms familiar from cognitive psychology under the heading of 'object permanence' (Piaget and Inhelder, 1969; Damon et al., 2006). This work suggests that infants have to learn that an object that disappears and comes back again is the same object – a piece of learning that generally speaking happens very early in development. In relation to issues of psychoanalytic interest, the infant might 'wonder', 'Is the breast that gives milk the same breast that sometimes is not available? Is the mother who goes away and the one who comes back the same person?' These are questions of great significance for the infant, perhaps even of life or death importance. The psychoanalytic idea is that, early on, they have to be dealt with carefully by using 'extreme' defences until the affect associated with them can be managed and psychological integration can be gradually achieved. Because the whole experience is highly charged, people tend to drift back into such extreme states when circumstances demand it – for example when something overwhelming and unbearable occurs. There is even a tendency to do this in situations of relatively mild assault on personal boundaries, such as being in a large crowd (at a football match or mass rally, for instance) or being under the influence of certain drugs. At such times, the capacity to experience the world as a whole is weakened and it is common to find a drift 'back' into what are seen as more 'primitive' ways of defending oneself.

The paranoid-schizoid position

The most clearly articulated theoretical version of this understanding of the relationship between psychotic and developmentally very early states of mind can be found in the work of Melanie Klein. Paradoxically, the Kleinian emphasis on the importance of what they call 'paranoid-schizoid' functioning also offers a way forward for the psychoanalysis of psychotic patients, and this has been an aspect of Kleinian practice that has made it highly influential. The argument involves a shift from seeing fragmentary states of mind as developmentally 'pre-historic', to understanding them as *foundational*. They do not simply represent a *failure* to achieve integration; they rather demonstrate the workings of basic mental mechanisms that are operative at all stages of life and that frequently make themselves felt in the consulting room. Because they are so pervasive, when they come to dominate a mind as they do in some psychotic states, they are familiar and potentially amenable to treatment – although Kleinians by no means underestimate the difficulties involved.

The previous chapter traced the development of the 'depressive position' as a move towards psychic integration and an appreciation of loss, guilt and responsibility. Kleinians see the achievement of this kind of psychological integrity as a life task, with mental health being characterized by the capacity to form loving, forgiving relationships based on it. However, it is neither a stable achievement nor does it appear from nowhere. It is underpinned by an earlier paranoid-schizoid phase in which powerful impulses towards splitting are dominant. This earlier phase has to be overcome, or worked through, for the depressive position to assert itself. But it is important not to see the paranoid-schizoid phase in totally negative terms. It also has a positive side, for instance in protecting the mind from extreme trauma and also in giving a great deal of energy to the psyche. The powerful ideas and affects associated with it are therefore continually drawn on throughout life as a resource, as well as being a potentially destructive threat. Put more simply, there is constant movement between the depressive position and the paranoid-schizoid position; the former dominates in a healthy person, but the latter is never very far away.

The paranoid-schizoid 'position', as the Kleinians term it, is a very complicated idea, which has the following characteristics:

- It is a developmental stage, occurring very early in the first year of life, which is retained as a way of functioning that is called on throughout later development and in adulthood. This is why it is termed a 'position', although it is also quite often referred to as a 'phase'.
- It is characterized by intense feelings of love and hate, attached to the workings of the life and death drives.
- It is governed mainly by the defences of splitting and projection:
  - The splitting is both of the ego and of the object, so that a loving element of the mind is separated from the destructive element and the 'good object' is kept apart from the 'bad object'. Processes of idealization and denigration throughout life are derivatives of this tendency.
  - The projection is a complicated process that begins with the rejection of the infant's own envious impulses, which are seen as deriving directly from the death drive. These envious impulses are experienced as dangerously destructive. In order to cope with them, they are expelled (projected) outwards and become attached to the external ('bad') object. This creates a paranoid environment for the child and places internal feelings of goodness at risk. As a consequence, loving impulses are also projected into the 'good object'.

- Experiences of a fundamentally caring environment, for example a mother who can survive the infant's 'attacks' without becoming depressed or punitive, lead the infant to view its destructive urges as gradually more manageable. This enables envy to be tempered by gratitude, hate by love, and an appreciation of the object as basically whole (both good and frustrating) emerges.
- *Introjection*, which refers to a process of absorbing objects and the impulses and emotions attached to them 'into' the mind, gradually takes place as a process of growing integration occurs. This then leads into the depressive position.

There are numerous elements in this 'model', some of the most important of which are laid out below. (The concept of projection will be dealt with in detail in Chapter 15.)

- **The bodily basis for psychological processes**
What is being described here is how very powerful unconscious urges are managed by equally potent defences; and these defences then become the mental mechanisms that govern the mind. They are built out of the infant's bodily experiences of taking in and giving out – of feeding and excreting – so that projection and introjection can be imagined as an extension of the infant's most elementary relationship with its world. As it matures, these bodily processes become mental representations of reality. This means that our most basic ways of thinking and feeling are forged in the image of those earliest physical experiences.

- **Envy as the manifestation of the death drive**
Klein's theory begins with adherence to a version of Freud's division between life and death drives, seen as inborn and initially very hard to manage. Although the life drive is always present, it is the death drive that dominates in early development, because it causes profound anxiety to the ego, which is fragile and tentative at the start. The death drive is a destructive urge, expressed psychologically in *envy*. Envy itself is worth taking seriously as a concept. Spillius et al. (2011, p. 166) define it as 'the angry feeling that another person possesses and enjoys something desirable, often accompanied by an impulse to take it away or spoil it.' Klein herself (1957, p. 176) states more strongly that it is 'an

oral-sadistic and anal-sadistic expression of destructive impulses.' In early infancy, envy is directed against the feeding breast and, according to Klein, it is absolutely inescapable, whether the breast is fulfilling or not. If the breast is unsatisfactory, the child hates it because it is felt to be mean and grudging; if the breast is satisfactory, its inimitable flow of goodness is envied, the child wishing hopelessly to own it. Thus, when envy is intense, the perception of a good object can be as painful as that of a bad one, for the better it is the more it gives rise to envious wishes. Envy destroys hope, because it is directed at the sources of goodness in the child's world. Its recurrence during psychotherapy, when the analyst might be envied precisely because she or he is able to be helpful, is both a necessary focus for work and a profound threat to progress, as the following brief vignette tries to show.

> A man plagued by feelings of insecurity and worthlessness comes to psychotherapy for help. Initially he seems responsive to the therapist's comments, but gradually it becomes obvious that nothing the therapist says is making any real difference to him. Tracing what happens in the session, it is clear that the patient 'rubbishes' the therapist's comments, and that the more potentially helpful they seem to be, the more intense is this rubbishing process. It seems as if he cannot bear the fact that the therapist has the ability to think clearly and constructively when he himself feels so damaged and empty inside. It is this envious response to the therapist's work that becomes the focus of the psychotherapy.

- *Splitting*

With envy being so rife and so damaging, the infant's ego has to call on some very powerful defences in order to survive. In particular, if the potential goodness of the psyche – the manifestation of the life drive in loving emotions – is to be protected, then it has to be kept separate from the potentially poisonous activities of envy. In early infancy it is therefore necessary for the infant to use splitting defences in order to protect the ego from being overwhelmed by envy. Only this way can the loving and grateful elements of mental life be preserved long enough for them to be strengthened, hopefully by experiences of a relatively nurturing environment. And it is only when loving impulses are strong enough that the child's mind can start to become integrated, and the depressive position can gradually come to shade the paranoid-schizoid one, calming things down.

Klein's emphasis on the foundational significance of splitting is actually a departure from the classical Freudian view. Freud believed that repression drove the formation of the unconscious and was the earliest real defence. Klein saw splitting as a more fundamental way in which intrapsychic conflicts are managed. The difference between them is that repression depends on the existence of a relatively strong ego capable of recognizing and repelling unwanted material from consciousness, but splitting is 'simply' a matter of holding things apart, rather desperately most of the time, and can be achieved at the behest of an ego which is literally just coming into being and is struggling for continued existence.

- *Extremes of splitting and psychotic fragmentation*

Failures of splitting and too much splitting are both destructive of mental progress. Because of the duality of the drives, the infant's mind is always at risk; this can be felt as emotional and cognitive confusion as well as being attacked by envious feelings. Consequently, in order to save the loving elements of the mind from being poisoned in this way, and also in order to create an ideal object to which the ego can aspire, loving and hateful elements of the mind have to be split from each other and projected outwards. Without this splitting, there would be no chance of moving forwards; but if the splitting is too intense and the environment not sufficiently caring to be able to build bridges across from 'bad' to 'good', it can become a fixed way of being in which it is impossible for ambivalence to occur. Instead, there exists pure hate in a persecutory world, and the love that feeds on gratification and generosity is forced into hiding in order not to be overwhelmed.

The conundrum here is that without splitting there can be no mind – one has to hold some things at bay in order to think about others – but with too much splitting, there is a failure to connect elements of inner and outer worlds. If splitting is too intense, the mind faces an increasing barrenness in which different elements become split off in order to preserve them from contamination by badness; and the outside world is experienced as constituted by fragmentary objects unable to make contact with each other. This extreme splitting hampers development and can form the prototype for psychotic breakdowns. For example, excessive anxiety can bring about too much of a split, leading to fragmentation of the ego, which results in its being broken up into unintegratable little bits. Hanna Segal (1973, p. 31) states about this, 'In order to avoid suffering the ego does its best not to exist, an attempt which gives rise to a specific acute anxiety – that of falling to bits and becoming atomised.' This is an example of how defences can cause psychic trouble even as they ward off something worse. In the work of the Kleinian analyst Wilfred Bion (1962), this process is theorized by the notion of 'bizarre objects', tiny bits of mind that are deliberately disconnected from one another to make them less vulnerable to attack. These bizarre objects have the effect of producing a psychological state that is desperately concrete and dangerous but also mysterious and confusing (nothing relates to anything else) – a prototypically psychotic experience.

Integrating the psyche

What Klein seems to be telling us in this apparently cataclysmic tale of inborn envy, splitting and fragmentation, is not only the Freudian story of a fundamental division in consciousness, but also how the activity of splitting is something in which the mind engages in order to be able to survive its own passion. Faced with the intensity of infantile emotion and with the difficulty of discerning 'good' from 'bad', love from hate, people lose themselves in fantasies of purity and difference. Here is the ideal, there the devil; here the all-good, there the one embodying evil. Not only, says Klein, are these emblems to be found or invented in the external world, but our inner lives become structured around such splits. We are consequently doubly divided beings, 'vertically' as Freud would have it, between conscious and unconscious (the conscious on the surface, the unconscious the hidden depth), but also 'horizontally', *in* the unconscious itself, between love and hate, life and death.

Klein stresses the innate character of envy and hence of splitting, but there is also an *environmental* role. An excess of bad experiences can fail to mollify the destructive urges of the infant, making the defences more and more extreme and self-damaging. A generous, calm and loving environment can ease the need for severe splitting and promote integration. For although gratification does provoke envy, which is why it is impossible to remove it completely and why it is so persistent throughout life, other emotions are also brought about by gratification: admiration, love and gratitude. The capacity for these positive feelings derives from a deep relationship with the good object, and is advanced when the proportion of gratifying experiences is greater than that of frustrating ones. This brings about an immensely positive state, the basis of integrated development. In one of her most important papers, 'Envy and Gratitude', Klein herself states (1957, p. 188):

> If the undisturbed enjoyment in being fed is frequently experienced, the introjection of the good breast comes about with relative security. A full gratification at the breast means that the infant feels he has received from his loved object a unique gift which he wants to keep. This is the basis of gratitude.

Hanna Segal (1973, p. 37) similarly comments that for the paranoid-schizoid position to be transcended in a reasonably unproblematic way, 'the necessary condition is that there should be a predominance of good over bad experiences. To this predominance both internal and external factors contribute.' This argument is similar to some of Winnicott's ideas about what is offered the child by a 'good enough mother', especially in the modification of aggression and the gradually emerging capacity to embody a secure, 'true' self. However, the Kleinians have a more extreme way of presenting such ideas, perhaps in tune with the violence that they think is at the source of so much of mental life. For example, in the following passage Bion (1963, p. 31) imagines this process from the point of view of the infant's subjective experience, trying to convey just how powerful are the forces to which the infant is subjected. Describing 'the feelings of the infant', he imagines a world of devouring objects and destructive feelings that all have to be ameliorated by the capacity of the 'good object' (the mother) to manage her own emotions and adopt a stance of accepting everything that comes from her baby, thinking about it and giving it back in a digestible form – a mental stance Bion elsewhere names as 'reverie'.

> The infant, filled with painful lumps of faeces, guilt, fear of impending death, chunks of greed, meanness and urine, evacuates these bad objects into the breast that is not there. As it does so, the

good object turns the no-breast (mouth) into a breast, the faeces and urine into milk, the fears of impending death and anxiety into vitality and confidence, the greed and meanness into feelings of love and generosity, and the infant sucks its bad property, now translated into goodness, back again.

The 'no-breast' referred to here is the antagonistic, depriving breast of the infant's fantasy. What Bion is bringing out in this complex and perhaps wild piece of writing, is the combination of internal and external processes that together produce the infant's mental structure. The mother, in her role as external object, is charged with the task of containing the child's bad feelings (the 'bad property' of Bion's vision) and translating them into new, more tolerable mental contents. It is her capacity to do this which allows the infant to accept back the destructive urges that had previously been felt as terrifying and to begin to own them as part of an integrated psyche. As Bion portrays it, in a move shared by many post-Kleinian analysts, the capacity to think is created through this interchange in which the quality of the interpersonal encounter with the 'object' is a crucial counterweight to the strength of constitutional drives.

If all this works out properly, the mind will gradually develop integrative properties that enable emotions to be more deeply felt and relationships to become rounded and secure. But the tendency towards splitting will never go away completely. It can be seen in psychotic states, as emphasized here, but also in many everyday encounters. It operates forcefully when people are worked up or under threat, when they are in rivalrous situations or when their environment causes them to lose a sense of the boundaries of their self. One can see it routinely in politics when specific groups are blamed for all that is going wrong, and also in the kind of violence that crops up between neighbours – the most common violence of all, both on a domestic and an international scale. The model the Kleinians put forward offers some hope in all these areas, most fully worked out in psychoanalytic psychotherapy where transference is understood as a process of projection that can be ameliorated through accurate interpretation, an idea that will be discussed in Chapter 17. However, they also promote a particular version of the 'tragic vision' of psychoanalysis: suffering due to destructiveness is always just a hair's breadth away.

Summary

- Initial psychoanalytic thinking on psychosis was that it was unlikely to be amenable to psychoanalytic treatment because it represented a failure to be able to relate to external objects in a sufficiently integrated way to make 'use' of them in therapy.
- This was theorized as a developmental issue, with psychotic processes being parallel to very early infantile mechanisms prior to the achievement of a sense of object wholeness and stability.
- Some post-Freudian psychoanalysts have been interested in how these kinds of 'primitive' mental processes may in fact be foundational for all mental mechanisms.
- Kleinian psychoanalysis has a very well delineated account in which splitting, projection and introjection are seen as fundamental psychological strategies laid down on the basis of early physical experiences and present throughout life.
- The Kleinian account of the 'paranoid-schizoid position' and its working through is a way of conceptualizing defences against very powerful destructive impulses that have to be managed through splitting and projection.
- Although this theory emphasizes biological bases for development, it places great weight on the capacity of the early environment to 'contain' the infant sufficiently for integration to occur.
- Evidence of splitting can be seen not only among individuals, but in many instances when idealization and denigration occur within and between social groups.

15

Projection and projective identification

Basic defences

The previous two chapters have laid out Kleinian theory in the context of the paranoid-schizoid and depressive positions. This facilitated a developmental account of how the mind gradually becomes integrated and how the child becomes capable of forming relatively intimate relationships with other people. Chapter 14 also explained that the paranoid-schizoid way of thinking is one that is never fully overcome, but 'regressed' to under circumstances in which the boundaries of selfhood are breached. The Kleinian account emphasizes the power of certain basic defences, notably projection and introjection, which are called on by the early ego in order to protect itself against the devastation potentially wrought by envy. These defences can be understood as fundamental mental mechanisms – that is, as the way the mind works in early infancy. They become overlaid by later cognitive and affective strategies, notably repression, but they retain their power throughout life, as the foundations on which mental activity is laid.

In some ways the idea of projection is very commonsensical and familiar, once one starts to reflect on the question of how it is that people can sometimes 'pick up' other people's feelings and even seem to know what others are thinking. It is important to be cautious here, as these intuitions are very often wrong – we think we know what others are thinking, but in fact we are deceived. But it is also clear that being intimately connected with others involves being affected by them. While most of the time this is probably through a kind of inner resonance with others' experiences, there is also the possibility of a more direct mechanism in which 'unconscious to unconscious communication' occurs. Projection is the most likely candidate as an explanation of this phenomenon: something is lobbed from 'inside' one person and felt within another, perhaps as a disturbance or as an excitement, as in sexual responsiveness; or at times as something that might make one feel mad.

Freudian projection

As with the material covered in the previous chapter, the concept of projection has been most fully developed in Kleinian psychoanalysis, although it is also drawn on heavily by analysts in the object relational and intersubjectivist schools. Indeed, it is fair to say that as psychoanalysis has become more and more interested in early relationships, in particular attending to ways in which the subjective experiences of baby and mother are linked, so there has been an ever-stronger need for concepts that can deal with the questions of influence (how one person's subjectivity impacts on another), unconscious communication and transfer of affects or emotions. The notion of projection provides the basis for understanding part of this process, as it offers a way of conceptualizing how people often 'expel' unwanted or threatening ideas into their environment. This usually means into other people, who come to embody the unwanted impulse. For example, a therapist might be seen by her patient as constantly critical and hostile when it is more the case that the patient is attributing his own (self-criticism) to her. Sometimes it is literally the 'environment' that receives projections as when it is experienced as full of persecutory elements that actually inhabit the mind of the person concerned. The frightening experience of being alone in the dark and hearing strange noises that seem to speak to one is a familiar example here. Various forms of personification and superstition ranging from seeing ghosts to attributing complex feelings to animals may similarly be the result of projection. But projection only goes so far; a more fully intersubjective approach requires other elements such as introjection and, especially, projective identification, which we will discuss below.

Freud introduced the term 'projection' very early on in his writing in order to explain how paranoia works. The idea is that it is normal for the mind to seek an external source for something painful or disturbing – for example a fire when one is getting too hot. Defensive projection is simply a way of misusing this normal mechanism when one has something painful in one's mind and attributes it to something outside. Laplanche and Pontalis (1973, p. 352) comment, 'although Freud recognizes projection in rather diverse areas he assigns it a fairly strict meaning. It always appears as a defence, as the attribution to another (person or thing) of qualities, feelings or wishes that the subject repudiates or refuses to recognize in himself.' The problem in paranoia, as Klein stressed in her description of the paranoid-schizoid position, is that this misattributed internal disturbance then comes back as a persecutory object. For instance, to continue the example of the critical patient mentioned above, once the therapist is experienced as hostile the patient has to face an important external 'object' who seems to be attacking him – even when, to an 'objective observer', she is not.

Although this approach is clear, it is not really sufficient to capture the psychoanalytic sense of projection as a means by which internal and external worlds are connected with one another. Freud's own idea of the ego being formed by the internalization of lost objects suggests a more complicated pattern in which what has been put out through projection is taken back in (differently) through introjective processes, so that the whole dynamic is more dialogical than one might think from a simple reading. In addition, as Laplanche and Pontalis point out (p. 353), there is some uncertainty in Freud's writing about what it is that is projected. Here there are at least three possibilities:

- *Cognition* in the sense of a misattribution of the cause of an event to something in the outside world rather than to ourselves.
- *Affect*, as when someone experiences another as full of hate when the hatred is actually a split-off feeling of her or his own.
- *Object* projection, as when the internal representation of a hated element becomes located in something external.

All these different ideas are brought together more fully in the Kleinian account.

Kleinian projections

As described in the previous chapter, Klein argued that infants are wracked by internal forces that their ego cannot control, and feel threatened with annihilation by those forces. As a defence against this, the envious impulses that come from the death drive are projected outwards into the external object; similarly, in order to protect the more loving elements of the personality against envy, they too are projected. Projection is felt to be a natural way of dealing with internal disturbance not only because, as Freud says, it is instinctive to seek an external cause of one's pain so that one can move away from it to protect oneself, but also because the infant's internal representation of the world is dominated by bodily experiences of ingestion and expulsion. Material things go in and out of the baby, so why should thoughts be any different? Because the object is itself split (in the fantasy of the infant), projection works to keep love and hate apart, allowing the former to be strengthened and the latter to be ameliorated. Splitting is of fundamental importance here, but so is projection.

There are of course negative consequences of this process, as the external world becomes a source of persecutory anxiety. However, under normal circumstances the gains outweigh the losses, because the external relocation of the destructive drive means that it is experienced as more controllable and also more amenable to mitigation by the actions of a loving object, the mother. In addition, the loving impulses of the infant are also projected, 'in order to create an object which will satisfy the ego's instinctive striving for the preservation of life' (Segal, 1973, p. 25). This makes an ideal object out of the breast, in which hope is invested and which has the function of keeping love alive. So long as the mother is basically stable and loving (which as Winnicott points out requires that she is properly supported too), the next stage of the cycle, introjection, can also occur. In this, the infant takes back in its own projected impulses, which are now experienced as more tolerable because they have been 'worked on' by the benevolence of the mother. At its most schematic, the capacity of the mother to survive the projection into her of the infant's destructiveness will mean that those destructive impulses are no longer experienced by the child as *actually* able to wreck everything. As noted earlier, it is this benevolent cycle that allows the infant gradually to form a more complex and integrated mind more capable of dealing with emotions and, especially, with ambivalence.

This general model is powerful as an account of the emergence of a complex internal mental structure during early infancy, and also as a way of conceptualizing some of the tasks of psychotherapy. As will be described more fully in Chapters 17 and 18, psychoanalytic psychotherapists very often see themselves as having to 'hold' the projections of their patients until such time as the patient is able to 'receive' them back again. For instance, a hostile patient may create an atmosphere in which the therapist feels persecutory; the therapist's task will be to avoid enacting this by staying calm and neutral, until the patient acquires the insight that the hostility is part of her or his own internal world. Projection is also a very widespread social phenomenon. It is the most common psychoanalytic explanation given for racism, the idea being that the racist is consumed by unconscious impulses that are felt to be unmanageable and disgusting; these are projected outwards onto classes of people made available by the social world, in the sense that they are already defined as outsiders or threats. So black people become the recipients of projections related to sexuality and bestiality, as these are the attributes foisted on them by the history of slavery and colonialism. Jews become embodiments of greed and conspiratorial seductiveness, associations that are firmly rooted in the long history of European antisemitism (Frosh, 2005).

Projective identification

The gradual transformation of psychoanalysis from a closed to an open systems theory, in which relationships are primary, has also meant that there is increasing interest in how these relationships become intense and perhaps particularly in how each one of us gets 'under the skin' of others. The Kleinian version of projection speaks quite clearly to this issue, describing the pattern of taking in and giving out that characterizes the cycles of introjection and projection. However, this is still to some extent a one-person account, focusing on what is projected from the individual into the object and then taken back in, even though there is a dialogical component through the idea that the containment offered by the object might make disturbing impulses more tolerable. It is with the notion of *projective identification* that psychoanalytic theory comes to grips with the intensity of elementary relationships with others. In particular, it helps to make sense of the way in which the *object* – the person who 'receives' the projections – is affected by what is coming at her or him. This means it is particularly well attuned to dyadic interactions, and it also offers quite profound ways of thinking about the processes by which contact with another person might change the self, which is obviously the key motif of psychotherapy. Projective identification, therefore, is an idea that links normal development, 'ordinary' unconscious communicational processes, and psychotic functioning within and outside therapy.

Projective identification is in some ways a bizarre concept. Perhaps this is forgivable as it is dealing with a set of phenomena that can themselves seem very hard to comprehend: the insertion of one person's feelings into another, the sense of being possessed and intruded upon by someone else's unconscious life, and so on. Of particular importance is the way in which projective identification adds a fourth component to the three types of projective content listed earlier – cognitive, affective and object. This time it is 'parts of the self' that are projected into the external object both for protection and as an act of aggression. This is supposed to be a normal event in early development, occurring before there is any clear differentiation between self and object (or it would not be fully possible). Because of the persistence of infantile feelings and mental processes throughout life, it operates just as noticeably and powerfully in adults, perhaps especially clearly in psychotherapy.

In its 'pure' form, projective identification appears to be solely negative. It is defined by Laplanche and Pontalis (1973, p. 356) as 'a mechanism revealed in phantasies in which the subject inserts his self – in whole or in part – into the object in order to harm, possess or control it'. In their *New Dictionary of Kleinian Thought*, Spillius et al. (2011) give projective identification a major entry and define it as:

Projective identification is an unconscious phantasy in which aspects of the self or of an internal object are split off and attributed to an external object. The projected aspects may be felt by the projector to be either good or bad. Projective phantasies may or may not be accompanied by evocative behaviour unconsciously intended to induce the recipient of the projection to feel and act in accordance with the projective phantasy. Phantasies of projective identification are sometimes felt to have 'acquisitive' as well as 'attributive' properties, meaning that the phantasy involves not only getting rid of aspects of one's own psyche but also of entering the mind of the other in order to acquire desired aspects of his psyche. (p. 126)

The sense is strong here of getting inside other people to dump unwanted elements of oneself in them or to 'steal' from them psychological attributes that one unconsciously desires for oneself. In an earlier version of the *Dictionary of Kleinian Thought*, Hinshelwood (1991, p. 184) identifies two aims of projective identification, one more benign than the other, but both of them clearly involving the 'use' of another as a relational partner with the self. Hinshelwood states that one of these aims is 'to evacuate violently a painful state of mind leading to forcibly entering an object, in phantasy, for immediate relief, and often with the aim of an intimidating control of the object', while the other is 'to introduce into the object a state of mind, as a means of communicating with it about this mental state.' Schematically, we have two functions of projective identification here:

1. To insert parts of the self into the other as a way of relieving internal anxiety and of mounting an envious assault.
2. To produce in the other a resonance, an unconscious understanding, which can form the basis of empathy.

These can be thought of as 'negative' (attacking) and 'positive' (communicational) functions, usually operating together and highly significant both in development and in psychoanalytic psychotherapy.

As implied by its name, as well as there being two alternative *aims* to projective identification, it also has two *components*: projection and identification with what has been projected. The projective component involves placing parts of the self into an external object either in order to deal with the anxiety these parts are producing (in the case of destructive elements) or so as to preserve something good and loving for safekeeping. The second component of projective identification, 'identification', is the process whereby the person feels her or himself to remain in contact with those parts of the self that have been projected out. Although there is always the risk of feeling depleted by projecting valued aspects of the self into the other (which is one reason why feelings of gratitude might provoke associated envious emotions), this aspect of projective identification is a way of communicating rather than just getting rid of feared parts of the self. In psychoanalysis, it therefore enables contact to be retained with the analyst's mind, conveying aspects of the patient's inner world. It is then the analyst's task to maintain a stance of free-floating attention in which she or he can receive, tolerate and think about any projections received from the patient, however threatening, so as to draw some of their sting and allow them to be re-introjected by the patient in a more manageable, 'digested' form. The parallels with early parenting are clear, with this kind of free-floating attention being exactly what Bion (1962) referred to as 'reverie': the ability to accept any projective identifications and to 'process' them in such a way that they are more liveable with.

Projective identification and psychosis

The Kleinian analyst Herbert Rosenfeld (1971) provides a detailed account of projective identification that emphasizes how it forms the basis of psychotic experience. He stresses that projective identification can result in the external object becoming infused with persecutory content that derives from the projector's own inner destructiveness. Under ideal situations this will be eased by the benevolence and good balance of the object, but if the object is actually hostile, or becomes so because it cannot manage the projections, the situation will escalate into a vicious cycle of splitting, projective identification, terror of introjection of the persecutory object, and more splitting and projective identification. This is exactly what will happen when the environment is genuinely persecutory – for example when a parent is too disturbed to manage the aggressive demands of the child. It can also occur in situations such as repeated fostering breakdowns, which might leave a child with the strong sense that she or he is inhabited by the kind of destructiveness that no one can tolerate. At its extreme, the psychotic consequence of this can be a mind in pieces, unable to use the object to help it put itself together again.

For Rosenfeld, there are different kinds of projective identification that need to be recognized in the analytic situation. The major distinction, as mentioned above, is between projective identification as a means of communication and projective identification as a way of expelling unbearable elements of the personality. The former is obviously more positive and underpins the capacity of people to intuit what is happening to someone they care about or are in an intimate relationship with. The 'evacuating' type of projective identification is, however, much more characteristic of the severely disturbed, psychotic patient. Rosenfeld (1971, p. 121) describes what happens:

> [T]he patient splits off parts of his self in addition to impulses and anxieties and projects them into the analyst for the purpose of evacuating and emptying out the disturbing mental content which leads to a denial of psychic reality. As this type of patient primarily wants the analyst to condone the evacuation process and the denial of his problems, he often reacts to interpretations with violent resentment, as they are experienced as critical and frightening since the patient believes that unwanted, unbearable and meaningless mental content is pushed back into him by the analyst.

Rosenfeld goes on to describe how projective identification can be a way in which the patient attempts to omnipotently control the analyst. Such a patient experiences her or himself as having entered into the analyst. This means not only that the ego–other boundary has been obscured, producing anxieties about the loss of self, but also that the patient sees the analyst as having been infected with her or his own madness. Rosenfeld writes (p. 122), 'The analyst is then perceived as having become mad, which arouses extreme anxiety as the patient is afraid that the analyst will retaliate and force the madness back into the patient, depriving him entirely of his sanity. At such times the patient is in danger of disintegration.' This is perhaps the worst type of projective identification, getting rid of the envious destructiveness in the mind at the expense of the mind itself. Little can remain here of optimism and hope, as the self flees from its fears into desperate fragments.

Projective identification is an unusual concept that often seems very abstract and formulaic as it tries to trace the movement of unconscious ideas from one person to another. It is sometimes hard to believe that it can relate to anything real. However, as we shall see in Chapters 17 and 18, it has turned out to be a very useful way of capturing some of the extreme situations that occur in the course of psychotherapy and to provide a vocabulary for considering what these mean and how they can be worked with. It might even be argued that psychoanalytic ideas of this kind are important tools for analysts and psychotherapists who, faced with the very difficult mental states of some of their patients, need guidance on how to stay sane.

Summary

- Projection and projective identification are defences that are also understood by some analysts, particularly Kleinians, as fundamental mechanisms by which the mind operates.
- Freud saw projection as a means of expelling disturbing material into the external world. He thought it was derived from the instinctive tendency to seek an external cause for pain in order to protect oneself against it.
- There is some uncertainty in Freud about whether the contents of projection are cognitions, affects or objects.
- Kleinian theory places great emphasis on projective processes as the earliest way in which the ego defends itself against the death drive. Splitting, projection and introjection form the essence of the infant's transactions with its environment.
- This can work in a benevolent cycle leading to greater psychological integration, but it also runs the risk of producing a paranoid state of mind.
- Projective identification is a specifically Kleinian concept conveying ways in which parts of the self are projected into an object and then identified with by the projector. It has various components, mainly divided into a communicational element that allows one person to intuit the unconscious life of another, and a destructive component that enviously attacks the object from the inside.
- Projective identification has shown itself to be a versatile concept used particularly to help understand psychotic mental states.

16
Lacanian psychoanalysis

Style and substance

I gave a brief outline of some elements of Lacanian psychoanalysis in Chapter 10, where I pointed out how surprisingly influential this approach has been. The 'surprise' is that such a difficult theory has been taken up so widely. It often seems extraordinarily complex and abstract, and much Lacanian writing – including the publications of Lacan himself – can appear wilfully obscure. Despite this, many Lacanian concepts have shown themselves to be of considerable value in conceptualizing clinical as well as non-clinical phenomena. Several of these concepts have been versatile enough to provoke new ways of thinking about human subjectivity.

Lacanianism is perhaps the most widely applied branch of psychoanalysis *outside* the consulting room. In the 1970s and 1980s, when it first began to be taken up in a serious way outside France, it was especially influential in film and literary studies, as part of the move towards 'post-structuralism' and the growing importance of continental philosophy and sociology (Coward and Ellis, 1977). It is probably fair to say that for some time after that, literary and philosophical engagements with psychoanalysis were confined mainly to readings of Freud and Lacan. This work produced some very provocative, albeit complex, interpretations of culture that combined well with other major 'deconstructive' movements of the time, even when these other movements were opposed either to psychoanalysis in general or to Lacanianism in particular. In a sense, they all spoke the same language. For instance, Jacques Derrida, the most important of the continental philosophers of the late twentieth century, produced a powerful critique of Lacanian literary analysis that nevertheless deployed many of its insights (Derrida,

171

1975). Feminists used Lacanian theory extensively (for example Mitchell and Rose, 1982; Grosz, 1990), but also created a strong opposition to it – again, however, using many of the concepts that Lacan had proposed (Clément, 1987). More recently, it is probably fair to say that the most powerful psychoanalytic interventions into social and political thought have come from Lacanians or critics who draw on Lacanian ideas, with the voluminous works of Slavoj Žižek being the outstanding example (see, for instance, Žižek, 1991, 2006b).

It has taken longer for Lacanian psychoanalysis to have an impact on clinical practice in the Anglo-American world, although for a considerable amount of time it has been a major player in psychoanalysis elsewhere, especially in Latin America as well as in France (Parker, 2011). However, with the emergence of Lacanian training programmes and the publication of a considerable amount of English-language clinical work (Fink, 1999), plus a few highly accessible first-hand accounts of the *experience* of being in a Lacanian psychoanalysis (Gunn, 2002), this way of thinking and working has become more widespread, and some Lacanian ideas have even begun to seep through into the mainstream of Anglo-American psychoanalytic practice. This is not to say that it is universally accepted, as there is still very considerable opposition to many aspects of Lacanianism from other psychoanalytic schools; but it has nevertheless become recognizable as a player in the psychoanalytic field.

One might actually have expected that after Lacan's death, in 1981, his influence would fade, because so much of it seemed to be due to his *style* – to the kind of performance he put on in his seminars and to the way he made himself embody a certain image of the psychoanalyst as learned, 'deep', obscure, provocative, pithy and prophetic. This style was controversial in Lacan's lifetime and certainly contributed to opposition towards him by many other analysts as well as those who felt mistreated and deceived by him – feminists perhaps being a particularly good example. Lacan's pronouncements on women never seemed particularly sensitive or supportive. There was also an irony in that while Lacanian theory developed a powerful critique of notions of psychoanalytic expertise and 'mastery', Lacan was somehow exempt from this. He was known as the 'Master' and his disciples acted precisely in that way towards him, as if every one of his utterances was somehow to be treated as the truth. Lacan may even have become impatient with this idolizing tendency among his followers. This is one explanation for his propensity to break up the 'schools' that formed around him (Roudinesco, 1990).

Despite this, Lacan's importance has grown rather than diminished in the post-Lacanian world. This is for numerous reasons, some of which I list below.

- Lacanianism opposes the dominant relational paradigm in psychoanalysis as well as being highly critical of Contemporary Freudianism and classical ego psychology. This means that it is one place to look for those who are interested in psychoanalysis but unconvinced by these approaches. It is perhaps especially attractive for analysts trying to release themselves from the Anglo-American hegemony in psychoanalysis.
- Lacanian style is not accidental, but expresses something important about the nature of psychoanalysis itself, and perhaps also about learning in general. Lacan was critical of traditional 'university' learning, which he argued represented the bureaucratizing of knowledge rather than the deepening of real understanding. For example, speaking to rebellious students in France in 1968 he said (Lacan, 1991, p. 198), 'Psychoanalysis is not something that can be transmitted like other forms of knowledge.' Psychoanalysis, he claimed, challenges what is usually taken to be knowledge. It stirs things up in a way that changes how everything is experienced, rather than reducing understanding to the kinds of things that can be tested in an examination. In suggesting that psychoanalytic knowledge might not be transmissible, therefore, he was not saying that the analyst 'has nothing to know', only that such knowledge cannot be taught by conventional means.
- Lacan embodied the way psychoanalysis represents a link in a primarily oral tradition of teaching in which the 'Master' passes on what he knows through testing and informing his pupils. This is why the seminar rather than the written word was the primary site of Lacan's teaching: learning takes place through the experience of being in the presence of one who has something to communicate. Both this point and the previous one mean that psychoanalysis proceeds through its effects rather than through some easy-to-communicate list of facts or concepts.

- Partly because of this approach to knowledge, Lacanianism has proved to be a rallying point for those who wish to maintain an oppositional perspective in psychoanalysis, and to use psychoanalytic ideas to think critically about social and political phenomena. Lacanian psychoanalysis tends to be disruptive and subversive, looking at what is being 'blocked' by received assumptions in all areas. It does not therefore promote a particular vision of how people should be, but instead takes apart the fixed ideas that it comes across whether in clinical work or elsewhere.
- Lacanianism emphasizes the place of language in the creation of the human 'subject', and this was very helpful in the context of a turn to language that ran right through the social sciences for at least two decades from the 1980s onwards. Through this means, Lacanian psychoanalysis became one of the philosophical and social theories drawn on by a wide range of thinkers who might also have been attracted to it by its relative difficulty and its broad philosophical and cultural references.

The complexity and difficulty of Lacanianism is such that it is impossible to give a very full account of it in this book. However, a few major concepts are briefly described in the rest of this chapter, partly to give a flavour of the approach but also become some of these ideas have gained widespread acceptance and have a great deal to contribute to new developments in psychoanalysis.

The subject

The notion of the 'subject' is not peculiar to Lacan, but rather is used widely in post-structuralist theory and in fact has its roots in the philosophy of Hegel. Nevertheless, the idea of the subject is used very effectively in Lacanian psychoanalysis to emphasize the way in which the 'person' is not in control of her or himself, but is rather a kind of alienated being at the mercy of certain kinds of internal and external forces. Whereas much psychoanalysis and psychotherapy is *humanistic* in its orientation, taking the person as its core interest (sometimes using terms like 'self' or even 'ego' to substitute for 'person'), Lacanianism places the locus of subjectivity *outside* the person. In this way it is probably closer to Freud's (1917a, p. 285) own view that the ego 'is not even master in its own house, but must content itself with scanty information of what is going on unconsciously in its mind.' What this nicely captures is the way in which the subject might be the source *of* action and meaning, but is also subject *to* forces that operate upon it, notably in the form of unconscious impulses and in the activities of what Lacanians call the 'big Other' of society.

The simplest way of illustrating the notion of the subject might be to return to the example of how people use language, given in Chapter 8 in the context of my description of psychosocial aspects of the Oedipus complex. The point was made there that people are *subjected to* language as well as being *subjects in* it. What this means is that:

1. Language makes certain meanings possible and has to be used in recognizable ways for people to become 'social subjects', able to communicate with one another and form relationships with society. It is not possible simply to invent one's own language. Rather, we are born into specific linguistic environments and have to give ourselves up to them. These environments have formed over long periods of time in the context of particular societies; they pre-date and post-date any individual language user. In this sense, language determines who we are – we are 'subjected to' it.

2. We use language creatively in order to speak, and often come up with completely new utterances that have never been spoken or heard before. This means that language users are not only subjected to language as it is; they also contribute to its development and have an impact on it. We are therefore subjects in the sense of being *agents* who can make something happen.

3. Lacanianism adds something else here, which is that when we speak we do not always say what we want to say, and it can even be argued that we *never want to say everything we say*. That is, our speech comes in part 'from the unconscious', perhaps especially in situations like that of psychoanalysis, when 'free' speech is encouraged. In this very important sense, we are *subjects of* the unconscious – subjected to forces outside the control of our 'selves' (the ego). When someone says, 'I didn't mean to say that,' they are consequently speaking the truth.

Language

For Lacanian psychoanalysis, language is not just an example of how the subject is affected by social and unconscious forces. It is central to understanding human consciousness and also psychoanalysis itself, which is seen as a 'practice of speech'. The first thing to note is that Lacan adopted a very modern view of language as *performative*. What this means is that language is understood not as something that merely reflects underlying thoughts (speech simply as putting ideas into words), but it *does things*. There was a substantial development of this view of language in the twentieth century, so much so that it has become quite orthodox. Rather than meaning coming first and being put into words in a more or less satisfactory way (which is often how we experience ourselves as language users), the emphasis here is on how language creates meaning, and is central in making things happen. It is worth noting that this is in fact an untheorized commonplace in psychoanalysis. If the 'talking cure' is to work, language must have powerful effects. Words are actions, in this account: as we speak, something new occurs.

Lacan takes this general idea and applies it to the psychoanalytic situation. To say that psychoanalysis is a practice of speech may seem obvious: after all, what happens in the analytic situation is simply that one person speaks to another. However, what Lacan does with this truism is very powerful, in two main ways.

1. Lacan opposes the idea that it is possible to know anything about the 'reality' that lies behind the patient's speech. Indeed, he recommends great caution over whether the analyst should ever claim to understand *anything*. In his seminar on 'Freud's Papers on technique', he says something very characteristic about what can and cannot be known.

   > What counts, when one attempts to elaborate an experience, is less what one understands than what one doesn't understand … How many times have I pointed it out to those that I supervise when they say to me – *I thought I understood that what he meant to say was this, or that* – one of the things which we should be watching out for most, is not to understand too much, not to understand more than what there is in the discourse of the subject. (Lacan, 1954, p. 73)

He goes on to say that psychoanalytic understanding is actually based on a 'refusal of understanding.' This is obviously paradoxical, but it becomes clearer if we realize that Lacan is objecting to the idea that there is some absolute *truth* that underlies the speech of the patient, and that the analyst can gain access to it through a correct interpretation of that speech. For Lacan, all that the analyst can know is the speech itself – the analyst has no access to anything else. This is contrary to most people's vision of psychoanalysis, which places it as an interpretive science committed to the possibility of finding meaning in everything. If a man keeps repeating an obsessional act, it is *because* he is warding off disturbing sexual thoughts. If a woman dreams of a lost child, it points to her own inner sense of abandonment and rejection. Lacan's warning is very precise here: it is not possible to understand more than 'what there is in the discourse of the subject.' In practice, this is likely to steer psychotherapy towards a focus on what is happening in the contact between therapist and patient, and in particular how words are being used and what effect they have.

2. Building on a complex set of ideas derived from structural linguistics, Lacan emphasizes the way meaning shifts about as a product of the different ways in which speech happens. This is part and parcel of the idea that language creates meaning rather than the other way around. As a person speaks, a mental representation is evoked in each listener and this has to be *translated* into something comprehensible. This translation is always approximate, just as the speech itself is always transitory and uncertain. In particular, when the subject (say, a patient in psychotherapy) uses the term 'I', it is not going to be clear exactly what this 'I' refers to. The meaning of 'I' shifts all the time; in a way, tracing how this happens is precisely what psychoanalysis is about. In the psychoanalytic situation, the analyst becomes interested in what is 'speaking in the subject' when the subject articulates itself as an 'I'. Truth can never be pinned down: there is always slippage between the words that are used and what arises from them.

Imaginary, Symbolic, Real

As outlined in Chapter 10, Lacan proposed three 'orders' of experience, through which psychic life becomes organized. Like the Kleinian depressive and paranoid-schizoid positions, these are both developmental phases and characteristic ways of relating to the world. These orders are the Imaginary, Symbolic and Real, and as a group they reflect the discrepancy between what can and cannot be known. Specifically, one might see the division between them like this:

- *Imaginary:* what is imagined to be true (the fantasy of an ego that can function autonomously and with integrity, of a subject who can fully know the truth).
- *Symbolic:* what can be symbolized and consequently manipulated, investigated and analysed (psychoanalysis itself operates in the domain of the Symbolic).
- *Real:* what can never be known, or can be known only at the edges or by its sudden appearance in moments of breakthrough.

The Imaginary

According to Lacan, the infant is born into an environment of loss, already cut off from something (the womb or the mother's immediate presence) but unable to articulate what this is. Even more importantly, the infant is immersed in a structure that is not of its own making. This structure consists, first, of what the parents desire of the infant, and secondly, what language and culture make possible. 'What does the (m)other want of me?' might be thought of as the foundational, unspoken question upon which the infant's emerging subjecthood is based. The idea is that the infant arrives as a biologically active but disorganized being in a setting where a lot is already expected of it (the parents' fantasies about their baby will play a large role here), but where everything is very confusing. All this means that the infant is initially at the mercy of its drives and unable to deal adequately with the overwhelming sense of disintegration produced by the combination of these drives, the loss or gap into which the infant feels itself to have fallen, and the desire of the 'other'. The infant consequently experiences a drive to prop itself up before it disintegrates completely. This drive is felt in the form of a wish for a missing object that it cannot adequately conceptualize – something taken away from it before it was known, but imagined as offering total security. This is a painful and potentially damaging state of psychic affairs, so it is no surprise to find the infant experiencing joy when it discovers something that makes it feel less broken apart and more whole. The 'something', according to Lacan, is the infant's own image in the mirror, pointed out to it by the mother.

The 'mirror phase' described by Lacan is the entry point to the Imaginary order. The idea is that the fragmentary infant catches a glimpse of itself in the mirror (the actual mirror or the 'mirror' of the mother's gaze) and identifies with this image, leaping with relief into the fantasy that because it can see itself as an entire *physical* being, it is also a whole *psychological* subject. The set-up here, in which the mother names the infant as whole, leading the infant to attach itself to what is after all a mere *image*, is one in which the emerging human subject is deceived, taken in by something. That is, Lacan's use of the 'mirror' term has nothing to do with the reality of the child's inner drives, but describes a specious representation of integrity, in which the mother presents her own vision *to* her infant but this is taken by the infant to be the 'truth'. The child's perception of the 'specular image' produces the fiction that she or he is whole and has a clearly ascertainable identity, when what is happening is really that the child is *identifying with* a vision that comes from elsewhere, from outside. This is taken by Lacan as the origin of the ego. In opposition to those who see ego development as the main way in which an infant progresses to stability and authenticity, Lacan claims that the ego is adopted as a kind of defence, an armour or shell supporting the psyche, which is otherwise experienced as in fragments.

The Imaginary is characterized by the narcissistic relation with the image, in which the fantasy is that wholeness and integrity can be achieved. This is carried over into a great deal of people's everyday functioning, highly visible when they act as if they absolutely 'know' themselves; or when they seek out something that will completely fill the gaps in their experiences. It is present in psychotherapy when patients imagine that therapists really understand them fully and can treasure and hold them and make them whole. Investment in this kind of Imaginary relationship is actually one source of disappointment in psychotherapy, when it becomes apparent that no such completely loving 'cure' is possible.

The Symbolic

It will perhaps be obvious that it is difficult to sustain the fantasy of complete Imaginary perfection. What happens developmentally, according to Lacan, is that the wholeness promised by the mirror is shattered by another step of alienation, in which the infant discovers that there is always something outside the perfect relationship that determines what form it can take. This 'structuring function' of an external force is clearly shown if we think about the limits of interpersonal communication. In the Imaginary order, the fantasy is that it is possible to have complete communication with another person without anything getting in the way. Total romantic love would be an example, in which each lover understands the other fully without there being any need for speech or going through the difficult process of working out what the other wants. Unfortunately, such blissful states are rare, if not impossible. Instead, we communicate with one another through complicated symbolic mechanisms, the predominant one being language.

As noted above, Lacanians see language as a structure that pre-exists the individual 'subject'. This means that it operates as a kind of regulatory *law*, making some things easy and other things difficult. The need to use language therefore interferes with the Imaginary fantasy, revealing that the relationship with the other is already organized by something outside it. This realization on the part of the infant is the moment at which she or he enters the Symbolic order. A third term is thereby introduced into the Imaginary self–other unity, from which time self and other cannot ever be in total, unmediated connection with one another. Instead, language and other symbols are used as the vehicles for communication; and as these have pre-established senses, they come *between* people in the same moment that they connect them. However, acceptance of the structure of language also allows the infant to find her or his 'voice' in the sense of being able to become a recognizable language user. The infant is thus placed in the circuit of human communication. Lacanians claim that refusing to accept the Symbolic is a refusal of reality in the sense that Freud meant it when describing psychosis. Living in an Imaginary world means not being able to tolerate the use of symbols, which are necessary for coping with the social environment. Nevertheless, giving up the fantasy of oneness is painful and never fully accomplished, as Imaginary experience is central to much of human consciousness.

The Symbolic order in Lacan is based on the Oedipal model put forward by Freud. As in the classical Oedipus complex, the Lacanian Symbolic is instituted through a sexual prohibition promulgated by the father and experienced by the child as the threat of castration. Because of its power, castration – the symbolic value of having or not having the phallus – becomes central to human subjects. This is why the Symbolic order is the provenance not only of language, but also of sexual difference. Indeed, in the large array of work influenced by Lacanian psychoanalysis, it is discussions around gender and sexuality that have been most prominent. For some authors (for example Grosz, 1990), the idea of the Symbolic gives leverage on questions about how patriarchy becomes 'internalized' by specific men and women. For others (for example Segal, 1999), it is another version of a traditional approach that treats women as 'lacking' and therefore as necessarily excluded by masculine culture.

The Real

The Real is made up of that which cannot be put into words, that abyss from which the subject flees into the arms of symbolization. Because the Real is unsymbolizable, it features as a lack at the centre of the human subject. On the other hand, at least in some readings, the Real underpins the sense that life is meaningful. It is, in a certain sense, that which precedes the various splits or moments of alienation enacted through the Imaginary and the Symbolic. The Real is not a mystical order outside the realm of experience; rather, it is what our psychological and social devices keep at bay. At certain times, it breaks through to link us with everything we have left out. But much of the time it pulses away as a threat, as that which can demolish all our attempts at identity-construction. In clinical settings, it makes itself felt when the subject's attempts at symbolization fall apart. Indeed, one of the foci of Lacanian psychoanalysis is the revelation that symbolization will always find a point at which it fails, and then something else will appear, breaking through the cracks in the defensive structure of the ego.

The four discourses

It is interesting to see how much of Lacanian thinking can be understood as a kind of prolonged meditation on the nature of knowledge. This is perhaps why there has been a lot of writing on the topic of Lacan and epistemology, much of it concerned with questions about what it means to 'refuse understanding' in the way described earlier in this chapter (for example Nobus and Quinn, 2005). It is also a very practical issue. The psychotherapist is asked by the patient to *understand* what might be at issue in the patient's difficulties, and her or his response to this demand will determine what happens in the therapy itself. The different possibilities here are elaborated very productively in a final set of Lacanian concepts to be considered here, known as the 'four discourses' (Lacan, 1991). These discourses are best thought of as ways in which knowledge is organized, and perhaps specifically as the answer to the question, 'how should the analyst respond?' Very schematically, the discourses are:

- *The discourse of the University*
As described above, this is the approach to knowledge that bureaucratizes it, so that it becomes a way of blocking true understanding. Instead, what happens in the 'university' discourse is that knowledge becomes a commodity that can be used (for example to gain qualifications) rather than an experience to be gone through. Treating counselling and psychotherapy as a kind of *technology* of skills (as in the 'scientific-practitioner model' adopted by many clinical psychologists) might be an example of the discourse of the University applied to the clinical situation.

- *The discourse of the Hysteric*
This is the approach to knowledge of the patient but also of the pupil and indeed of any subject seeking full understanding. It is characterized by endless questions appearing in the form of demands for answers, and it positions the other as the one who must (or is 'supposed to') know these answers. It is thus the basis for the kind of transference in which the patient acts as if the therapist knows what she or he should do to get better, even if the therapist is 'refusing' to share this knowledge. The discourse of the Hysteric will always be restless because complete understanding of the unconscious is unattainable.

- *The discourse of the Master*

The Master is paired with the Hysteric as the one who acts as if, or maybe believes, she or he is in possession of the truth. The Master is provoked by the Hysteric to provide solutions to questions, and comes to fill, precariously, the position of the 'one who knows'. This kind of expertise is always false because no one can be in full possession of the truth, and in analysis it is a trap because it suggests that the analyst holds the secret of the 'cure'. It is, however, a very powerful lure for anyone in a position in which they are supposed to demonstrate expert understanding. Outside the consulting room, it may for example be a useful way of understanding the behaviour of financial market analysts who believe they are fully in control of the market even when their investments and trading methods are demonstrably disastrous.

- *The discourse of the Analyst*

As one might expect, this is the ideal discourse – something that should perhaps provoke scepticism, given Lacanianism's supposed opposition to ideals, which are seen as Imaginary constructs. Nevertheless, what it references is the analyst's ability to step aside from the place of mastery; that is, to acknowledge that no one has full knowledge of the unconscious, and all one can do is reveal this non-knowledge. In the clinical setting, the therapist adopts the discourse of the Analyst when it becomes clear that she or he is occupying the position of the 'subject supposed to know' at the patient's behest. At this point, the therapist becomes aware of being not the one who *really* knows, but the one who is actually merely performing a function for the patient. The analytic task becomes that of revealing that there are no complete answers, only a stream of more or less productive questions.

These four discourses have wide application, but they are focused most strongly on the situation of the psychoanalyst in psychotherapeutic practice. This leads us on to a broader introduction to the core psychoanalytic concepts that apply to the therapeutic relationship.

Summary

- Lacanian psychoanalysis has become increasingly important both in terms of its influence on psychoanalytic practice and as a repository of theoretical concepts that challenge the assumptions made by many other schools of psychoanalysis.

- It promotes the idea of psychoanalysis as a 'teaching' that is different from other modes of knowledge.
- It has been widely applied outside the consulting room, particularly in the arts and social sciences and in political critique.
- There are numerous Lacanian ideas that are proving productive both in clinical thinking and in the application of psychoanalysis to these other disciplinary areas. These ideas include:
  - the notion of the 'subject';
  - the relationship of the subject to language;
  - the three 'orders' of Imaginary, Symbolic and Real;
  - the 'four discourses' of the University, the Hysteric, the Master and the Analyst.

17

Interpretation and transference

Interpretation

It follows from the psychoanalytic assumption that there is an unconscious dimension to mental life that what we hear when someone tells us something, and what we see when we observe their behaviour, cannot necessarily be taken at face value. Instead, psychoanalysis proposes that something else is going on 'underneath' the surface, and this 'something else' is nearer to the true meaning of the speech or action. The act of identifying this something else is an act of *interpretation*. For psychoanalysts, what is being described here is the process whereby the unconscious ideas lying behind the surface of a patient's speech are gradually uncovered. This process is often thought of as the heart of psychoanalytic practice. Indeed, Laplanche and Pontalis (1973, p. 227) state that, 'Psychoanalysis itself might be defined in terms of it, as the bringing out of the latent meaning of given material.'

Sandler, Dare and Holder (1973, p. 110) usefully suggest a definition of interpretation as a communication from the analyst with a specific intended effect on the patient. Their formulation is: 'all comments and other verbal interventions which have the aim of immediately making the patient aware of some aspect of his psychological functioning of which he was not previously conscious.' What is made clear here is that an interpretation is a verbal statement and that it has a specific aim: not to demonstrate the *analyst's* understanding, but to increase the insight of the *patient*. So long as this is the case, it is an interpretation – whether or not it is actually successful in achieving that aim. There is a useful set of discriminations here. The therapist might believe she or he understands something about the patient but choose not to offer an interpretation until the patient feels ready to hear it. An interpretation might be made, but it can be wrong or misplaced, or mistimed – it might, therefore, not achieve its aim, but it will still be (a 'bad') interpretation. From this quite a lot of technical variations emerge, for instance between those analysts who believe that interpretations should be built up slowly in order not to frighten a patient off, and those who argue that interpretations should be as 'deep' as possible from the start, so that a patient can quickly recognize that her or his anxiety can be safely named. Where classical analysts concentrate on interpretations that gradually uncover defences to allow careful exploration of the anxieties lying behind them, Kleinians are much more inclined to deal directly with the anxieties themselves, arguing that change does not come about through increased knowledge becoming available to the ego, which can then control conflicts more effectively, but through repairing splits at an unconscious level. Such analysts are likely to concentrate less on the patient's history (though they will treat this seriously) and more on the way in which she or he behaves in the session. There are even some analysts (many Lacanians, for instance) who object to the idea of interpretation altogether because of its assumption that something real or true is being identified at work 'beneath' the surface of the patient's talk. For them, it makes more sense to talk about 'interruptions' that force the patient to start thinking along new lines but which make no particular claim to know the 'true meaning' of the patient's speech.

Something that is not always appreciated about psychoanalytic interpretations is how linked they are to the therapeutic situation. This is an issue that will be returned to in Part III of this book, because it calls into question some of the claims that theorists have made when interpreting artistic, literary or social material through psychoanalytic lenses. Here, the important point is that psychoanalysis recognizes that the interpersonal context in which an interpretation takes place will make a considerable difference to its effect. This is in many respects obvious from everyday life. If someone you dislike says something about you ('you've made yourself look good today'), you might hear this as a sarcastic attack. If exactly the same words are used by someone you trust and who cares for you, they might feel reassuring and supportive. In the therapeutic context, how the therapist's comments are heard will similarly be heavily influenced by the view the patient has of the relationship that has built up between them. A patient who feels positive towards her therapist might understand an 'interpretation' such as 'You are finding it hard to talk to me today' as an invitation to examine the difficulty in speaking about something that is on her mind. A patient in the grip of the idea that the therapist is critical and cruel could hear the same interpretation as a persecutory attack. This relational context is known in psychoanalysis as the *transference*.

Transference as an inner model of relationships

Transference refers to the form that the relationship between patient and therapist takes in the course of psychoanalysis, and it has become central to the psychoanalytic and psychodynamic understanding of therapeutic processes. For Freud, what is 'transferred' are feelings that properly belong elsewhere, usually attached in some way to persons or situations of long ago, and never fully dealt with. This means that it offers a window into the unconscious assumptions that a patient might have and a way of using the microcosm of the therapeutic encounter to throw light on how a person approaches their important relationships. For example, people who have regular difficulties with authority, perhaps rooted in their difficult relationship with their father, might quite quickly and forcefully show resentment towards the constraints of the therapeutic situation, or might fantasize that the therapist is bullying and bossy, or might become overly deferential and timid. Someone who unconsciously believes that the only way to survive is to be attractive and alluring might sexualize the transference very strongly.

For Freud, the idea of transference gradually became more important, as he observed how his patients related to him in ways that were inappropriate or excessive to the reality of the situation. Specifically, Freud came to see himself as being the recipient of 'transferred' thoughts and feelings that really belonged to important figures in the past, usually the patient's parents.

In his 'Dora' case study, Freud defined transference as:

> new editions or facsimiles of the impulses and phantasies which are aroused during the progress of the analysis; but they have this peculiarity, which is characteristic of their species, that they replace some earlier person by the person of the physician. (1905, p. 116)

It is worth noticing a few things about this definition.

- It is based on an analogy in which there is an original text and then a 'new edition or facsimile'.
- The new edition is a kind of translation of the original, in which the earlier person towards whom the 'impulses and phantasies' were directed is replaced by the analyst. This might be thought of as like an updating of a novel in which the situations are changed but the original plot is retained.
- Thought of this way, the analytic relationship becomes a framework within which the patient relives the original plot without realizing it. This opens the way for an understanding of psychoanalysis as a kind of interpretation or translation process, in which the patient is helped to see how her or his way of relating to the new environment is governed by a storyline that was originally developed for a different one.
- The analyst's interpretations of the 'new edition' might then become a means for the original to be made sense of, and the patient to be freed from its unconscious grip.

One question that arises from this immediately is whether in highlighting the role of transference in psychoanalysis, it is being assumed that it is a special kind of relationship that involves different mechanisms from those that occur in 'everyday life'. Usually, there is some degree of reciprocity in what happens between people, which can perhaps be thought of as a way in which reality can be tested out. So if we approach a new acquaintance with expectations that come from our past relationships, as we are almost bound to do, these can be quite quickly adjusted as we come to experience the real presence of the new person. For example, perhaps a child feels intimidated by his bullying father and expects the new male teacher he encounters in school to be similar. He might then immediately act fearfully towards him. If the teacher is in reality bullying and authoritarian, the child's expectations of authority figures as antagonistic and frightening might be strengthened. If, however, the teacher turns out to be sensitive to the child's anxieties and to act towards him kindly and carefully, the child might learn to discriminate between his internal model of an authority figure and this particular one. Under favourable circumstances, he might even come to see his father as the exception rather than the rule. More generally, whenever we meet people and engage with them, we might mix our inner expectations, derived from earlier experiences, with the actuality of what happens now. This can lead either to seeing the new person as similar to past 'objects', or to seeing them as different, perhaps exceptional. We might then alter our inner model of what to expect.

The notion of an inner model of relationships derived from early experience when dependence is great and the intensity of attachments very strong is a widespread and quite convincing one. It is also reasonable to move from this to the idea that this model might be used as a kind of unconscious template whenever people start to build new relationships. If the template is very rigid, it can force all relationships to come out the same, so that, for example, a person's experience of an authority figure might be always of a punitive father against whom she or he must rebel aggressively; or maybe a potential love partner is always assumed to be seductive and untrustworthy, like some unreliable mothers. If, however, the template is flexible enough, it can shift, allowing relationships to become different from those of the past. The question is, what is it that might occur in the new situation that can facilitate this shift in the template?

One obvious answer to this is that the new relationship might be so strikingly different to the original one that it challenges the assumptions on which the template is based. This presumably happens a great deal, but it is perhaps exactly a difficulty with perceiving these differences that contributes to the formation of the kinds of longstanding difficulties that might bring someone into psychotherapy. For example, a very powerful set of unconscious assumptions about being worthless might lead a person to seek out relationships that confirm those assumptions, or perhaps to turn every relationship into such a confirmation. So when a friend is kind, it is interpreted as pity; when the kindness then turns into annoyance, this is taken as proof of the worthlessness assumption; and when the friend gives up and breaks the relationship, this is further evidence that the person can never be valued or loved. Under these circumstances the potential 'reality' of the new relationship might never have a chance to bite, as everything that happens is already interpreted in terms of the pre-existing template.

Psychoanalysis as a special relationship

It is here that psychoanalysis takes a possibly counterintuitive turn in its own understanding of transference and what to do with it. In the psychoanalytic situation there is obviously some kind of reality. Analysts cannot avoid revealing something about themselves. They will be young or old, male or female, black or white; they will sometimes be alert and sometimes sleepy; they will unavoidably show interest in some things more than they do in others. Sometimes they will be ill; they might have a specific accent or some kind of visible disability. All these things might both provoke transference responses (it is probably easier, for example, to have a maternal transference towards an older woman than to a young man) and also allow these responses to be tested (the capacity of the analyst to listen without interruption might feel very strange to someone whose mother always butted in and allowed no space for thought). But the key psychoanalytic tactic will nevertheless be to try to reduce these 'reality' elements to a minimum, so that the transference can become clearer.

The idea here is that in 'ordinary' life, the reality of the situation modifies or obscures the transference quite quickly. In psychoanalysis, precisely because the analyst is a kind of 'non-present presence', the transference is much more explicit and obvious, and hence available to interpretation. If, for example, the analyst never does much except listen and make gentle, tentative comments, then if the patient experiences that analyst as hostile, punitive and judgemental it is a fair bet that something else is going on in the patient's mind that has not got to do with the reality of the analyst's behaviour. Why should the analyst's silence be interpreted as hostile judgement rather than supportive listening? The answer here is, 'because of the transference'; and the reserve (Freud called it 'abstinence') of the analyst is what makes that so apparent.

Not all analysts would accept this general characterization. For instance, Lacanians are more likely to argue that the term 'transference' should be reserved for what goes on in the consulting room, which means that other instances where one's past experiences influence present relationships are seen as different, less intense perhaps or less saturated with unconscious fantasies. Others object to the premise that therapists can ever be 'neutral', a point which will be returned to in the next chapter. There is also debate about whether everything that happens between the patient and the analyst is an effect of transference, or whether there are some nontransference ('real') elements of the analytic situation that are also important. This debate can be seen at work in the differences between analysts who restrict themselves to transference interpretations, which are interpretations that try to unpick what is going on in the relationship with the patient, and those who are willing to speak about other things, for example to give advice or comment on what a patient has said about the external world.

Nevertheless, there is a wide consensus among analysts that transference is core to understanding the analytic relationship, and that this understanding is in turn central to the practice of therapy. It is this focus on transference that makes psychoanalytic psychotherapy into a special relationship. Unlike in other situations, the transference is encouraged rather than alleviated. Also unlike what happens in most relationships, it is commented upon by the therapist, who tries to help the patient understand what is happening and how it relates to their unconscious relational template. In addition, there are times when what Freud calls a 'transference neurosis' forms, in which 'all the patient's symptoms have abandoned their original meaning and have taken on a new sense which lies in a relation to the transference' (Freud, 1917a, p. 444). This means that the patient enacts the salient elements of her or his neurotic difficulties in the therapy itself – coming late, getting angry, having palpitations, going deaf. The therapist is therefore able to engage with them directly, making interpretations and allowing unconscious conflicts to be examined and resolved in a kind of laboratory situation that can then be generalized to the patient's life as a whole. None of this is commonly found outside the peculiar situation of the analytic consulting room.

Developments in transference

Spillius et al. (2011, p. 515) note how the valuing of transference has developed from Freud's initial view of it as a problem, to its current centrality. The sequence they give is that transference has been seen historically as:

- A form of resistance to analysis by making the working relationship into an emotional one.
- The re-enactment of the past, giving a new clarity to the psychoanalytic reconstruction of the details of childhood experiences, especially traumas.
- The externalization of current unconscious fantasy.
- A complex set of relationships of the patient with the analyst.

The classical Freudian view of transference is that it is based on *displacement* of an unconscious idea from the object to which it was once attached onto the person of the analyst. The theme that runs through Freudian thinking on this is that there is a question of reality-perception at work: the patient *mistakenly* takes the analyst for the original object, usually the parent. The analyst's interpretations are consequently aimed at identifying the 'mistake' and helping patients to gain insight into how it occurs and how it influences their general functioning. The transference involves what Sandler et al. (1973, p. 46) call '"inappropriate" thoughts, attitudes, fantasies and emotions which are revivals of the past.' Even with the scare quotes around 'inappropriate', the implication here is of something unreal and out of touch. The presumption is that over time it is possible to put the analytic relationship onto a firmer footing of reality, with less displacement and more accurate positioning of the past as indeed the *past*.

If transference is understood in this way, the psychotherapeutic task becomes one of encouraging a better sense of reality in the patient, and hence of strengthening the ego so that it can discriminate more accurately between fantasy and reality. Newer developments in thinking on transference, however, have tended to suggest that such discriminations are very difficult to make. For these analysts, transference is not an irrational process that can be put right, but rather a description of what happens in all relationships.

They are all imbued with fantastic elements; the difference in psychoanalysis is simply that it becomes possible to acknowledge this openly and examine what its effects might be.

One effect of this disinclination to differentiate too clearly between reality and fantasy is to break down the distinction between what is and is not transference. This is one characteristic of Kleinian thinking that has also been influential in other forms of contemporary psychoanalysis. For instance, Hanna Segal (1981, p. 8) asserts that all aspects of the patient's communications in the session contain 'an element of unconscious phantasy', even if they appear to be concerned with external facts or other things that are not specifically to do with the analytic relationship. This is, she writes, 'equivalent to saying that all communications contain something relevant to the transference situation.' On an unconscious level, the patient is talking about these things in the context of the transference, and hence is using them in order to deal with anxieties stirred up by the transference relationship.

> For example, a patient might be talking about his worries about his child's schooling. Whatever the reality of this, the analytically relevant question is what it reveals about the relationship with the therapist. Perhaps he has chosen this topic because he feels that he has not got a good enough therapist to help him with his own 'exams', that is, with facing the demands of his life. Or maybe the therapist's apparent capacity to think and stay calm is bringing up in him feelings of envy and these are hinted at in his thoughts on schooling – for instance in envy towards people who can afford to buy elitist educational provision. Or it might be simpler than that: in talking about his child, the patient might be expressing the child in himself, or might be fleeing from a discussion of his own vulnerabilities.

From this, it can hopefully be seen why, as Hinshelwood (1991, p. 465) notes, 'The practice of Kleinian psychoanalysis has become an understanding of the transference as an expression of unconscious phantasy, active right here and now in the moment of the analysis.' Kleinians argue that the psychological mechanism underpinning transference is not displacement, as the Freudians suggest, but *projection and projective identification* (processes described in

Chapter 15), whereby aspects of the patient's personality are externalized into the mind of the analyst. In this model, what is happening in the consulting room is that elements of the patient's self as well as current emotions and fantasies are being projected into the relationship with the analyst, in order primarily to deal with anxiety, but also enabling therapeutic activity to occur. Kleinians still maintain a historical focus in the sense that they are interested in the infantile origins of a patient's way of being. However, what is distinctive about the Kleinian view of the transference is how it focuses not on the misfit between 'then' and 'now', but rather on current emotions and self-representations, infused of course by past experiences but nevertheless alive and growing *now*.

Once one has moved from a displacement to a projection model of transference, it becomes easier to imagine how a fragmented mind of the kind seen in psychosis might be worked with in psychoanalysis. This is because displacement assumes a significant level of mental organization. The person has a thought, feeling or impulse that is directed towards an object (for example 'everyone I love abandons me'), and this becomes redirected to another object, but is still a relatively integrated idea. In contrast, projection and especially projective identification emphasize the way aspects of the mind are split off and then projected into the analyst, either for safekeeping or as a way of expelling intolerable parts of the self. The role of the analyst in this then becomes that of a 'container' of disintegrated bits of the patient; and the analytic work is focused on thinking through these bits so they can become tolerable and meaningful, and can then be recovered by the patient.

Negative transference

Although Freud was alert to the way in which patients might harbour aggressive or denigratory feelings towards the analyst, he understood transference primarily as an idealizing love relationship that could cause trouble if it were not analysed fully. Kleinians, on the other hand, as a function of their interest in the destructiveness that is basic to the psyche, have focused on the negative transference, the complex of hostile feelings which the analysis will raise for the patient and which accordingly will be directed against the analyst. Because these destructive, envious elements are so powerful and so fundamental to psychic trouble, they have to be worked through if the personality is to be recuperated and integration is to occur; otherwise, they will simply obliterate the patient's loving potential. The negative transference both enacts the envy and makes this working through possible – but only if the analyst is capable of surviving the patient's attacks, continuing to think and be reliable and non-punitive, just as is required of the mother of early infancy.

The fundamental task of analysis is to enable integration of the personality to occur through overcoming splits in the psyche, which are perpetuated by unresolved primitive conflicts. The appropriate method is to analyse both sides of the early love–hate conflict as they are replayed in the positive and negative transference (Klein, 1952). Destructive and loving feelings can by this means gradually be brought together. Especially, it will be essential for the patient to have the experience of projecting hostile feelings into the analyst and having them 'contained', so that they can lose some of their sting and be given back, through the analyst's interpretation of the negative transference, in a more meaningful and less devastating form.

Freud (1907, p. 90) commented that, 'The process of cure is accomplished in a relapse into love.' This has given rise to the idea that psychotherapy might work as a 'cure through love' – the unconditional love that the mother should have given to her infant being replaced by the therapist's love for the patient. It should be clear from the account above that this is far from the ideal of contemporary psychoanalysis, which understands that the therapeutic situation is not one in which a previously failed love is replaced by a now real (or realistic) one. Instead, psychoanalysis is saturated with unconscious fantasies and these are often horrible. The task of the analyst is to love the patient only in the sense that she or he is committed enough to the analytic task to stay in the room, to stay sane and thoughtful, in the face of these attacks. Something destructive always has to be faced if people are to feel that it is possible to live with their unconscious impulses. This places great demands on the therapist's ability to deal with extreme mental states, an issue which will be discussed in the next chapter.

Summary

- Freud saw transference as a *displacement* of impulses that were originally directed towards important objects (the parents) onto the person of the analyst.
- Although it was first seen as a problem, it rapidly became clear that transference is the key to analytic work. This is because it dramatizes in the here-and-now of the analytic encounter what are the core unconscious templates for all the patient's relationships.
- Freudian psychoanalysts conventionally conceptualized the task of analysis as aiding the patient's insight into the way these unconscious templates might be determining their behaviours and ideas. It was therefore a practice of ego building, allowing clear distinction between reality and fantasy.
- Kleinians and some others have emphasized the pervasiveness of transference in analysis and conceptualized it as based on the *projection* of mainly unwanted thoughts and elements of the personality into the analyst. This raises the possibility of an analytic practice based on containing these projections and working on them through interpretations until they can be introjected back into the patient in a modified and less damaging form.
- Kleinians also emphasize the importance of negative transference, seen as the emergence in analysis of the patient's envious impulses, which have to be managed if the personality is to move towards more integration.

18
Psychotherapeutic relationships

Psychoanalysis as a relational practice

There is a widespread idea that psychoanalytic psychotherapists work by sitting in a chair behind a couch and very occasionally pronouncing some interpretive truth about the patient. This has some validity: the chair and couch actually exist, although most therapists also work in face-to-face contact, especially with 'non-analytic' patients who come to see them fewer than three times weekly. The passivity also has something to say for it – it is true that analysts tend to listen more than they speak, and to choose their words carefully. There is no physical activity, no advice or prescriptions, no behavioural exercises. Most analysts do not manage to avoid making some noninterpretive comments, such as asking questions or announcing when holidays will be, but these are kept to a minimum and may themselves come out as interpretations – that is, from the point of view of a patient locked in a negative transference, even a gentle question might be received as a kind of critical interpretation.

This last point is not a trivial one and it highlights what has happened in psychoanalytic thinking about therapy over the past few decades. For Freud, the relational elements of the analytic encounter were less important than the interpretive ones. Psychoanalysis had the flavour of a kind of detective story in which the truth of the unconscious was hunted through the clues thrown off by the patient's speech. He certainly understood that transference operated, but its significance took a long time to dawn on him. Even once this had happened, he was not inclined to emphasize the idea of psychoanalysis as a relationship between two people. Most importantly, he saw emotionality in the analyst's response to the patient as something regrettable, basically produced by incompletely analysed elements of the analyst's personality. The preferred analytic stance was that of neutrality. This was not an unsympathetic stance, but rather distant and professional, with an emphasis on maintaining clarity of thought and a kind of studied rationality.

Psychoanalysts still strive for neutrality. They avoid becoming over-involved with the patient or overtly judgemental. However, the theory and practice of psychoanalysis has moved on to recognize that whatever the analyst does or does not do, a relationship will form, and this has to be worked with. Indeed, in many respects one might argue that there has been a shift in psychoanalysis from being an *interpretive* practice to being a *relational* one. What this means is that whereas the original emphasis was on an increase in a certain kind of knowledge ('insight') *supported by* the transference relationship, many analysts now see the effects of the relationship itself as primary. This is reflected in the common idea from within relational and Kleinian thinking that a representation of the analyst might be internalized by the patient as a 'good object', or that the patient might end analysis identifying with the analyst's mind in the sense of developing a capacity to think without being flooded by anxiety. Such notions present what happens in the consulting room as an engagement between two human 'subjects' in which each is deeply involved, even if one of them (the patient) is perhaps affected more than the other.

Countertransference

Growing awareness of the importance of the relationship in psycho-analytic thinking is reflected in the way the concept of countertransference has become increasingly central. Countertransference is defined by Laplanche and Pontalis (1973, p. 92) as 'The whole of the analyst's unconscious reactions to the individual analysand – especially to the analysand's own transference.' This definition really conflates two different aspects of countertransference, both of them important but relating to differing theoretical and practical approaches:

1. Countertransference as the analyst's transference.

2. Countertransference as a response to the patient's transference.

Countertransference as the analyst's transference

For Freud, countertransference was a term used to describe an inter-ference in the analyst's thinking that came from unresolved uncon-scious elements in the analyst her or himself. Freud (1910b, p. 145) commented, 'no psycho-analyst goes further than his own complexes and internal resistances permit.' Sandler et al. (1973, p. 62) identify this comment with the Freudian view of countertransference, which 'was seen as a sort of "resistance" in the psychoanalyst towards his patient, resistance due to the arousal of unconscious conflicts by what the patient says, does or represents to the analyst.' These uncon-scious conflicts could prevent the analyst getting a clear view of the patient's troubles, and in particular might inhibit the separation of the patient's transference feelings from realistic aspects of the situa-tion. The source of countertransference would then be unanalysed aspects of the analyst's own personality, and as such the task would be to reduce the effects of these unanalysed conflicts as far as humanly possible. Sandler et al. (ibid.) go on to elaborate:

> [If] a psychoanalyst had not resolved problems connected with his own aggression, for example, he might need to placate his patient whenever he detected aggressive feelings or thoughts towards him in the patient. Similarly, if the analyst is threatened by his own uncon-scious homosexual feelings, he may be unable to detect any homo-sexual implications in the patient's material; or, indeed, he may react with undue irritation to homosexual thoughts or wishes in the patient, may sidetrack the patient on to another topic, etc. The 'counter' in counter-transference may thus indicate a reaction in the analyst which implies a parallel to the patient's transference (as in 'counterpart') as well as being a reaction to them (as in 'counteract').

Moore and Fine (1990) similarly state, 'Under the influence of countertransference, analysis takes on an unconscious, conflicted significance for the analyst instead of being a reality-adapted, conflict-free activity.' They suggest that the analyst might under such circum-stances identify with the patient or react over-strongly to elements of the patient's presentation. From this predominantly Freudian perspec-tive, therefore, countertransference is a problem for the analyst that comes from her or his own unconscious life and makes it harder to relate to the patient rationally and neutrally. In terms of technique, the task of the analyst would be 'to reduce manifestations of counter-transference as far as possible by means of personal analysis so that the analytic situation may ideally be structured exclusively by the patient's transference' (Laplanche and Pontalis, 1973, p. 93).

Countertransference as a response to the patient's transference

Melanie Klein herself adhered roughly to the view of countertransference outlined above, in which it was understood as something to be dealt with by more analysis for the analyst. However, beginning in the 1950s, Kleinians have been at the forefront of the development of an understanding of countertransference as a key source of knowledge for the analyst about what is coming 'from' the patient in the form of projections. Countertransference becomes both an indicator of what is happening in the patient's unconscious life, and a tool for the analyst to trace the fluctuations that occur during therapy. In this vein, Spillius et al. (2011, p. 288) note that one of the original papers presenting this view of psychoanalysis, Paula Heimann's (1950) work 'On counter-transference', 'defines countertransference as "an instrument of research into the patient's unconscious" and says that "... the analyst's countertransference is not only part and parcel of the analytic relationship, but it is the patient's creation, it is a part of the patient's personality".'

The idea here is that the analyst has an unconscious reaction to the specific qualities of the patient, and that the analyst needs to cultivate the capacity to register, recognize and understand this reaction and use it as a *guide* to the patient's transference. In a slightly later paper, Heimann (1960) argues that by reflecting on the counter-transference, the analyst will have a good idea of what is happening in the analysis itself. For example, by 'comparing the feelings roused in himself with the content of the patient's associations and the qualities of his mood and behaviour, the analyst has the means for checking whether he has understood or failed to understand his patient' (p. 10). Here, the argument is that the analyst will have feelings called up by the analytic process, that while some of these will relate to the analyst's own state of mind, many will also be connected to the patient's mental state. Tracking these feelings carefully, which means accepting and reflecting upon them, will allow the analyst to understand what is happening both 'inside' the patient and in the analytic relationship.

> In the course of a prolonged psychotherapeutic relationship, a therapist finds herself consistently feeling empty and bored. Reflecting on this, she thinks that it is an unusual state of mind for her to be in and wonders if it has to do with the way the patient is treating her. The patient, a man, seems to act as if the therapist hardly exists. He never asks her anything, rarely reacts directly to her interpretations, and talks as if he has to do all the work in therapy by himself. The therapist, tracking her own responses, comes to believe that her feelings have to do with the patient's resistance to being in a relationship with her. It is as if he has shut down, or emptied out, all possibility of a link with her, making the therapy 'empty'. The therapist's own sense of futility is therefore a response to the way in which she is being treated, but may also be a kind of representation of the patient's feelings that he has unconsciously 'put into' her.

What the therapist feels

The second understanding of countertransference, as a response to the specific qualities of the patient, has become very influential in Kleinian and object relational psychoanalysis, despite having various problems attached to it. Not the least of these is how exactly a therapist might learn to distinguish between the first and second types of countertransference, that is, between those moments when she or he is responding to aspects of the patient that bring up personal 'stuff' for the therapist, and those other times when what is being felt is truly coming from the patient. If a therapist is bored and sleepy, is this because: (1) the therapist is tired or depressed, or (2) something in the patient reminds the therapist of her or his own depressed mother, or (3) the *patient's* depression has been projected 'into' the analyst? If it is either of the first two possibilities, then commenting on the patient as depressed would be a way in which the analyst imposes her or his own neurosis on the patient. On the other hand, if the material really does come from the patient, then finding a way to speak about it carefully and sensitively could lead to the patient feeling recognized and 'contained' and be a route through to thera-peutic progress. In truth, it is highly likely that all these components operate during therapy, perhaps even at the same time. A particular therapist may be especially responsive to depression in a patient because the therapist has that tendency her or himself; but this does not mean that the patient's depression is not really there. If the thera-pist is sufficiently aware of how all this works, it might be possible to hold her or his own depression at bay and retain the necessary analytic approach towards the patient.

What is being described in this view of countertransference as a genuine response to a patient's unconscious conflicts is a way in which something that is 'inside' the patient becomes lodged 'in' the analyst, who can then feel and think about it. The mechanism here is that of projective identification: an element of the patient's mental life has been projected into the analyst and is held onto in some way. As described in Chapter 15, projective identification can have various qualities. The important thing is that it both alerts the analyst to something going on in and with the patient, and provides powerfully emotional evidence of what that thing might be. Hanna Segal (1981, p. 82) comments, 'We see the patient not only as perceiving the analyst in a distorted way, reacting to this distorted view, and commu-nicating these reactions to the analyst, but as also doing things to the analyst's mind, projecting into the analyst in a way which affects the analyst.' This also clarifies what the therapeutic work might be, some-thing that was examined particularly influentially by Wilfred Bion and other Kleinian analysts, who use a strong developmental analogy. In this view, outlined earlier in Chapter 14, the mother is required to receive the projections and projective identifications of the infant, to 'feel' them inside her (so she registers the baby's agitation as an inner sense of anxiety herself), and then to think about what they mean and respond accordingly, in a loving and calm way. Similarly, the therapist has to contain the projections of the patient, reflecting on their impact and significance. The therapist must keep alert and thoughtful, in a state of 'reverie' (Bion, 1962). By means of both the analyst's stability and interpretive accuracy, the patient comes to feel contained and more able to think. In this way, psychoanalysis becomes a rela-tional event whereby the working out of transference and counter-transference go on together. The patient's projections – whether emotions or parts of the self – become the central data for feeling, reflection and interpretation. What the therapist does with these, how she or he infuses them with parts of her or his own self, is crucial to the progress of the therapy.

This image of the interpersonal encounter embedded in the transference–countertransference cycle is very influential. Its implication is that there is an intimate link between patient and psychotherapist centred on the capacity of the therapist to feel unconscious resonance with the patient. The therapist's task becomes that of acting as a receptacle for the patient's unconscious fantasy while remaining anchored in the therapist's own self, so as not to enact the patient's disorder. The therapist does not simply observe and interpret the patient's unconscious life from the outside. Instead, an intersubjective dialectic occurs. Spillius et al. (2011, p. 292) put it like this:

> In recent years it has steadily emerged how sensitive patients are to the analyst's feelings and the analyst's methods of coping with those feelings, defensive or otherwise. Because one of the implications of the cycle of projective and introjective identifications is that the process of modification is in the analyst, who is required to have the stability of mind to cope with extremely difficult anxieties without becoming overly disturbed himself, it is in fact the patient's perceptions of the analyst's ability to modify anxiety that is really the important component.

The therapist picks up through the countertransference what is happening hidden in the patient's mind; the patient is constantly monitoring the therapist for evidence of whether the parts of her or himself that have been projected into the therapist are being contained and cared for, or are creating panic. The whole outcome of analysis depends on this dialectic being a benevolent one.

The 'analytic third'

Building on the idea of transference and countertransference as entwined with each other, relational psychoanalysts have become increasingly interested in the work that patients and analysts do together to make something new happen. Some of this thinking uses the idea that projective identification is a major feature of the transference–countertransference dialectic. Other work is more directly derived from Winnicott's notion of a transitional space that can be created as an 'in-between' area for creativity and play. For example, Jessica Benjamin (2004) describes such a transitional space as a kind of 'thirdness' – neither just the patient nor solely the analyst, but a meeting point that is outside them both yet also includes them. She distinguishes between some different kinds of 'third', two of which are especially relevant here.

• The 'third in the one', which is the capacity of the mother or the therapist to appreciate what can be created *with* the infant or patient. In therapy, this involves continuing to value and communicate with the patient even when the patient is destructive. It is in essence the ability to hold in mind the patient, the therapist and the relationship between them.

• The 'one in the third', which is close to the Winnicottian idea of transitional space (see Chapter 10). This links the patient and the therapist in such a way as to produce something new. It is a space for meeting and reflection, owned by neither party but an aspect of them both. The idea here is that what happens in analysis does not take place solely within the patient nor inside the therapist. Instead, the analytic relationship itself becomes a space into which unconscious material is projected, to be worked on imaginatively. In a way, both patient and therapist lend aspects of themselves to the situation, and if things go well each participant can then 'take back' elements of her or his unconscious world, now modified by the impact of projections from the other.

For Benjamin, these ideas show how much the analyst is actively present in the therapeutic encounter. Similarly, some very influential work by Thomas Ogden has stressed the intersubjective dimension of analysis, supplementing the idea that there is an analyst and a patient with the notion that there is *also* an analyst–patient couple. As briefly noted in Chapter 12, Ogden is interested in holding in tension the individual subjectivity of patient and analyst with an appreciation of the area of their mixing together – the third. In a paper published in 2004, Ogden links this with the process of projective identification, showing among other things how much Kleinian thinking has recently permeated the world of American psychoanalysis. He is interested in how projective identification 'has the effect of profoundly subverting the experience of analyst and analysand as separate subjects' (p. 189). His main point is that analysis works when the 'third' of the analytic relationship, which Ogden calls a 'new intersubjective entity', allows both analyst and patient to think new thoughts and feel new feelings. This on its own is not enough, however. The patient and analyst must also become able to let go of the third without destroying or denying it. They must be able to hold it in play while also returning to their individual subjective positions. Ogden states the necessary conditions for this as follows:

> The generative freeing of the individual participants from the subjugating third depends upon (1) the analyst's act of recognizing the individuality of the analysand (for example by means of his accurate and empathic understanding and interpretation of the transference-countertransference), and (2) the analysand's recognition of the separate individuality of the analyst (for example through the analysand's making use of the analyst's interpretations). (2004, p. 191)

The analyst and the patient have different roles in this relationship, but they are both involved, and their willingness to participate in it is crucial for change.

Lacanian ideas on intersubjectivity

The emphasis in this chapter has been on the relational elements of the psychoanalytic encounter, and this is a fair reflection of the general trend of much contemporary psychoanalysis. However, it is worth returning briefly to an alternative view, which is suspicious of all talk of the use of the therapist's self or of intersubjective connection. As described in Chapter 16, Lacanian psychoanalysts argue that the 'discourse of the Analyst' is one that reveals the 'discourse of the Master' as a kind of empty space; that is, it aims to give back to the patient the realization that one has somehow to find a way to acknowledge one's desire without the help of any magic 'cure'. This is reflected strongly in Lacanian understandings of how transference might work. The key idea here is that of the psychoanalyst in the transference as 'the subject supposed to know' (Lacan, 1972–3, p. 139), with the emphasis on 'supposed to'. The analyst fills the space people give to all imaginary sources of knowledge and help, but this is different from *actually* knowing anything. Dylan Evans (1996, p. 197) explains:

> [The] analyst is often thought to know the secret meaning of the analysand's words, the significations of speech of which even the speaker is unaware. This supposition alone (the supposition that the analyst is the one who knows) causes otherwise insignificant details (chance gestures, ambiguous remarks) to acquire retroactively a special meaning for the patient who 'supposes'.

The patient invests hope in the analyst, but not just that; what defines transference is an unconscious belief that all that is wrong in the patient's life can be eased away by the analyst's words of wisdom. This, however, is in Lacanian terms an 'imaginary' state of mind. In actuality, there is no such capacity residing in anyone, and a great deal of trouble is caused by thinking that there is. Lacan is opposed to psychoanalytic versions of cure that hold that the analyst either does know the difference between real and unreal (the classical view) or can become a 'good object' inside the patient (roughly, the Kleinian and object relational view). Rather, the end point of the Lacanian transference, the point at which it is 'dissolved', comes when the patient realizes not just that the analyst has no answers, but that *no one* possesses the answer to the question of existence. The 'subject supposed to know' is only *supposed* to know because of the fantasies generated about authority and knowledge itself. Because of all this, Lacanians tend to be suspicious of approaches that seem to make the relationship between therapist and patient too central. Analysts need to be suspicious of their own feelings, because of the seductions of the appeal to mastery, and concentrate instead on the details of the patient's speech.

This viewpoint is not the dominant one in contemporary psychoanalysis, which tends to emphasize more flexible modes of practice based on the idea that the work of psychotherapy depends on the quality of the therapeutic relationship and the skill with which it can be reflected upon by both therapist and patient. It is this relational approach that is also most influential in psychoanalytic psychotherapy and psychodynamic counselling. The move towards more flexible, self-reflexive practice can only be good, as it makes psychotherapists more accountable and responsive to their patients' needs, and in principle at least more humble about their own. Nevertheless, it is worth holding in mind the question that the Lacanian critique raises. In placing so much weight on the therapeutic relationship, is there a danger that psychotherapy might be reduced to 'love'? And if this happens, does it risk becoming what Freud (1930) once called a mode of 'consolation' rather than a means through which people are challenged to change?

Summary

- Psychoanalytic theory has increasingly recognized how psycho-analysis operates in practice through the *relationship* of analyst and patient.
- The concept of countertransference is often applied to the analyst's participation in this relationship.
- For Freud, countertransference was really the analyst's transfer-ence – the issues raised in the analyst by the patient, which produce a neurotic response on the part of the analyst and there-fore interfere with treatment.
- Kleinians and some later relational psychoanalysts have developed a view of countertransference as the analyst's specific response to the patient's transference. The analyst absorbs the patient's projec-tions and reflects on them, gaining in this way a strong sense of what the patient is feeling. From the patient's point of view, the analyst's capacity to reflect on this and offer back the projections in a modified form allows greater integration of the personality to occur. Transference and countertransference are thus envisaged as a relational cycle or dialectic. Projective identification may be the mechanism at the heart of this.
- Some contemporary analysts have used the idea of the 'analytic third' to convey the notion of an intersubjective space in which the unconscious ideas of both patient and analyst are pooled, allowing something new to occur.
- Not all analysts are convinced of the value of an intersubjective or relational approach. Lacanians argue that analysts are related to by their patients as 'subjects supposed to know', and that their task is to help patients come to the realization that there is no outside other in whom one can invest that kind of magical ability to cure.

PART III

Wider applications

19
Psychoanalysis, art and literature

Applying psychoanalysis

Although many of the examples of applications of psychoanalytic theory used in this book to date have been based on the contact between analysts and their patients, others have been used to try to show how psychoanalysis has contributed to understanding social situations. In this last section of the book, I will give a brief outline of some of the issues that arise when applying psychoanalysis 'outside the clinic', specifically in the arts and humanities and in some of the social sciences. It is not possible to do this large topic full justice in such a small space, but it is still important to engage with it. As it happens, there are many who claim that the *main* significance of psychoanalysis is now in these areas, as a kind of tool for cultural analysis rather than as a therapeutic system.

Psychoanalysis has its origins in the consulting room, but from early on Freud was interested in how it could be 'applied' elsewhere. This was for two main reasons. First, he was concerned about establishing the scientific accuracy of psychoanalysis and thought that evidence from patients could be usefully supplemented by other kinds of data, notably from artistic and cultural material. He was very impressed with the intuitive understanding that artists and some philosophers had of the unconscious, and believed that if he could show similarities between his own theories and their work, he would be presenting evidence supportive of the claims made by psychoanalysis. Secondly, Freud saw psychoanalysis as a contribution to scientific enlightenment and hence to the advancement of civilization and so sought opportunities to demonstrate the insights it could provide in the widest possible social and cultural arenas.

211

Peter Gay (1988, pp. 312–13) suggests that what mattered to Freud in applying psychoanalysis in these areas, 'was less what he could learn from art history, linguistics and the rest than what they could learn from him; he entered alien terrain as a conquistador rather than a supplicant.' This marks one of the areas of controversy about the use of psychoanalysis 'outside the clinic': does it pay sufficient heed to the specific conditions and traditions of the other disciplines in whose terrain it treads? For example, when dealing with art does it attend to what artists and art historians say or does it launch in with its own 'better' knowledge of the unconscious motivations for their work? In the case of a novel, can we read a piece of writing as an expression of unconscious urges, like a dream, or do we have to take account of the genres and technical ways in which writers work? Much applied psychoanalysis has not been sensitive enough to these issues, but to be fair to Freud he did realize that, whatever his own pleasure in cultural speculation, there might be limits to what his new approach could do.

Early forays into literary and artistic theory by Freud and his circle (for example Freud, 1907) had a significant impact on biographically oriented work and also in opening out a domain of interpretive activity that was new in its orientation and its possibilities. In some areas, such as art history, literary criticism and film studies, the effect of psychoanalysis since then has been profound, provoking rich seams of research that touch on fundamental questions of structure, motivation, representation and response (for example Ehrenzweig, 1967; Mulvey, 1989; Stonebridge, 1998; Žižek, 1991, 2006b). Despite fluctuations in the extent to which psychoanalysis is regarded as having cultural currency, it continues to be a significant intellectual resource in the humanities and social sciences, with especially influential recent deployments in some major works on art and politics, sexuality, violence and war (for example Žižek, 2006a; Rose, 1996; Butler, 2009). This shows very cogently how psychoanalysis has migrated out of the clinic and become one of the most significant tools available to those who wish to understand the social world.

In this chapter, two examples of psychoanalysis applied to the arts will be presented, those of film and literature. This leaves out a lot: for example, beginning with Freud's own work on art and sculpture (for example Freud, 1910a, 1914) there has been a considerable amount of interest in applications of psychoanalysis in these areas. Perhaps even more importantly, there is a long history of 'psychobiography' in which the work of creative artists is examined psychoanalytically through analysis of their biographies. Freud's (1910a) account of Leonardo da Vinci is the classic instance of this, with its proposal that Leonardo's creativity was a manifestation of his repressed homosexuality, itself linked to the speculative history of his relationship with his mother. The problem here, repeated in a lot of applied psychoanalytic work, is partly that there is usually very limited evidence for such biographical explanations (certainly very much less than would be available for patients in therapy) and that the meaning of this material cannot be tested in any 'live encounter'. Psychobiography also tends to be *reductive* in the sense of not attending sufficiently to the specifics of the social and cultural contexts of artists' lives, including the particularity of their crafts.

Cinematic origins

One problem with the notion of 'applying' psychoanalysis is that it suggests that one well-formed discipline is going to be used to elucidate the obscurities of another – for example that psychoanalysis has insights into art history that the historians themselves may not have – and that as a general theory it can be stretched across widely disparate areas of intellectual activity. Not only does this neglect the specifics of *psychoanalysis'* conditions of emergence and the question of the limits of its applicability; more to the point it neglects the specifics of the disciplines to which it is being applied. For example, can psychoanalysis speak of literature without using literary tropes? Is it fair to import it into music or art without deep knowledge of the conventions and technical apparatuses of those two immensely rich terrains? Did psychoanalysis 'cause' cinema, which grew up at exactly the same time, or was the direction of effect the other way around, or mutual?

This last example is a particularly good one, as it reminds us of the extent to which psychoanalysis arose at a certain time and was connected with other new inventions and discoveries of its period. Like psychoanalysis, cinema has always dealt with illusions, fantasies and dreams. Gabbard (2001, p. 1) describes this mutuality well:

> In 1895 there were two auspicious births. The Lumière brothers invented a rudimentary film projector, signifying the birth of the

cinema, and *Studies in Hysteria* appeared, inaugurating the new science of psychoanalysis. Throughout the twentieth century the two new disciplines have been inextricably linked. As early as 1900 a writer would describe his psychotic episode in terms of 'the magic lantern' effects of the nickelodeons … In 1931 the American film industry was already being called a 'dream factory', reflecting the close resemblance between film imagery and the work of dreams.

Gabbard (2001, pp. 4–5) is cautious about how useful psychoanalysis is for exploring cinema, noting that, 'Obviously, when one applies a psychoanalytic lens to the text of a film, one cannot hope for a definitive reading. A more modest goal is to emphasize how clinical psychoanalytic theory can illuminate what appears to be happening on the screen and the manner in which the audience experiences it.' The term 'illuminate' here reveals the complexities of the situation. 'Illumination' is precisely the activity of cinema, and one might argue that the vocabulary and technology of film are exactly what is needed to help us understand psychoanalysis itself. That is, maybe it is only among a population that is used to the play of images on a screen, out of which a narrative is made, that the distinction between conscious perception and unconscious significance makes sense. More likely, both cinema and psychoanalysis depend on the same modern capacity to read surfaces and imagine depths. This is shown in the degree of engagement that film audiences have with the two-dimensional images that they know have nothing behind them – a situation rather different from that operating in the older form of representation, theatre, where people mask themselves and pretend to be something other than what they are, but are nevertheless demonstrably present (Metz, 1977). That is, cinema plays on the way people are seduced into believing in a certain kind of 'apparatus' that fills out empty images as if they have real substance. Similarly, psychoanalysis depends on identification with its own 'apparatus' (the couch, the consulting room, the texts of Freud, and so on) to convince its adherents that there is something at work beneath the surface of speech and behaviour. Its dreamscape is cinematic, and perhaps without film we could neither imagine it so thoroughly nor find it so convincing. Most importantly, in both cases what is worked on is fantasy; both film and psychoanalysis make this central to human psychic life.

Psychoanalytic film criticism has a relatively short history in comparison with psychoanalytic literary criticism, even though the use of psychoanalytic ideas in films occurred from early on. This is perhaps simply because cinema itself only became an object of academic scrutiny in the 1950s. Despite this, there is an enormous literature on film and psychoanalysis, and there have been some major developments in theory that have implications both for cinema and for psychoanalysis itself. The main thing to note here is that although there is a strong tradition of using psychoanalytic ideas to interpret the actions of film characters, this is not the main thrust of contemporary work. As will be described below in relation to psychoanalysis and literature, the idea that the motivations of a fictional character can be understood by subjecting her or him to analysis is in relative disrepute: such characters do not have a 'real' psychic life, nor of course do they have a childhood. They might be used illustratively, as when someone speculates on the effects of Norman Bates's traumatic history in Hitchcock's (1960) *Psycho* – but Bates, being a fictional character, is not actually motivated by unconscious complexes of this kind. This does not, however, mean that nothing can be learnt from such analyses. For instance, in his *Pervert's Guide to Cinema*, Slavoj Žižek (2006c) has enormous fun in exploring a huge variety of films. Along the way, he gestures briefly towards a standard Oedipal interpretation of Hitchcock's (1963) *The Birds*. In this, the birds are seen as embodying an eruption of libidinal eroticism into the intense mother–son incestuous bond that the romantic lead, Melanie, breaks into. Žižek refers to the son (Mitch) being split between 'his possessive mother and the intrusive girl', but he is not really doing an analysis of Mitch, he is rather using the film to illustrate the way in which desire works. The Oedipal structure channels and contains desire; *The Birds* is an exploration of what happens when this containment is under unbearable strain. Similarly, Žižek's (2006b) analysis of Ridley Scott's (1979) *Alien* does not interpret the creature as a simple manifestation of the unconscious of the film's *characters*, but rather reads it as the Freudian drive or the Lacanian Real breaking into the film itself. It speaks to audiences because it embodies something they already, unconsciously, know.

This moves us away from attempts to analyse either the characters in films or what they might represent, and to the question of how film works on audiences. This is again a very rich and complex area, but some major ideas produced by psychoanalytically informed theorists are summarized below.

- *Film as allowing audiences to work through anxieties*

Classical psychoanalysts working within the Freudian tradition have tended to see films as providing opportunities for audiences to face their desires and anxieties. The model here is very much that of the dream, which expresses in a 'compromise-formation' the unconscious impulses that cannot be allowed full expression in consciousness. Epitomizing this perspective, Gabbard (2001, p. 14) claims that 'audiences do not attend films merely to be entertained. They line up at the local multiplex to encounter long-forgotten but still powerful anxieties that stem from universal developmental experiences. They seek solutions to problems in the culture that defy simple answers or facile explanations. The screen in the darkened theatre serves as a container for the projection of their most private and often unconscious terrors and longings.' A consequence of this idea is that the concepts employed to make sense of films are similar to those used for dream analysis but also for therapeutic work. For instance, in examining the attraction of horror films, Gabbard uses language redolent of the vision of the therapeutic situation as a place in which people's terrors can be faced without the usual feared consequences. 'Part of the appeal of the horror and science fiction genres,' he writes (p. 8), 'is related to the audience's vicarious mastery of infantile anxieties associated with earlier developmental crises. The audience can re-encounter terrifying moments involving early anxieties while keeping a safe distance from them and knowing that they can survive them.' The cinema is thus a kind of therapeutic space in which the imagination is allowed to confront the unconscious and live.

- *Film as providing objects of desire*

This idea has been developed particularly by feminist film critics influenced by Lacanian film theory. The best known example here is Laura Mulvey, whose 1975 article 'Visual Pleasure and Narrative Cinema' is probably one of the most influential academic film papers ever written. Intriguingly, the article is set up as a political rather than a filmic intervention; Mulvey writes (p. 14), 'Psychoanalytic theory is ... appropriated here as a political weapon, demonstrating the way the unconscious of patriarchal society has structured film form.' What she is especially interested in is the way the woman in films is made the object of a male gaze, which she argues is part of the structure of cinema itself in a patriarchal society. Mulvey claims (p. 19) that 'In a world ordered by sexual imbalance, pleasure in looking has been split between active/ male and passive/female. The determining male gaze projects its fantasy onto the female figure, which is styled accordingly.' The female is usually the erotic element in a film, and this, claims Mulvey, makes her *static*, a still point around which the narrative has to move. 'The presence of woman is an indispensable element of spectacle in normal narrative film,' Mulvey writes (ibid.), 'yet her visual presence tends to work against the development of a story-line, to freeze the flow of action in moments of erotic contemplation.' The consequence here is that the viewer identifies with the male gaze as active, moving the story forward, but enjoying the woman as spectacle. Patriarchal assumptions are reinforced and played out in relation to this 'scopophilic' gaze, scopophilia being a term used in psychoanalysis to denote erotic pleasure in looking.

- *Film as providing identificatory objects*

The idea that audiences might gain enjoyment from identifying with the protagonists in a film is a strong and obvious one. Mulvey argues that this aspect of film viewing is actually in tension with the scopophilic one mentioned above. Where the scopophilic drive is alienating in the sense that one stands outside and *looks*, the identificatory one links the ego to the object and so is *immersive*. Mulvey suggests that in mainstream film this depends on having 'a main controlling figure with whom the spectator can identify' (1975, p. 20) and that this places the viewer (whether male or female) in the masculine (active) position. Sometimes, however, this identification breaks down, for example when the female spectator finds herself totally averse to the male protagonist, or where a film works explicitly to disrupt gender assumptions and calls into question the sexualized identifications of the viewer. Famous examples here include Neil Jordan's (1992) *The Crying Game*, in which the discovery of the 'actual' gender of one of the lead characters disrupts the assumptions about gender and sexuality that have powerfully structured the film to date. Kimberly Peirce's (1999) *Boys Don't Cry* has some similarities with Jordan's film, but perhaps even more powerfully shatters straightforward gender identifications through its portrayal of masculine homophobic violence.

- *Cinema as a symbolic apparatus*

Finally here, there is some important work on how film criticism itself offers a way of challenging the identificatory and ideological processes at work in cinema. This particular argument has a lot of different sources, but one major one is in Lacanian film theory, which identifies the enjoyment of cinema as being primarily in the realm of the Imaginary (see Chapter 16). Critical analysis draws the viewer away from this Imaginary position and inserts a third term – theory – into the relationship with film, revealing how it is structured and so drawing the experience into the Symbolic. This makes psychoanalytic film theory itself into a kind of therapeutic intervention. Just as the analyst helps the patient put things into words and so come to terms with them, so the film theorist allows the viewer to achieve some distance from the unconscious effects of the film, and therefore understand and manage them better.

There is a great deal more that could be said about film and psychoanalysis, with much important recent writing that explores the place of gaze and desire in highly critical ways (for example Copjec, 2000). However, the key point here is to note how productive psychoanalysis has been in developing an account of what it might mean to be a *viewer* of film, rather than as a way to interpret film narratives themselves. This is also true of a second area to be briefly considered here, that of psychoanalysis and literature.

Literature and dreams

Psychoanalysis has always been controversial as a method of literary analysis, particularly among writers and critics who regard it as a colonizing discipline trying to tell the 'truth' of literature without necessarily appreciating its specificity, including its aesthetic properties. There is certainly a lot for such critics to get their teeth into, as psychoanalysts have not been coy about applying their clinical insights to literature. Sometimes, as with Freud, this is because they admire creative writing and wish to understand it better; but often they seem simply unable to resist the temptation to speculate freely about literary characters or their authors, perhaps rejoicing in them as 'patients' who cannot answer back. The most outrageous instances of psychoanalytic 'reading in' to literary productions treat them as somehow transparent indicators of the mental state and psychobiographical attributes of the author. Examples here include Marie Bonaparte's (1933) early study of Edgar Allen Poe, which identified necrophilia as a pathological personality state underpinning Poe's writing, or Ernest Jones's (1910) study of *Hamlet* as Oedipal drama. The limitations of this approach and of the parallel tendency to treat literary characters as real have been well recognized for a long time. Maud Ellmann (1994) makes the key point. 'Hamlet,' she writes (p. 3), 'has the disadvantage that he can never contradict his psychoanalyst. Unlike a real analysand, he cannot lie down on the couch and free associate about his dreams or recapitulate the trauma of his infancy. Amusing as it is to speculate about his early history, Hamlet *never had a childhood.*'

As in Bonaparte's and Jones's early studies, there is a tradition of treating literary texts as equivalent to dreams, offering a 'royal road' through to the neurosis of their authors. There are numerous problems with this. For one thing, the biographical detail needed to inform psychoanalytic formulations and the opportunity for testing interpretations in the context of clinical transference relationships are not available even if one accepts the premise that a literary work might be akin to a dream. In the case of the dream, each element might open out associations *in the dreamer* that can be subjected to psychoanalytic work; in the literary example, no such associations are available, with the consequence that it is commonly the *analyst's* associations that are substituted for the author's. Moreover, while an author might well 'inhabit' her or his writing in ways that give rise to biographical curiosity, any interpretive account of a text in terms of the character or psychopathology of the author is undermined by the way writers *craft* their work. Writers work with their material in ways that are derived from the history of their profession. Even when they challenge and depart from this history (and even, one might say, if they are influenced by psychoanalysis in doing so), it is in relation to the practice of writing that this happens, not the practice of free association.

What has made a profound difference to the reception of psychoanalysis in literary criticism has been a shift of attention from the 'psychological truth' of the text to the way in which knowledge is constructed *in the relation between* the material itself and the reader. This has been commented on almost since the beginning of applied psychoanalysis, but is expressed especially clearly by Shoshana Felman (1982) in a famous examination of the 'and' in the phrase 'psychoanalysis *and* literature'. Felman points out that psychoanalysis' approach to literature has been one of attempted mastery, in which interpretation is the key to unlock the 'real meaning' of a literary piece. The alternative to this, she argues, is to seek a way in which psychoanalysis and literature can genuinely invest in each other as equals – not one mastering the other, either as psychoanalysis speaking the truth of literature or as literature exposing the narrative assumptions of psychoanalysis, even though both disciplines do have something to say to the other from these 'expert' positions. For Felman, the issue is one of using psychoanalysis and literature to provoke each other, so that the theoretical heritage of both disciplines is enhanced. Felman (p. 8) writes, 'In view of this shift of emphasis, the traditional method of *application* of psychoanalysis to literature would here be in principle ruled out. The notion of *application* would be replaced by the radically different notion of *implication*.' What she means by this is that the concern of psychoanalysis in relation to literature should be to examine what each discipline does to the other, how the strategies of reading involved in textual and clinical work draw on one another and produce new ideas. It is this question of *reading* that is perhaps central: not just the masterful analyst reading the patient's discourse for its unconscious significance or the sophisticated literary critic reading the text for its nuances and resonances, but the awareness present in both disciplines that reading is a process of involvement that draws the reader in. It is a productive process that changes the reader or analyst as much as it explores any text.

Psychoanalysis as literature

The struggle to develop psychoanalysis, usually coded as an attempt to find a scientific basis for this complex depth psychology, is also a development within the broad disciplinary nexus known as the 'humanities'. This recognizes it as an attempt to refine consciousness in relation to human motivation and desire, and to express this refinement in recognizable terms within its own literary genre. In this context, psychoanalysts who recommend the development of literary capacities as a way of mastering technique have something useful to say, not only because of what there is to be learnt from the practice of literature, but also because working *reflexively* in this way leaves psychoanalysis itself open to challenge and change. For example, the leading psychoanalyst Thomas Ogden (1999) describes powerfully (using a Robert Frost poem as an example) how there may be parallels between 'the way he listens to the language of the poem and the way he and his patient speak with and listen to one another' (p. 49). For Ogden, the lesson of poetry for the consulting room is not to use language 'poetically', but rather to cultivate a mode of listening and speaking that is attuned to the question of 'what it is "that's going on here" in the intrapsychic and intersubjective life of the analysis, the "music of what happens" in the analytic relationship' (p. 50). Ogden argues that both poetry and psychoanalysis make possible forms of 'human aliveness' and the discipline of listening to one can enhance that of listening to the other. In this account the task of the analyst is no longer to unearth the truth of what lies behind the patient's or the poem's words; it is simply to find a way to listen and respond that brings 'feelings and ideas to life in words that will advance the analytic process' (p. 66). This moves the discipline towards more of a focus on intersubjectivity, with responsiveness rather than knowingness being a core attribute of the analyst.

It will be obvious from this discussion that psychoanalysis has had problems with its analyses of film and literature and (by extension) other artistic forms. Despite this, it has contributed significantly to a cultural industry that takes seriously the way in which art works its effects on audiences. In particular, psychoanalysis provides tools for examining the unconscious investments that people have in artistic material – the patterns of desire and identification that lure audiences in and make the play of images and words seem meaningful. Psychoanalysis can offer numerous concepts to help here, for example the Oedipus complex, repression, scopophilia, projection and identification. It can also benefit from its engagement with the arts, particularly by responding to the challenge that artistic perceptions make to psychoanalysis' own received assumptions and modes of practice.

Summary

- Freud originated a tradition of 'applied' psychoanalysis that addresses issues outside the clinical situation.
- This tradition both seeks support for psychoanalysis through accumulation of a wider range of evidence than would be available in the consulting room, and seeks to show the utility of psychoanalysis as an instrument for providing explanations of social and cultural phenomena.
- There are three main kinds of intervention that Freud made in artistic and literary criticism:
  - To use artistic examples as ways of providing evidence for psychoanalytic claims.
  - To increase understanding of artistic and literary creations by offering psychoanalytic interpretations of them.
  - To provide insights into how biographical features of an artist might explain that artist's work.
- All these interventions offer stimulating insights, but all are made problematic by questions such as whether psychoanalysis engages sufficiently with the traditions of the art forms it is investigating, and whether the 'psychological reductionism' to which it is prone gives a distorted view of what art is really about.
- Examples from psychoanalytic film criticism and the encounter of psychoanalysis with literary studies suggest that the most productive theoretical concepts are those that focus on how the art work has its effects on its audience.
- Psychoanalysis can also draw on literature and art to enhance its own theory and practice.

20
Politics and society

Psychoanalysis as social theory

Many of the issues that arise in relation to the arts also emerge in social science disciplines such as social psychology, philosophy, politics, history and law. These particularly involve the use of psychoanalytic interpretations and concepts to make sense of social phenomena. As his fame grew, Freud was increasingly expected to pronounce wisely on the social issues of his time. This was the origin, for example, of the exchange with Einstein that became the paper *Why War?* (Freud and Einstein, 1933), in which Einstein professed belief in an inbuilt human destructiveness that paralleled Freud's notion of the death drive. More generally, the contribution of psychoanalysis to theorizing on some major early twentieth-century themes, such as the origins of civilization and the 'conflict' between society and the individual, seems to have been seen as an important test of the standing of psychoanalysis. If psychoanalysis is an account of the sources of human trouble, then surely it should be able to comment on how and why these troubles are so often inflicted in and by society. Especially after the First World War, which clearly revealed people's extraordinary capacity for self-deception and violence, any psychology that claimed to explain the depths of human nature must also be able to say something novel about so-called human 'civilization'. Over the course of psychoanalysis' development, it has made many controversial attempts to do just that.

The quality of psychoanalysis' social interventions has been variable and has often been subject to some important criticisms, especially in relation to its tendency to be reductionist in the sense of trying to explain social phenomena in psychological terms (for example Segal, 1999). Psychoanalysis has also faced challenges from sympathetic critics who worry about its tendency to slip into normative assumptions around race (for example Brickman, 2003) and sexuality (Mitchell, 2002). Nevertheless, psychoanalysis continues to contribute strongly to the understanding of social phenomena. There have been powerful examinations of racism (Rustin, 1991), fascism (Bollas, 1993), social identities (Butler, 2005) and most recently, postcolonial situations (Khanna, 2004). This work draws on a wide range of psychoanalytic ideas, including, for instance, Klein (in the case of Rustin), object relations theory (Bollas) and the French psychoanalyst Jean Laplanche (Butler). Khanna's book embraces postcolonial thinking on psychoanalysis deriving in large part from the writings of Franz Fanon (1952); other writers in the area have used Lacanian theory quite extensively – for example Derek Hook's (2012) provocative analysis of apartheid. Over all this hangs the vast array of Lacanian work produced by Slavoj Žižek (for example 2011), which is the subject of great controversy as well as bringing Lacanian psychoanalysis into the academic celebrity mainstream. This wide range of sources suggests that psychoanalysis is alive as a resource for critical social thought even while debate continues to rage about the implications of different psychoanalytic ideas. As a way of offering a necessarily brief summary, here is a short list of some psychoanalytic concepts that have proven helpful for social analysis.

Repression: Fundamental to some early psychoanalytic political thinking (for example Marcuse, 1955) is the idea that oppressive societies 'repress' their subjects in the sense of denying them access to their desires. It continues to have some currency when applied for instance to ways in which the break-up of totalitarian states can unleash powerful antagonisms that have been previously kept at bay.

Projection: This is a widely used idea for explaining some of the mechanisms of social hatred, particularly racism (Rustin, 1991) and war (Segal, 1995). The argument is that virulent hatred arises from unconscious destructive impulses that are projected outwards onto external objects made vulnerable by social forces. So, for example, racist assumptions about black 'bestiality' are derived from historical constructions of black people as non-human slaves, but are also fuelled by the racist's own sexual terrors.

Identification: This is a crucial idea when it comes to discussions of social identity and refers to the way people unconsciously mould themselves in the light of external structures that provide them with models of various kinds. For instance, 'diasporic identities' are often created through identifying with the cultural and religious values and histories of specific groups, as they are mediated by myths, stories and personal relationships (Hall, 1990). Many gender theorists see identification as the central mechanism whereby gender identity forms, with lively debates about whether gender identifications are primarily same-sex (girls identifying with their mothers, for instance) or whether multiple cross-gender identifications are routine features of development (Benjamin, 1998).

Internalization: This relates to the material on loss and melancholia mentioned in Chapter 13. The notion that there might be something 'ungrieved' that is held by people and cultures as a kind of 'living-dead' entity is proving fruitful both in studies of gender and sexual identities (Butler, 1997) and postcoloniality (Oliver, 2004).

Castration: This is a more complex and contentious issue, relating to the Lacanian idea that at the core of human subjecthood is a state of 'lack' produced by the impossibility of desire ever being fulfilled. Žižek (2008) and others have used this powerfully to examine how such lack might drive violence in the social sphere. For instance, Žižek shows how the sensation of lack might be covered over by the fantasy that 'aliens' have *stolen* something from 'us', a fantasy that is often at work in racism.

This short list is hopefully enough to show that psychoanalysis offers something important in the field of social thought. Arguably, it is the most developed vocabulary and theoretical system that we have to link what might go on 'within' each one of us with what happens 'outside'. It can therefore be a genuinely psychosocial approach, offering a way of understanding the intensity of emotion, the pervasiveness of fantasy and the frequently profound irrationality of social life. In the rest of this chapter, I give three very brief examples of how this might work in some applied areas.

Authority and social regulation

As we have seen in Part I, one premise of Freudian psychoanalysis is that there is a clash between what the individual might wish for and what society might allow. Classical psychoanalysis proposed that sexual wishes have to be moderated, because let loose they would undermine the capacity of all of us to function rationally in a peopled world. As a consequence, Freud had to think about how the conditions of society affect the individual, what constraints are beneficial or harmful, and what painful restrictions are essential. The refinement of his views about the processes through which repression operates, and in particular the emergence of the concept of the superego, led to a more nuanced understanding of how certain social processes might find their way 'into' the mind of the individual. For instance, the description Freud gives of how the superego emerges as a consequence of the Oedipus complex is in essence a *social* account of development (see Chapters 7 and 8). It suggests that as a result of the 'law' laid down by the father, a new mental structure is formed. This structure, the superego, is made up mostly of the prohibitions and moral judgements attributed to the father. In other words, what was initially an external authority becomes an internal one. So society controls the individual through a process in which its authority is internalized.

This fundamental idea is one source of psychoanalysis' attraction to some legal scholars, interested in how the law both polices behaviour and invites transgressions (for example Cornell, 2000). Psychoanalysis might suggest that the prohibition of criminality helps make it exciting, by promoting it as exotic, exceptional and dangerous. Crime can therefore become addictive. It can also be a way of dealing with guilt, rather than the more conventional other way around. That is, a person who feels guilty for unconscious reasons may commit a crime in order to have an obvious *reason* to feel guilty. He or she may even wish to be punished by an external authority, and hence have her or his guilt alleviated. This idea, often attributed to Winnicott (1965), was expressed first by Freud himself (1916). Discussing patients who commit crimes, he noted that 'such deeds were done principally because they were forbidden, and because their execution was accompanied by mental relief for their doer. He was suffering from an oppressive feeling of guilt, of which he did not know the origin, and after he had committed a misdeed this oppression was mitigated. His sense of guilt was at least attached to something' (p. 332). Freud describes these people as 'criminals from a sense of guilt.'

Civilization

For Freud, the development of social structures was due primarily to individuals' need for protection. Fearful of the forces of nature, of the weakness of the body and of the actions of other people, individuals form together in groups in order to defend themselves. These groups become what Freud termed 'civilization', defined as 'the whole sum of the achievements and the regulations which distinguish our lives from those of our animal ancestors and which serve two purposes – namely to protect men against nature and to adjust their mutual relations' (Freud, 1930, p. 89). However, just as psychological defences can cause problems even while they protect the ego against the ravages of unconscious life, so civilization is a compromise between the need of people to live together and the fundamentally asocial demands of the unconscious. This means that people always have to give up something for the sake of social survival; in this sense, society is opposed to the individual even though it is also essential to life. Civilization is a necessary evil that always brings unhappiness.

Late in life, Freud (1927) produced an extensive review of one of society's major 'institutions', religion, explaining it as an 'illusion' whereby the pains of life are ameliorated. The details of this are revealing in that they show how devoted an adherent Freud was of a 'rationalist' perspective that refused any mystical consolations or illusions. For Freud, religion was precisely such an illusion, built on infantile dependence – the need for protection and the wish that this will be offered by a powerful, superior being who has sought one out. Freud recognized the appeal of this, but was also certain that it was time for religious illusions to be overcome and that by blocking a true understanding of reality they were doing great damage. 'Surely infantilism is destined to be surmounted,' he wrote (Freud, 1927, p. 48). 'Men cannot remain children for ever; they must in the end go out into "hostile life". We may call this "education to reality".' The task of psychoanalysis in exposing the roots of religion is parallel to its task when faced with neurotic patients. Just as a patient's symptoms will have developed for good reason, to protect the ego against what might seem to be something worse, so a society's symptoms, including the development of religion, will have defensive functions. But these defences have a tendency to turn destructive, which is what makes them into symptoms. They cause too much further unhappiness and they need to be outgrown.

There is some recent psychoanalytic work that is much more sympathetic towards religion than was Freud (Black, 2006). However, Freud was in the mainstream of much of the thought of his time in believing in a basic opposition between individual and society. There are obvious problems with this view, particularly in its neglect of the *enjoyment* offered by social connections. Religion, for instance, might at times bind people together positively and not simply defend them against painful reality. The Freudian tendency, however, is to see the individual's drives as 'basic' and to understand society as set up solely in order to control them. This has some contradictory implications for social change. On the one hand, it was the source for some famous radical thinking examining how the drives could be let free in a revolutionary, non-repressive society (for example Marcuse, 1955). On the other, it suggested to more socially conservative analysts that the task of the individual is to *adapt* to the constraints of 'reality'.

This view was characteristic of ego psychology in post-war America, resulting in a great deal of criticism of that form of psychoanalysis from more radical theorists (Jacoby, 1975). Ego psychology was seen as socially conformist because of its interest in how the ego could be strengthened so that the drives could be made to fit in with the requirements of the social environment. Yet the argument here is not straightforward. For example, ideas like the Kleinian one that there is a basic destructive drive (the death drive) at work in each person and that this needs to be managed appropriately can have socially reformist implications. Michael Rustin (1995) argues in this vein that, by starting with destructiveness and moving towards reparation (see Chapter 15), Kleinian theory poses the question of what needs to be done *relationally* in order for aggression and violence to be survived, and damage and loss made good. We ignore human destructiveness at our peril; acknowledging it but also understanding how it is produced within a social context should lead us to think about how society can be organized to minimize its effects.

The psychoanalytic idea of a containing environment for potentially destructive but also loving urges is present in a different way in work drawing on Winnicottian ideas of security and trust (see Chapter 12).

For instance, Axel Honneth (1996) suggests that healthy maturation is dependent on an accurate and sustaining experience of recognition from the parent. Recognition involves responding to children in such a way that they gain self-awareness as separate but loved beings, with entitlements and a capacity to make their needs felt. With such recognition, children gain security and trust and a strong sense of identity; without it, they will feel fragile and disempowered. Early relational experiences of care are thus the source for the kind of emotional stability and security of selfhood that is necessary for sustaining social life. This turns into a sociological theory when Honneth proposes that entire social groups can feel unrecognized and cut off from sources of validation in society. Claims for *social* recognition may then become the fuel for social struggle and collective resistance. Thus, an essentially *emotional* state (the demand for recognition rather than, for example, for resources) leads to political activity.

This kind of thinking about how social conflict and the possibilities for reconciliation are based in experiences of security and trust, has stirred up a great deal of debate. Does psychoanalytic theory offer a link between the intimacies of the supposedly personal sphere (the parent–child encounter) and social action? If it does, it might explain the passion with which people struggle for fairness and equality, for recognition of themselves and for all the other elements that go into an 'identity politics'. On the other hand, the problems of reductionism that plague most psychological accounts of social and political relationships remain. In other words, if theorists are not very careful, they can end up explaining the whole of social life on psychological grounds without attending fully to features of the social itself (class, race, gender and sexual orientation being among the most obvious) that have their own independent and profound effects.

Gender and sexual difference

This challenge to psychoanalysis can also be seen in some other areas of social scientific application of psychoanalytic thinking, where the role of psychoanalysis has been questioned even when its concepts are being deployed. The most important instance of this kind is that of gender and sexual difference, to which psychoanalysis has attended from the start. For Freud, sexual difference was the 'bedrock' of psychoanalysis, beyond which it could not go (Freud, 1937, p. 252). For him, this meant that no analytic work would shake the fundamental human tendency to reject femininity and aspire to masculinity. This clearly conservative view was contested from very early on, in the work of psychoanalytic writers of the 1920s and 1930s, some of whom attributed it to Freud's own neurotic failings. However, especially since the publication in 1974 of Juliet Mitchell's book *Psychoanalysis and Feminism*, psychoanalysis has also been drawn upon by many theorists in a search for theoretical leverage on gender and sexuality. Mitchell's position was a radical one in that she was a recognized feminist scholar who took issue with the feminist orthodoxy of the time, which viewed psychoanalysis as a powerful agent for perpetuating patriarchy. Mitchell did not deny the patriarchal elements in psychoanalytic thinking, dealing extensively in her book with notions such as penis envy and the specifically feminine 'difficulties' with the Oedipus complex. However, she argued that psychoanalysis need not be seen as perpetuating women's supposed 'inferiority', but rather contributes to understanding patriarchy and its effects in a way that no other approach can do. Those aspects of feminine psychology that were widely seen as biologically determined were viewed by her as socially constructed, and psychoanalysis was turned to as a theory that might explain how such constructions become embedded in people's psyches as part of an unconscious mental structure. It might even be said that Mitchell put the unconscious on the contemporary feminist map. She demonstrated how radical changes in sexual politics require not only political interventions (she drew heavily on Marxist theory in her book), but also ways of engaging with the unconscious dynamics of gender 'internalized' from a patriarchal society.

Mitchell's promotion of psychoanalysis as a sexually progressive discipline has not gone unchallenged by other feminists, even those working as psychoanalysts or psychoanalytic psychotherapists. Virginia Goldner (2003), for example, in a widely read paper, argues that most Freudian thinking on gender and sexuality is now woefully out of date. With the exception, she claims, of 'a band of Euro-Lacanians and a few surviving True Believers', Freud's ideas on women are now seen as deriving from his own 'ambivalent homophobia, casual misogyny, and traditional family values' (pp. 113–14).

The issue of 'penis envy' no longer has much resonance outside stand-up comic routines. Even the object relational idea that girls, because of their close ties with their mothers, struggle with issues of autonomy and separation while boys trip up over intimacy, draws on highly traditional images of appropriate ways of being feminine and masculine. Characteristically, such critics would say, what is omitted here is any real analysis of the social mechanisms that ensure these gender assumptions remain dominant. What has replaced psychoanalytic orthodoxy, as Goldner (ibid.) lists it, is the work of 'Contemporary feminists, gay and lesbian scholars, queer theorists, and generations of psychoanalysts looking for better ideas about sex and gender.'

Despite this healthy critique of psychoanalytic platitudes, contemporary gender theory is almost unimaginable without psychoanalytic input. Serious writers on gender and sexuality such as Judith Butler and Lynne Segal routinely deploy notions of unconscious life. Indeed, in Butler's case, the centrality of psychoanalysis to her thinking has been very marked (for example Butler, 2005). Importantly, the key concepts she uses are not those put forward by Freud and later analysts to explain sexual difference but rather the psychoanalytic formulation of more general mental mechanisms, particularly the identificatory ones described in Freud's (1917b) *Mourning and Melancholia*. Butler (1997) suggests, for instance, that the fragility of heterosexual masculinity derives from a kind of melancholic identification. The ideas here are complex, but one important notion is that the 'straight' man's sexual identity is built on an unconscious repudiation of *homosexuality*. This 'lost' homosexual identity is never properly acknowledged, so it can never be fully mourned and given up. The result is a kind of haunting of masculinity by an unresolved grief.

It can perhaps be seen that psychoanalysis enters the fray and holds its own not so much because of widespread adoption of its specific theories of sexual difference, but because of the sophistication and versatility of its conceptual lexicon. This might be a general point about its involvement in the field of social theory. Grand psychoanalytic accounts of how society works are not that helpful, because society is not a psychological entity. But careful tracing of how unconscious material is influenced by, and expressed in, the social domain is essential for understanding how each of us is constructed in and by the cultural and social environment in which we live. It also helps to explain why society itself shows so much evidence of being saturated by passionate feelings and unconscious desires.

Summary

- Freud was interested in how psychoanalysis could make sense of the 'suffering' of individuals in society, and participated in a tradition in which psychoanalysis has been used actively in social and political theory.
- Two fundamental premises to be found in Freud, especially in his later work, are:
  - There is an opposition between the drives, represented psychologically by unconscious ideas and wishes, and society, which has to control these drives in order to protect people from one another.
  - There are important mental mechanisms whereby the constraints of society are 'internalized' so that they are felt to arise from within the individual. Conscience as an internalization of authority via the superego is an example here.
- These assumptions have both socially conservative and progressive possibilities and have been used in both ways by later theorists.
- There have been many recent developments in social theory using psychoanalytic concepts, in particular drawing on object relational perspectives on security and trust; Kleinian ideas on destructiveness; and Lacanian notions of desire and lack.
- Despite concerns over psychological reductionism, the versatility of psychoanalysis in theorizing how apparently 'internal' and 'external' states are connected has made it applicable to a wide range of social contexts.

Conclusion

This book has introduced many of the major ideas to be found in psychoanalytic theory. It began by considering the question of why we might still find this theory important and worth studying, and it is to this issue that I want to return in this brief concluding note. Psychoanalysis has been the subject of considerable criticism over the years, much of it excessive but some of it well founded. What I am aiming at here, however, is not any kind of balanced consideration of the strengths and limitations of psychoanalysis, though I hope some of my views on this have emerged during this book, and they are developed more fully elsewhere (Frosh, 2006, 2010). Rather, I want to offer a more subjective set of summary assertions about why psychoanalytic theory is worth engaging with even at a time when, for the reasons given in Chapter 1, it is under various kinds of attack.

- *Psychoanalysis provides a vocabulary for reflexive self-understanding*

Despite Freud's own belief that the deepest unconscious urge is for rest, there is overwhelming evidence that what drives people on is a wish actively to understand themselves and the world around them. Decades of psychoanalytic as well as cognitive psychological research has shown that young infants are oriented towards their social world and are apparently 'hardwired' to form relationships with other people (Stern, 1985). This propensity stays with us throughout life and fuels interest in counselling and psychotherapy, settings in which relationships are the basis for therapeutic change. It is also, arguably, what provokes us to reflect seriously on art, literature and philosophy, and possibly to develop scientific knowledge. We are interested not only in controlling the world, but also and possibly more fundamentally in comprehending it and our place in it.

Psychoanalysis attaches itself to that bit of this desire for understanding that is directed inwards, at ourselves. Why do we do what we do? What sense can we make of our dreams or our psychological symptoms? Why do people get addicted to things that are bad for them? What kinds of relationships help us and what other kinds damage us? How can we come to terms with our limitations and enjoy our successes without guilt? How can we cope with loss? Finding ways to approach these questions and others like them means, first, recognizing that they are important; secondly, having some kind of vocabulary to articulate them clearly; and thirdly possessing a conceptual scheme to offer at least preliminary answers. Psychoanalysis is not the only way into this, but it is a powerful and well-developed system that offers both a general theoretical framework and a set of specific explanatory concepts. The general framework emphasizes the existence of an unconscious dimension to mental life. The specific concepts include the various ideas described in this book, ranging from repression and the other defence mechanisms through to transference and counter-transference. Above all, psychoanalysis encourages us to think about the reasons for our actions and asserts that engaging in this kind of thinking is a central aspect of what it means to be human.

- *Psychoanalysis helps to produce the modern human 'subject'*
I argued in Chapter 1 that an important complication in assessing the validity of psychoanalytic claims is that people make sense of themselves by using the cultural ideas available to them (often called 'discourses' in contemporary social theory). This kind of reflexivity also means that powerful social theories *produce* the phenomena that they study. Psychoanalysis certainly seems to work in this way and to be one major source of contemporary self-understanding, and therefore of the modern 'subject'. There are others, of course: religion is still important in forming many people's consciousness of themselves; the scientific framework that emphasizes the physical basis of biology and psychology also has a powerful effect. Psychoanalysis features alongside these and other discourses, producing the idea that we have unconscious lives and the associated issues that arise from this. For example, the importance of early relationships in forging lifelong psychological tendencies is a notion that is not unique to psychoanalysis, but has been immeasurably more strongly impressed on people by its cultural influence. As

a consequence, we attend more closely than we might otherwise do to the conditions under which children develop, with implications for social and educational policy as well as for our own behaviour and our judgements of others'.

- *Psychoanalysis helps to break down the opposition between 'individual' and 'social' prevalent in the social sciences*

The distinction between the individual and the social is one that developed over a long period of time and was institutionalized academically through a kind of division of labour that arose between sociology and psychology towards the end of the nineteenth century. It is still an unstable distinction, as is evident in discussions about families and groups. Are we talking about individuals bundled together or social forms with their own structural characteristics? It is probably obvious that both perspectives are 'true' to the extent that they encompass real elements of the 'psychosocial' formation of these entities. For example, groups contain individuals who might each have their own hopes and needs; but they also function quite predictably as a consequence of such organizational characteristics as their size, structure (egalitarian versus hierarchical, for instance) and leadership styles (authoritarian versus democratic). We can go further than this, however, in arguing that the social and individual always go together. People are 'inhabited' by the social relationships they encounter and heavily influenced by social mores and the construction of desires (think of the effects of advertising and 'celebrity culture' as just two instances). Conversely, the social field is saturated with fantasies and desires, as is evident in the way violence between social groups can erupt and be sustained by imagined slights or terrors that have little justification from historical reality (for example Rose, 1996).

A problem here is that it is very difficult to develop concepts that work across the deeply embedded social–individual divide. Psychoanalysis offers an important source of such concepts. For example, projection and introjection, key ideas especially but not uniquely in Kleinian theory, deal explicitly with the question of how what seems to be 'inside' can at the same time be 'outside'. Because of this, they are particularly useful when thinking about groups (for example Turquet, 1994) and situations in which the external world seems to become flooded by feeling (Frosh, 2011). The Lacanian notion of the 'Symbolic' (see Chapter 16) is another example, because it provides a way of thinking about how each one of us becomes 'humanized' by entry into a specific social order.

- *Psychoanalysis shows how fantasy and emotion are vital to human psychology, and how they play out on the social and political stage as well*

This has already been touched upon above, but it is worth emphasizing it here. Academic psychology has for many years emphasized cognition over emotion. Sociology similarly has rarely engaged with the affective or emotional elements of social life, although there have been some recent attempts to do this, largely influenced by psychoanalysis (for example Roseneil, 2006). Political, legal and economic theory has again been highly rationalistic, despite some early interventions from major writers who were also willing to use psychoanalysis (for example Kelsen, 1924; Keynes, 1930). Yet the emotional dimension of social, political and economic realities is very strong, as responses to the banking crises of the first decade of the twenty-first century have made clear. Some powerful work has begun to be articulated in this field, much of it drawing on psychoanalysis. Slavoj Žižek's writings on violence and Judith Butler's on vulnerability have been mentioned in earlier chapters (Chapter 20 in particular); their 'debate' on ethical violence is also of considerable importance for social theory (see Frosh, 2010). Michael Rustin's (1991) work on racism alongside that of Joel Kovel (1995) and others is exemplary. Žižek (1994, p. 78), writing about the explosion of violence in post-Yugoslavian Bosnia, makes the point strongly, when he asserts that 'war is always also a *war of fantasies*.' Similarly, Jacqueline Rose (2007) shows in detail how the psychoanalytic notion of 'resistance' can be used to help understand the resistance to *political* change. These are not add-ons to political and social thought; they rather stake the claim that psychoanalytic categories need to be installed at the core of sociopolitical theory if a full account of social phenomena is to be attempted.

- *Psychoanalysis offers powerful concepts for exploring different forms of social violence, including racism, sexism and homophobia*

Extending the point above, psychoanalysis is a potent addition to the conceptual armoury for exploring manifestations of social hatred.

This is despite the way it has itself not been immune to these hatreds, especially in its retrograde stance on homosexuality (Mitchell, 2002; Frosh, 2006) and its more than occasional evidencing of antisemitic rhetoric (Frosh, 2005). Even in such instances, psychoanalysis can be turned against itself to explore how these elements function. For example, homophobia is widely interpreted as a response to homosexual tendencies within the homophobic person, alongside anxieties about sexual and identity dissolution that make these tendencies hard to acknowledge. The noted psychosexual researcher Robert Stoller (1985) observed this long ago, commenting 'Is it improper to suggest that some analysts' problems in understanding homosexuality have – to put it delicately – psychodynamic roots?' (p. 182). This might also be the case for psychoanalysis' uncertainty with regard to its Jewish heritage.

More generally, however, what I am arguing here is that psychoanalysis provides concepts that can explain how it is that the social field can be saturated with what seem to be 'irrational' states of mind. Examples are given above, but the particular accounts it can give of sexism, racism and homophobia should also be stressed. Hatred of the woman; disdain for the 'different' racialized other; revulsion towards gay and lesbian people – these are all states of mind that can be theorized psychoanalytically as arising from unconscious complexes, desires and anxieties and that link up powerfully and destructively with political features of the social landscape.

- *Psychoanalysis has a set of values that challenge the 'quick fix' technological approaches to therapy that are increasingly prevalent*

Moving away from social applications, there is something important that psychoanalysis stands for in the psychotherapeutic situation. As noted in Chapter 1, the emphasis in most health systems is now on brief, focused psychotherapeutic approaches, usually with a strong cognitive-behavioural component. In itself, this is not necessarily a trend to be denigrated. After all, it is fair enough that health service providers try to make rational decisions about which modes of effective intervention can reach the largest number of people most quickly. Short-term work might help sufficient numbers to overcome relatively mild or moderate difficulties, and give others a psychological boost that enables them to pick up the threads of their life again, at least for a while. Psychoanalytic psychotherapy is an important basis for some of these short-term interventions, and indeed there is a long and distinguished history of brief psychodynamic interventions (Coren, 2009). Nevertheless, the usual preferred modality of psychoanalytic work is longer term and where possible more intense (that is, several sessions per week). This is based on a different value system from brief interventions. It suggests a number of things about the attitude we might take up towards people seeking help, and perhaps also to people generally. It implies that understanding and facilitating change in a person's psychological world is a complex process, not easily done and not likely to be achieved quickly by simple interventions. Relatedly, it promotes a view of individuals as worth the 'investment' we put into them. After all, if we consider what it takes to bring up a child – how much time, money, planning and emotional energy goes into it – why should we spare the attention someone might need to help them deal with severe difficulties? This is not simply an economic argument, of course, but an ethical one. Psychoanalysis implies that it should be central to the principles of an ethical society that it takes seriously the mental states of its subjects and offers them what they need to make the best of themselves.

- *Psychoanalysis asks painful questions of reality and insists that we do not back away from the answers*

Finally, there is something very obvious yet very difficult that psychoanalysis presents us with. It deals primarily with extreme states of mind, with passionate feelings and troubled ways of being. These states of mind are located not just in 'disturbed' people but, to a greater or lesser extent, in every one of us. There is a very strong inclination to look away from them and try to pretend they do not exist, or do not matter. But they are real. We see confirmation of this not only in the amount of clear psychological distress there is in society, but also in the extremes of hatred and destructiveness that surround us. We can choose to hide this from ourselves, and much of the time we do – the psychoanalytic concepts of repression and splitting explicitly tell us how we do this, and to some extent justify our actions. But there is a price to pay, which psychoanalysis calls the 'return of the repressed'. Things that are not properly dealt with come back to haunt us, and eventually to make life harder and harder to bear. Psychoanalysis is not afraid to look into the heart of these ghostly returns; this has always been part of its appeal, and perhaps part of the trouble it causes. It is another element of its ethical tendency. It argues that repressed, unconscious ideas are part of the 'truth' of each one of us. There is nothing more important than this truth, in the psychoanalytic vision, however unstable that truth might be and however hard to pin down. Looking the monster in the face, is how it might be described; a horrible experience at times, but a necessary one if life is to be lived ethically, and to the full.

Recommended reading

My brief list of texts given here is aimed at readers who wish to follow up some of the material given in this book. It is obviously by no means comprehensive; a full list of the sources on which I have drawn is in the References. There is a vast literature on psychoanalysis. Much of it has now become accessible through the **Psychoanalytic Electronic Publishing** system (http://www.pep-web.org), which contains the searchable full text of a range of major psychoanalytic journals from 1913 onwards together with many classic psychoanalytic texts, and the Standard Edition of the complete works of Freud in German and English. PEP is only really affordable through an institutional subscription but is a very valuable resource if it is available to you.

My own previous work includes *The Politics of Psychoanalysis* (Palgrave Macmillan, 1999), which introduces psychoanalytic theory from a social perspective; *For and Against Psychoanalysis* (Routledge, 2006), which assesses the standing of psychoanalysis; *Hate and the Jewish Science* (Palgrave Macmillan, 2005), looking at psychoanalysis and antisemitism; and *Psychoanalysis Outside the Clinic* (Palgrave Macmillan, 2010), which deals with applications of psychoanalysis in literature, social psychology, politics and psychosocial studies.

Histories of psychoanalysis

Borch-Jacobsen, M. and Shamdasani, S. (2012) *The Freud Files: An Inquiry into the History of Psychoanalysis.* Cambridge: Cambridge University Press.
A critical account of the myth-making tendencies of psychoanalytic history.

Gay, P. (1988) *Freud: A Life for Our Time.* London: Dent.
The standard 'life of Freud'.

Makari, G. (2010) *Revolution in Mind.* London: Duckworth.

An account of the origins of psychoanalysis up until about 1939, emphasizing its roots in the scientific culture of the time.

Roudinesco, E. (1990) *Jacques Lacan and Co.: A History of Psychoanalysis in France, 1925–1985*. London: Free Association Books.
A gossipy insider's account of psychoanalysis in France.

Zaretsky, E. (2004) *Secrets of the Soul*. New York: Knopf.
A sociological history from a mainly American perspective.

Dictionaries and encyclopaedias

Evans, D. (1996) *An Introductory Dictionary of Lacanian Psychoanalysis*. London: Routledge.
An excellent introduction to Lacanian terms.

Laplanche, J. and Pontalis, J.-B. (1973) *The Language of Psychoanalysis*. London: Hogarth Press.
The most important of psychoanalytic dictionaries, focusing on Freud and influenced by Lacanian thought.

Sandler, J., Dare, C. and Holder, A. (1973) *The Patient and the Analyst*. London: Maresfield Reprints.
A classic account of major Freudian ideas.

Skelton, R. (2006) *The Edinburgh International Encyclopaedia of Psychoanalysis*. Edinburgh: Edinburgh University Press.
An up to date if slightly idiosyncratic dictionary giving space to cultural applications.

Spillius, E., Milton, J., Garvey, P. and Couve, C. (2011) *The New Dictionary of Kleinian Thought*. London: Routledge.
A new version of an important dictionary with extended accounts of key Kleinian concepts.

Freud's writings

Freud, S. (1917) Introductory Lectures on Psycho-Analysis. *The Standard Edition of the Complete Psychological Works of Sigmund Freud, Volume XVI (1916–1917): Introductory Lectures on Psycho-Analysis*, 241–463.

Freud, S. (1933) New Introductory Lectures On Psycho-Analysis. *The Standard Edition of the Complete Psychological Works of Sigmund Freud, Volume XXII (1932–1936): New Introductory Lectures on Psycho-Analysis and Other Works*, 1–182.
These two books lay out Freud's ideas in an accessible way.

Freud, S. (1905) Fragment of an Analysis of a Case of Hysteria. *The Standard Edition of the Complete Psychological Works of Sigmund Freud, Volume VII (1901–1905): A Case of Hysteria, Three Essays on Sexuality and Other Works*, 1–122.

Freud, S. (1909a) Analysis of a Phobia in a Five-Year-Old Boy. *The Standard Edition of the Complete Psychological Works of Sigmund Freud, Volume X (1909): Two Case Histories ('Little Hans' and the 'Rat Man')*, 1–150.

Freud, S. (1909b) Notes Upon a Case of Obsessional Neurosis. *The Standard Edition of the Complete Psychological Works of Sigmund Freud, Volume X (1909): Two Case Histories ('Little Hans' and the 'Rat Man')*, 151–318.

Freud, S. (1918) From the History of an Infantile Neurosis. *The Standard Edition of the Complete Psychological Works of Sigmund Freud, Volume XVII (1917–1919): An Infantile Neurosis and Other Works*, 1–124.
These references are to Freud's four classic case histories: 'Dora', 'Little Hans', the 'Rat Man' and the 'Wolf Man'.

Contemporary Freudian, attachment and neuro-psychoanalytic approaches

Fonagy, P. and Target, M. (2003) *Psychoanalytic Theories: Perspectives from Developmental Psychopathology.* London: Whurr.
An important and comprehensive statement of advances in these areas.

Kleinian and object relational psychoanalysis

Greenberg, J.R. and Mitchell, S.A. (1983) *Object Relations in Psychoanalytic Theory.* Cambridge, MA: Harvard University Press.
A classic description of object relations and Kleinian theories.

Klein, M. (1957) Envy and Gratitude. In M. Klein, *Envy and Gratitude and Other Works*. New York: Delta, 1975.
One of Klein's longest essays, developing the idea of envy and the death drive.

Phillips, A. (1988) *Winnicott*. London: Fontana.
A very clear account of Winnicott's work.

Segal, H. (1973) *Introduction to the Work of Melanie Klein*. London: Hogarth Press.
A highly influential account of Klein's theories.

Lacanian psychoanalysis

Fink, B. (1999) *A Clinical Introduction to Lacanian Psychoanalysis*. New York: Harvard University Press.
Quite a difficult book, but a very astute rendering of Lacanian practice.

Grosz, E. (1990) *Jacques Lacan: A Feminist Introduction*. London: Routledge.
An important intervention into theory that also does a very good job of explaining Lacanian ideas.

Parker, I. (2011) *Lacanian Psychoanalysis: Revolutions in Subjectivity*. London: Routledge.
A highly theorized account that develops thinking on the social and clinical context of Lacanian work.

Žižek, S. (1991) *Looking Awry*. Cambridge, MA: MIT Press.

Žižek, S. (2006) *How to Read Lacan*. London: Granta.
Both these books are very accessible yet stretching introductions, using many examples from popular culture.

Psychoanalytic psychotherapy

Bateman, A., Brown, D. and Pedder, J. (2010) *Introduction to Psychotherapy*. London: Routledge.
This book provides a broad overview of psychoanalytic psychotherapy and related approaches, with clinical examples.

Coren, A. (2009) *Short-Term Psychotherapy: A Psychodynamic Approach*. Basingstoke: Palgrave Macmillan.
A persuasive presentation of short-term psychoanalytic psychotherapy, with many clinical examples.

Gunn, D. (2002) *Wool-Gathering or How I Ended Analysis*. London: Routledge.
An often hilarious personal account of Lacanian analysis.

Ogden, T.H. (2004) The Analytic Third: Implications for Psychoanalytic Theory and Technique. *Psychoanalytic Quarterly*, 73, 167–95.
A highly influential clinical paper that is also very accessibly written.

Spurling, L. (2009) *An Introduction to Psychodynamic Counselling*. Basingstoke: Palgrave Macmillan.
An excellent, clear introduction to the theory and practice of this psycho-analytic style of work.

Literary, social and political applications

Butler, J. (2009) *Frames of War*. London: Verso.
A set of essays drawing in part on psychoanalytic themes, by one of the world's leading social theorists.

Mitchell, J. (1974) *Psychoanalysis and Feminism*. Harmondsworth: Penguin.
Although now rather dated, this was the most influential feminist inter-vention into psychoanalysis of modern times.

Mulvey, L. (1989) *Visual and Other Pleasures*. London: Macmillan – now Palgrave Macmillan.
A classic account of psychoanalysis and cinema.

Rose, J. (2007) *The Last Resistance*. London: Verso.
This book, like much of Jacqueline Rose's work, both explores psychoa-nalysis and uses it in political and literary criticism.

Rustin, M. (1991) *The Good Society and the Inner World*. London: Verso.
Written from a Kleinian perspective, this includes one of the best avail-able psychoanalytic accounts of racism.

Stonebridge, L. (1998) *The Destructive Element: British Psychoanalysis and Modernism*. London: Macmillan – now Palgrave Macmillan.
A very compelling exploration of psychoanalysis and modernism, focusing on Britain.

Žižek, S. (2008) *Violence*. London: Profile Books.
A relatively easy to read yet highly provocative account of violence drawing on Lacanian ideas.

References

Ainsworth, M. and Wittig, B. (1969) Attachment and Exploratory Behavior of One-Year-Olds in a Strange Situation. In B. Foss (ed.) *Determinants of Infant Behavior*. London: Methuen.

Althusser, L. (1969) Freud and Lacan. In L. Althusser (1971) *Essays on Ideology*. London: Verso.

Anzieu, D. (1986) *Freud's Self-Analysis*. London: The Hogarth Press.

Benjamin, J. (1998) *Shadow of the Other: Intersubjectivity and Gender in Psychoanalysis*. New York: Routledge.

Benjamin, J. (2004) Beyond doer and done to: An intersubjective view of thirdness. *Psychoanalytic Quarterly*, 73, 5–46.

Bion, W. (1962) *Learning from Experience*. London: Tavistock.

Bion, W. (1963) *Elements of Psychoanalysis*. London: Karnac.

Black, D. (ed.) (2006) *Psychoanalysis and Religion in the Twenty-First Century*. London: Routledge.

Blass, R. and Carmelli, Z. (2007) The case against neuropsychoanalysis: On fallacies underlying psychoanalysis' latest scientific trend and its negative impact on psychoanalytic discourse. *International Journal of Psychoanalysis*, 88, 19–40.

Bollas, C. (1993) *Being a Character*. London: Routledge.

Bonaparte, M. (1933) *The Life and Works of Edgar Allan Poe*. New York: Humanities Press, 1971.

Borch-Jacobsen, M. and Shamdasani, S. (2012) *The Freud Files: An Inquiry into the History of Psychoanalysis*. Cambridge: Cambridge University Press.

Bowlby, J. (1969) *Attachment and Loss Volume 1: Attachment*. London: Hogarth Press.

Bowlby, J. (1973) *Attachment and Loss Volume 2: Separation, Anxiety and Anger*. London: Hogarth Press.

Bowlby, J. (1980) *Attachment and Loss Volume 3: Loss, Sadness and Depression*. London: Hogarth Press.

Breuer, J. and Freud, S. (1895) Studies on Hysteria. *The Standard Edition of the Complete Psychological Works of Sigmund Freud, Volume II (1893–1895): Studies on Hysteria*, i–vi.

Brickman, C. (2003) *Aboriginal Populations in the Mind*. New York: Columbia University Press.

Butler, J. (1997) *The Psychic Life of Power*. Stanford: Stanford University Press.

Butler, J. (2005) *Giving an Account of Oneself*. New York: Fordham University Press.

Butler, J. (2009) *Frames of War*. London: Verso.

Clément, C. (1987) *The Weary Sons of Freud*. London: Verso.

Cohen, S. (2001) *States of Denial: Knowing about Atrocities and Suffering*. Oxford: Polity.

Copjec, J. (2000) The orthopsychic subject: Film theory and the reception of Lacan. In E. Kaplan (ed.) *Feminism and Film*. Oxford: Oxford University Press.

Coren, A. (2009) *Short-Term Psychotherapy: A Psychodynamic Approach*. Basingstoke: Palgrave Macmillan.

Cornell, D. (2000) *Just Cause: Freedom, Identity, and Rights*. New York: Rowman and Littlefield.

Coward, R. and Ellis, J. (1977) *Language and Materialism*. London: Routledge and Kegan Paul.

Damon, W., Eisenberg, N. and Lerner, R. (2006) *Social, Emotional, and Personality Development*. New York: Wiley.

Derrida, J. (1975) The Purveyor of Truth. *Yale French Studies*, 52 (Graphesis: Perspectives in Literature and Philosophy), 31–113.

Ehrenzweig, A. (1967) *The Hidden Order of Art*. London: Weidenfeld and Nicolson.

Ellmann, M. (1994) Introduction. In M. Ellmann (ed.) *Psychoanalytic Literary Criticism*. Harlow: Longman.

Erikson, E. (1956) The problem of ego identity. *Journal of the American Psychoanalytic Association*, 4, 56–121.

Evans, D. (1996) *An Introductory Dictionary of Lacanian Psychoanalysis*. London: Routledge.

Eysenck, H.J. (1985) *Decline and Fall of the Freudian Empire*. Harmondsworth: Viking.

Fairbairn, W.R.D. (1944) Endopsychic structure considered in terms of object-relationships. In W.R.D. Fairbairn, *Psychoanalytic Studies of the Personality*. London: Routledge and Kegan Paul.

Fanon, F. (1952) *Black Skin, White Masks*. London: Pluto Press.

Felman, S. (1982) To open the question. In S. Felman (ed.) *Literature and Psychoanalysis: The Question of Reading: Otherwise*. Baltimore: Johns Hopkins University Press.

Fink, B. (1999) *A Clinical Introduction to Lacanian Psychoanalysis*. New York: Harvard University Press.

Fonagy, P. (2008) The mentalization-focused approach to social development. In F. Busch (ed.) *Mentalization*. London: The Analytic Press.

Fonagy, P. and Target, M. (2003) *Psychoanalytic Theories: Perspectives from Developmental Psychopathology*. London: Whurr.

Fonagy, P. and Target, M. (2007) The rooting of the mind in the body: New links between attachment theory and psychoanalytic thought. *Journal of the American Psychoanalytic Association*, 55, 411–56.

Freud, A. (1936) *The Ego and the Mechanisms of Defence*. London: Hogarth Press, 1948.

Freud, A. (1966) *Normality and Pathology in Childhood*. Harmondsworth: Penguin.

Freud, S. (1895) Letter from Freud to Fliess, January 1, 1896. *The Complete Letters of Sigmund Freud to Wilhelm Fliess, 1887–1904*, 158–62.

Freud, S. (1900a) The Interpretation of Dreams. *The Standard Edition of the Complete Psychological Works of Sigmund Freud, Volume IV (1900): The Interpretation of Dreams (First Part)*, ix–627.

Freud, S. (1900b) Letter from Freud to Fliess, June 12, 1900. *The Complete Letters of Sigmund Freud to Wilhelm Fliess, 1887–1904*, 417–18.

Freud, S. (1905) Fragment of an Analysis of a Case of Hysteria. *The Standard Edition of the Complete Psychological Works of Sigmund Freud, Volume VII (1901–1905): A Case of Hysteria, Three Essays on Sexuality and Other Works*, 1–122.

Freud, S. (1907) Delusions and Dreams in Jensen's Gradiva. *The Standard Edition of the Complete Psychological Works of Sigmund Freud, Volume IX (1906–1908): Jensen's 'Gradiva' and Other Works*, 1–96.

Freud, S. (1909a) Analysis of a Phobia in a Five-Year-Old Boy. *The Standard Edition of the Complete Psychological Works of Sigmund Freud, Volume X (1909): Two Case Histories ('Little Hans' and the 'Rat Man')*, 1–150.

Freud, S. (1909b) Notes Upon a Case of Obsessional Neurosis. *The Standard Edition of the Complete Psychological Works of Sigmund Freud, Volume X (1909): Two Case Histories ('Little Hans' and the 'Rat Man')*, 151–318.

Freud, S. (1910a) Leonardo da Vinci and a Memory of his Childhood. *The Standard Edition of the Complete Psychological Works of Sigmund Freud, Volume XI (1910): Five Lectures on Psycho-Analysis, Leonardo da Vinci and Other Works*, 57–138.

Freud, S. (1910b) The Future Prospects of Psycho-Analytic Therapy. *The Standard Edition of the Complete Psychological Works of Sigmund Freud, Volume XI (1910): Five Lectures on Psycho-Analysis, Leonardo da Vinci and Other Works*, 139–52.

Freud, S. (1914) The Moses of Michelangelo. *The Standard Edition of the Complete Psychological Works of Sigmund Freud, Volume XIII (1913–1914): Totem and Taboo and Other Works*, 209–38.

Freud, S. (1915a) Instincts and their Vicissitudes. *The Standard Edition of the Complete Psychological Works of Sigmund Freud, Volume XIV (1914–1916): On the History of the Psycho-Analytic Movement, Papers on Metapsychology and Other Works*, 109–40.

Freud, S. (1915b) Repression. *The Standard Edition of the Complete Psychological Works of Sigmund Freud, Volume XIV (1914–1916): On the History of the Psycho-Analytic Movement, Papers on Metapsychology and Other Works*, 141–58.

Freud, S. (1915c) The Unconscious. *The Standard Edition of the Complete Psychological Works of Sigmund Freud, Volume XIV (1914–1916): On the History of the Psycho-Analytic Movement, Papers on Metapsychology and Other Works*, 159–215.

Freud, S. (1916) Some Character-Types Met with in Psycho-Analytic Work. *The Standard Edition of the Complete Psychological Works of Sigmund Freud, Volume XIV (1914–1916): On the History of the Psycho-Analytic Movement, Papers on Metapsychology and Other Works*, 309–33.

Freud, S. (1917a) Introductory Lectures on Psycho-Analysis. *The Standard Edition of the Complete Psychological Works of Sigmund Freud, Volume XVI (1916–1917): Introductory Lectures on Psycho-Analysis*, 241–463.

Freud, S. (1917b) Mourning and Melancholia. *The Standard Edition of the Complete Psychological Works of Sigmund Freud, Volume XIV (1914–1916): On the History of the Psycho-Analytic Movement, Papers on Metapsychology and Other Works*, 237–58.

Freud, S. (1920) Beyond the Pleasure Principle. *The Standard Edition of the Complete Psychological Works of Sigmund Freud, Volume XVIII (1920–1922): Beyond the Pleasure Principle, Group Psychology and Other Works*, 1–64.

Freud, S. (1921) Psycho-Analysis and Telepathy. *The Standard Edition of the Complete Psychological Works of Sigmund Freud, Volume XVIII (1920–1922): Beyond the Pleasure Principle, Group Psychology and Other Works*, 173–94.

Freud, S. (1923) The Ego and the Id. *The Standard Edition of the Complete Psychological Works of Sigmund Freud, Volume XIX (1923–1925): The Ego and the Id and Other Works*, 1–66.

Freud, S. (1924) Neurosis and Psychosis. *The Standard Edition of the Complete Psychological Works of Sigmund Freud, Volume XIX (1923–1925): The Ego and the Id and Other Works*, 147–54.

Freud, S. (1925) Negation. *The Standard Edition of the Complete Psychological Works of Sigmund Freud, Volume XIX (1923–1925): The Ego and the Id and Other Works*, 233–40.

Freud, S. (1926) Inhibitions, Symptoms and Anxiety. *The Standard Edition of the Complete Psychological Works of Sigmund Freud, Volume XX (1925–1926): An Autobiographical Study, Inhibitions, Symptoms and Anxiety, The Question of Lay Analysis and Other Works*, 75–176.

Freud, S. (1927) The Future of an Illusion. *The Standard Edition of the Complete Psychological Works of Sigmund Freud, Volume XXI (1927–1931): The Future of an Illusion, Civilization and its Discontents, and Other Works*, 1–56.

Freud, S. (1930) Civilization and its Discontents. *The Standard Edition of the Complete Psychological Works of Sigmund Freud, Volume XXI (1927–1931): The Future of an Illusion, Civilization and its Discontents, and Other Works*, 57–146.

Freud, S. (1933) New Introductory Lectures On Psycho-Analysis. *The Standard Edition of the Complete Psychological Works of Sigmund Freud, Volume XXII (1932–1936): New Introductory Lectures on Psycho-Analysis and Other Works*, 1–182.

Freud, S. (1937) Analysis Terminable and Interminable. *The Standard Edition of the Complete Psychological Works of Sigmund Freud, Volume XXIII (1937–1939): Moses and Monotheism, An Outline of Psycho-Analysis and Other Works*, 209–54.

Freud, S. and Einstein, A. (1933) Why War? *The Standard Edition of the Complete Psychological Works of Sigmund Freud, Volume XXII (1932–1936): New Introductory Lectures on Psycho-Analysis and Other Works*, 195–216.

Frosh, S. (2005) *Hate and the Jewish Science: Nazism, Anti-Semitism and Psychoanalysis*. Basingstoke: Palgrave Macmillan.

Frosh, S. (2006) *For and Against Psychoanalysis*. London: Routledge.

Frosh, S. (2010) *Psychoanalysis Outside the Clinic*. Basingstoke: Palgrave Macmillan.

Frosh, S. (2011) *Feelings*. London: Routledge.

Gabbard, G. (2001) Introduction. In G. Gabbard (ed.) *Psychoanalysis and Film*. London: Karnac.

Gay, P. (1988) *Freud: A Life for Our Time*. London: Dent.

Gellner, E. (1985) *The Psychoanalytic Movement*. London: Paladin.

Giddens, A. (1991) *Modernity and Self-Identity*. Cambridge: Polity.

Goldner, V. (2003) Ironic Gender/Authentic Sex. *Studies in Gender and Sexuality*, 4, 113–39.

Greenberg, J.R. and Mitchell, S.A. (1983) *Object Relations in Psychoanalytic Theory*. Cambridge, MA: Harvard University Press.

Grosz, E. (1990) *Jacques Lacan: A Feminist Introduction*. London: Routledge.

Grünbaum, A. (1984) *The Foundations of Psychoanalysis: A Philosophical Critique*. Berkeley: University of California Press.

Gunn, D. (2002) *Wool-Gathering or How I Ended Analysis*. London: Routledge.

Guntrip, H. (1973) *Psychoanalytic Theory, Therapy and the Self*. New York: Basic Books.

Hall, S. (1990) Cultural Identity and Diaspora. In J. Rutherford (ed.) *Identity: Community, Culture, Difference*. London: Lawrence and Wishart.

Heimann, P. (1950) On Counter-Transference. *International Journal of Psychoanalysis,* 31, 81–4.

Heimann, P. (1960) Counter-transference. *British Journal of Medical Psychology,* 33, 9–15.

Hinshelwood, R. (1991) *A Dictionary of Kleinian Thought.* London: Free Association Books.

Hinshelwood, R. (1995) Psychoanalysis in Britain: Points of cultural access, 1893–1918. *International Journal of Psychoanalysis,* 76, 135–51.

Honneth, A. (1996) *The Struggle for Recognition: The Moral Grammar of Social Conflicts.* Oxford: Polity.

Hook, D. (2012) *A Critical Psychology of the Post-Colonial: The Mind of Apartheid.* London: Routledge.

Jacoby, R. (1975) *Social Amnesia.* Sussex: Harvester.

Jahoda, M. (1977) *Freud and the Dilemmas of Psychology.* London: Hogarth Press.

Jones, E. (1910) The Oedipus-complex as an explanation of Hamlet's mystery: A study in motive. *The American Journal of Psychology,* 21, 72–113.

Kelsen, H. (1924) The conception of the state and social psychology – with special reference to Freud's group theory. *International Journal of Psycho-Analysis,* 5, 1–38.

Keynes, J. (1930) *A Treatise on Money.* London: Macmillan for the Royal Economic Society, 1971.

Khanna, R. (2004) *Dark Continents: Psychoanalysis and Colonialism.* Durham: Duke University Press.

Klein, M. (1952) The origins of transference. In M. Klein (1975) *Envy and Gratitude and Other Works.* New York: Delta.

Klein, M. (1955) The psychoanalytic play technique. In M. Klein (1975) *Envy and Gratitude and Other Works.* New York: Delta.

Klein, M. (1957) Envy and Gratitude. In M. Klein (1975) *Envy and Gratitude and Other Works.* New York: Delta.

Kovel, J. (1995) On racism and psychoanalysis. In A. Elliott and S. Frosh (eds) *Psychoanalysis in Contexts.* London: Routledge.

Lacan, J. (1954) The topic of the imaginary. In J. Lacan (1975) *The Seminars of Jacques Lacan, Book I: Freud's papers on Technique 1953–1954.* Cambridge: Cambridge University Press.

Lacan, J. (1972–3) God and the *jouissance* of the woman. In J. Mitchell and J. Rose (eds) (1982) *Feminine Sexuality.* London: Macmillan – now Palgrave Macmillan.

Lacan, J. (1991) *The Other Side of Psychoanalysis: The Seminar of Jacques Lacan Book XVII.* New York: Norton, 2007.

Laplanche, J. and Pontalis, J.-B. (1973) *The Language of Psychoanalysis.* London: Hogarth Press.

Luckhurst, R. (2002) *The Invention of Telepathy.* Oxford: OUP.

Main, M. and Goldwyn, R. (1990) Adult attachment ratings and classification system. In M. Main (ed.) *A Typology of Human Attachment Organization Assessed in Discourse, Drawings and Interviews.* New York: Cambridge University Press.

Makari, G. (2010) *Revolution in Mind.* London: Duckworth.

Marcuse, H. (1955) *Eros and Civilization.* Boston: Beacon Press.

Masson, J. (1984) *Freud: The Assault on Truth.* London: Faber and Faber.

Metz, C. (1977) *Psychoanalysis and Cinema: The Imaginary Signifier.* London: Macmillan – now Palgrave Macmillan, 1982.

Mitchell, J. (1974) *Psychoanalysis and Feminism.* Harmondsworth: Penguin.

Mitchell, J. and Rose, J. (eds) (1982) *Feminine Sexuality.* London: Macmillan – now Palgrave Macmillan.

Mitchell, S. (2002) Psychodynamics, homosexuality, and the question of pathology. *Studies in Gender and Sexuality*, 3, 3–21.

Moore, B. and Fine, B. (1990) *Psychoanalytic Terms and Concepts.* New Haven: Yale University Press.

Mulvey, L. (1975) Visual pleasure and narrative cinema. In L. Mulvey (1989) *Visual and Other Pleasures.* London: Macmillan – now Palgrave Macmillan.

Mulvey, L. (1989) *Visual and Other Pleasures.* London: Macmillan – now Palgrave Macmillan.

Nobus, D. and Quinn, M. (2005) *Knowing Nothing, Staying Stupid.* London: Routledge.

Ogden, T. (1994) The analytic third: Working with intersubjective clinical facts. *International Journal of Psychoanalysis*, 75, 3–19.

Ogden, T. (1999) 'The music of what happens' in poetry and psychoanalysis. *International Journal of Psychoanalysis*, 80, 979–94.

Ogden, T. (2004) The analytic third: Implications for psychoanalytic theory and technique. *Psychoanalytic Quarterly*, 73, 167–95.

Oliver, K. (2004) *The Colonization of Psychic Space.* Minneapolis: University of Minnesota Press.

Parker, I. (2011) *Lacanian Psychoanalysis: Revolutions in Subjectivity.* London: Routledge.

Phillips, A. (1988) *Winnicott.* London: Fontana.

Piaget, J. and Inhelder, B. (1969) *The Psychology of the Child.* New York: Basic Books.

Popper, K. (1959) *The Logic of Scientific Discovery.* London: Hutchinson.

Potter, N. (ed.) (2006) *Trauma, Truth and Reconciliation: Healing Damaged Relationships.* Oxford: Oxford University Press.

Rose, J. (1996) *States of Fantasy.* Oxford: Clarendon Press.

Rose, J. (2003) Apathy and accountability: The challenge of South Africa's Truth and Reconciliation Commission to the intellectual in the modern world. In J. Rose, *On Not Being Able to Sleep*. London: Verso.

Rose, J. (2007) *The Last Resistance*. London: Verso.

Rosenfeld, H. (1971) Contribution to the psychopathology of psychotic states. In E. Spillius (ed.) (1988) *Melanie Klein Today: Volume 1, Mainly Theory*. London: Routledge.

Roseneil, S. (2006) The ambivalences of angel's 'arrangement': A psychosocial lens on the contemporary condition of personal life. *The Sociological Review*, 54, 846–68.

Roth, A. and Fonagy, P. (2005) *What Works for Whom: A Critical Review of Psychotherapy Research*. London: Guilford Press.

Roudinesco, E. (1990) *Jacques Lacan and Co.: A History of Psychoanalysis in France, 1925–1985*. London: Free Association Books.

Rustin, M. (1991) *The Good Society and the Inner World*. London: Verso.

Rustin, M. (1995) Lacan, Klein and politics: The positive and negative in psychoanalytic thought. In A. Elliott and S. Frosh (eds) *Psychoanalysis in Contexts*. London: Routledge.

Sandler, J., Dare, C. and Holder, A. (1973) *The Patient and the Analyst*. London: Maresfield Reprints.

Segal, H. (1973) *Introduction to the Work of Melanie Klein*. London: Hogarth Press.

Segal, H. (1981) *The Work of Hanna Segal*. New York: Jason Aronson.

Segal, H. (1995) From Hiroshima to the Gulf War and after: A psychoanalytic perspective. In A. Elliott and S. Frosh (eds) *Psychoanalysis in Contexts*. London: Routledge.

Segal, L. (1999) *Why Feminism?* Cambridge: Polity.

Seshadri-Crooks, K. (2000) *Desiring Whiteness: A Lacanian Analysis of Race*. London: Routledge.

Solms, M. and Turnbull, O. (2002) *The Brain and the Inner World*. New York: Other Press.

Spillius, E., Milton, J., Garvey, P. and Couve, C. (2011) *The New Dictionary of Kleinian Thought*. London: Routledge.

Stern, D. (1985) *The Interpersonal World of the Infant*. New York: Basic Books.

Stoller, R. (1985) *Observing the Erotic Imagination*. New Haven: Yale University Press.

Stonebridge, L. (1998) *The Destructive Element: British Psychoanalysis and Modernism*. London: Macmillan – now Palgrave Macmillan.

Turquet, P. (1994) Threats to identity in the large group. In L. Kreeger (ed.) *The Large Group*. London: Karnac.

Winnicott, D.W. (1958) The capacity to be alone. *International Journal of Psychoanalysis*, 39, 416–20.

Winnicott, D.W. (1965) *The Maturational Processes and the Facilitating Environment: Studies in the Theory of Emotional Development.* London: The Hogarth Press.

Winnicott, D. (1969) The use of an object. *International Journal of Psychoanalysis*, 50, 711–16.

Winnicott, D.W. (1971) *Playing and Reality.* London: Tavistock Publications.

Winnicott, D.W. (1975) *Through Paediatrics to Psycho-Analysis.* London: The Hogarth Press.

Zaretsky, E. (2004) *Secrets of the Soul.* New York: Knopf.

Žižek, S. (1991) *Looking Awry.* Cambridge, MA: MIT Press.

Žižek, S. (1994) *The Metastases of Enjoyment* London: Verso.

Žižek, S. (2006a) Philosophy, the 'unknown knowns,' and the public use of reason. *Topoi*, 25, 137–42.

Žižek, S. (2006b) *How to Read Lacan.* London: Granta.

Žižek, S. (2006c) *The Pervert's Guide to Cinema.* P. Guide Ltd (DVD).

Žižek, S. (2008) *Violence.* London: Profile Books.

Žižek, S. (2011) *Living in the End Times.* London: Verso.

Index